The Many Faces of the City

Exploring the Metropolis

Edited by Stefan Litz

The Many Faces of the City

Exploring the Metropolis

Edited by Stefan Litz

COMMON GROUND

First published in 2021
as part of the *Global Studies* Book Imprint
doi: 10.18848/978-0-949313-12-6/CGP (Full Book)

Common Ground Research Networks
60 Hazelwood Dr.
University of Illinois Research Park
Champaign, IL
61820

Library of Congress Cataloging-in-Publication Data

Names: Litz, Stefan, editor.
Title: The many faces of the city : exploring the metropolis / edited by
    Stefan Litz.
Description: Champaign, IL : Common Ground Research Networks, [2021] |
    Includes bibliographical references. | Summary: "This reader presents a
    collection of several essays highlighting different aspects of the urban
    condition. Contributions range from chapters that use literature to
    explore the city to chapters that focus on specific aspects like, for
    example, urban shopping malls or different types of maps that may be
    used to visualize structure and dynamic flows in the metropolitan
    context. It also contains chapters that critically discuss problematic
    trends including fortification and monitoring of urban space. The
    collection also includes chapters that deal with morphological questions
    related to urban growth and development. It also features contributions
    that focus on the urban poor and their experience of living in the city.
    This book is a great starting point to explore the metropolis and to
    critically reflect about specific challenges large urban agglomerations
    are facing in many parts of the world"-- Provided by publisher.
Identifiers: LCCN 2020050817 (print) | LCCN 2020050818 (ebook) | ISBN
    9780949313102 (hardback) | ISBN 9780949313119 (paperback) | ISBN
    9780949313126 (adobe pdf)
Subjects: LCSH: Urbanization--Social aspects. | Cities and towns--Social
    aspects. | Sociology, Urban.
Classification: LCC HT151 .M359 2021 (print) | LCC HT151 (ebook) | DDC
    307.76--dc23
LC record available at https://lccn.loc.gov/2020050817
LC ebook record available at https://lccn.loc.gov/2020050818

Cover Photo Credit: Phillip Kalantzis-Cope

Table of Contents

Chapter 1

Introduction: Exploring the Many Faces of the Metropolis

Stefan Litz

Introduction

When Goethe made his famous first trip to Italy in 1787, he stayed for several months in Rome. He was mainly interested in exploring what was for him the capital of the world and the capital of arts. But he was also enjoying socializing with various artists and bohemians *incognito*. Goethe was, for the most part of his stay in Rome, first and foremost simply an unknown nobody or stranger. In his book, reporting his journey and experience in Italy, Goethe (1992) highlighted that even an intellectually less sophisticated individual can thrive to some degree within the wide range of diverse circles and individuals in a large city. On the other hand, even the intellectually most sophisticated individual (and for sure he saw himself as such a person) cannot fully enjoy life in a small place where almost everyone knows everyone else. It is important to stress that Rome, at Goethe's time, was a relatively small city with no more than 100.000 inhabitants. However, during its heydays, centuries earlier in antiquity, Rome was already called home by more than one million individuals. Nevertheless, Rome was, in contrast to the tiny town of Weimar (where Goethe spend much of his life) an amazingly large city. For Goethe, and for so many other individuals after and before him, the urban environment creates a unique physical and social condition that makes it quite distinct from smaller and less densely settled places like towns and villages. The special socio-economic environment of the city was also reflected in a legal principle during the early medieval times that enabled serfs who ran away from their feudal lords to legally gain freedom after being able to stay (and survive) for one year and one day in a city. However, the *statutum in favorem principum* ("Statute in Favor of the Princes") officially ended this customary law for the territory of the Holy Roman Empire in 1231/32.

In any case, the large metropolis has fascinated people since centuries if not millennia as the cities first emerged to be the centers of commerce, science, learning, politics etc. The urban condition certainly has significantly changed over the centuries, the antique city and the medieval city looked very different, and (post)modern metropolitan life may be experienced once again very different by individuals and social groups that dwell in the cities of the world. The city has therefore many faces and this book provides a collection of some selected essays that shed light on the city while offering different perspectives. This book is supplementing a variety of existing readers that bundle selected articles dealing with the specifics of city life like, for example, the readers edited by Kasinitz (1994), Sorkin (1992), LeGats & Stouts (2016), Lin & Mele (2013), and Duneier et al. (2014). In the following part of this introduction, I will now briefly introduce the essays that are featured in this book and highlight their key arguments.

At the beginning of the book, two essays are discussing representations of the urban experience in literature. Marcella Livi employs Franz Kafka's famous depiction of space as an odd or strange experience of space, buildings and rooms. It is primarily the experience of physical barriers and mazes but also the development of mental barriers that are horrifying the individuals in the stories that Kafka was narrating. Livi focuses particularly on two books: Kafka's *The Process* and the *Wedding Preparations in the Country*. Modern city life experience is often, as Livi points out, faked and not real or distorted and perceived as twisted and frightening like the space and rooms depicted by Kafka. Livi also points out, that urban space is actually not a space that surrounds or envelopes humans but the ever moving human bodies (and one could add, other moving objects, too) are a central part of the dynamics of urban space and its perception. It is the uncertainty and unpredictability of what may happen in the ever changing public but also private space that characterizes much of modern urban city life. Of course, life is also unpredictable in rural communities but less so since individuals know each other and many proceed in their daily life with the same routines and take the same routes at the same time, like the philosopher Immanuel Kant was known to make his strolls always at the same time. What may seem to some a trusted space and a predictable experience of urban space may, in fact, turn out for others to be an unorthodox subjective experience of space and surfaces. In addition, the various "ghostly systems" that Kafka mentioned, interrupt communication and make it difficult if not impossible to establish reliable, solid or meaningful relationships. Ghostly systems were, at Kafka's time, the telegraph and the telephone as Livi points out and, today, they are machines that open the virtual realm that connects humans only indirectly. Already some hotels and motels exist where guests are unlikely to meet any staff as everything is managed by electronic systems. Robots and AI are the next versions of "ghostly systems" that we may encounter more frequently in the cities in this world. It is the fear of the unfamiliar and unpredictable that makes the experience of urban life so difficult and perhaps a haunting experience to some.

Kalpana Bora Barman and Rohini Mokashi-Punekar focus in their contribution on the experience of life in the city of Bombay (India). For this, they utilize Henry Lefebvre's concept of the social production of space that distinguishes between the three levels: "representations of space", "representational space" and "spatial practices". The different novels and narrations they employ to explore the social production of space highlight that, in the same physical space, a multiplicity of worlds may exist. In the first novel, written by Chandra, the underworld of Bombay is explored focusing on the experience of life in "kholi". "Kholi" are small shanty dwellings that are often illegally erected in slums or in derelict parts and hidden corners of the city where those who are living in the "underworld" attempt to create a somewhat "normal" life. But equally important to physical markers of space are verbal markers indicating that the speakers belong to different worlds. In addition to Chandra, the authors also discuss Shroff's collection of short stories *Breathless in Bombay*. The book narrates the life of individuals who have a hard time to economically survive around the "dhobi ghat". "Dhobi ghat" are the traditional laundry or washing areas in Bombay. The remark of the authors, that naming of streets, quarters etc. defines ownership and power and renders certain things and individuals visible and others invisible are highlighting subtle aspects of policing. Ranciere (1999), in fact, defines "police" widely as a term that includes any practices that helps to preserve the dominance of the establishment and suppresses alternative voices or renders the underclass "invisible".

Adishree Panda explores in her essay the practice and reality of "jugaad" in urban planning in India. The term "jugaad" is used in Hindi to label make-shift problem solutions relying on basic tools or material that need to be either free as they are recycled or very cheap. Panda is focusing on the urban poor and how they attempt to make a living with very limited means in the urban context in India. For example, a broken or non-existing shower head may be replaced by using a plastic water bottle that is connected to the water pipe with tape and has small holes on the bottom where the water will pour out. Even though anyone can use "jugaad" techniques at times, most likely they are the urban poor. Panda highlights that those techniques are reframed as innovative and useful techniques for urban planning – cheap material is being used or redeployed in order to accomplish an important task. These activities entail transformative powers that help to change the living conditions especially of the urban poor while requiring only minimal financial resources. Panda points out that, from a social justice perspective using Rawls (1971) theory of justice, urban planning needs to include "jugaad" activities as legitimate means to improve the urban living conditions. This will help that the urban poor and their needs will be better recognized, they and their needs will be better included in urban planning and they may participate more in the planning process and, finally, it will also help that some resources (even though very modest) will be better redistributed between the various social groups in the city.

Tommaso Durante's article looks at how the idea of the global citizen is being created or reinforced by displaying images that emphasize the global over the national and the local in the city. His contribution highlights the ideational component of the globalization process in an urban context. Durante is concerned with the question how the idea of creating the identity of a global citizenry is being shaped by images and slogans. Based on field research, he has created a repository of photos of images (images of images so to speak) from which several are printed in this book. Durante demonstrates how those images may help to reinforce the idea of an existing global social community and the identity of being world citizens. In this respect, Durante analyzes, for example, the "Globe Trotter" suitcase that seems to evoke the idea of belonging to the class of world citizens. Buying one of those suitcases demonstrates and expresses, for Durante, that the owner belongs to the wealthy and highly mobile class of the cosmopolitan or global citizens. In the urban context, according to Durante, whether those cities may be belonging to the network of the global cities (Sassen 2001) or not, the global imaginary is omnipresent and coexist with images and slogans that rather emphasize the local, regional or the national aspect of existence. Durante therefore sheds light on the various images and slogans that may influence our mental perception of urban life in many if not all cities around the world. Even though his contribution focuses on the "global message" that may be in contrast with the "local message", many other dichotomies could be identified that may be expressed by images and slogans in the urban context: messages of safety vs. fear, messages of progress vs. stagnation, messages of hope vs. resignation etc.

Nick Dunn argues in his essay that the city can be analyzed by focusing on various layers of information exchange that continuously occur in the "networked city" (Castells 2000) by looking at specific information flows. He points out that the evolution of the city from being a place with a single-center with clear boundaries, mostly created in ancient and medieval times and solidified by walls and other defense structures and fortifications, to the suburbanization that led to urban sprawl, resulted in a more fuzzy differentiation between the center and the periphery. Poly-centric large metropolitan structures eventually emerged and may be identified in many large cities around the globe. The contemporary polycentric physical reality in many cities is further differentiated by additional layers of a likewise polycentric virtual reality. Dunn calls them "networks of abstracted space" and provides some examples of how the virtual and the physical urban space (including the flow of information and other type of traffic) may be mapped. Dunn is, for example, discussing Lisa Jevbratt's visualization of internet traffic in cities in order to "disclose latent structures" as well as Stanza's maps of cities based on sound type and structure as well as their change over time in different parts of the city. The question is whether the everchanging various virtual layers and the physical layers of the city are structurally separate or are somehow integrated. Dunn argues that, whether separate or integrated, urban planners and analysts must focus on the "multi-layered landscape" of the city to better understand structure and dynamics.

Steven Nardi and Munehito Moro's article is also concerned with multilayers in cities and highlights the fact that, while focusing on Bejing in China as an example, many cities in the world may feature different maps depending on which historical time of the city one may focus on. For Beijing, they identify a first map that maps the remains of the classic imperial city while highlighting buildings and other structures that relate to the ancient imperial history of the city with, of course, the "forbidden city" in the center. The second map would highlight buildings and infrastructures of Beijing that were constructed during the time when it was the political center of Maoist China. It includes structures like, for example, the "Great Hall of the People". The third map of Beijing is based on highlighting its redevelopment as a capitalist postmodern city that includes infrastructure, parks and buildings like, for example, the

"Beijing National Stadium" or the "Bird's Nest". Referring to Edward Soja's notion of the "third space", the authors further point out that what we see today in Beijing (and really in many other cities around the world) and on the maps is actually a mélange of the real and the simulated. Many of the "historical" buildings are actually not the original structures but reconstructions of the original even though we are not (made) aware of this fact. For example, the damaged "Gate of Heavenly Peace" in Bejing was secretly reconstructed in the 1970 without anybody noticing it. One could add that, for example, much of the world famous Rothenburg o.d.T. in Germany, a global tourist destination, appears to be the renovated original medieval romantic town. In fact, the town was largely reconstructed after WW II due to heavy destructions. In any case, as Nardi and Moro point out, the three different maps related to the three different epochs of the city, and the real and simulated, are intertwined and create, in Zizek's terminology, a parallactic reality. Nardi and Moro highlight in their contribution further how these different maps and the "parallactic reality" of Beijing has been instrumentalized for the opening ceremony of the Olympic Games in Beijing in 2008.

Andrew Marton and Terry McGee's essay is also focusing on urban China but on rapid urbanization of large urban agglomerations on China's East coast. Next to providing a historical comparison of urbanization processes in a range of Asian countries that are categorized according to the rate of urbanization, the authors focus on the particular features and challenges of the urbanization in China. Marton and McGee balance their discussion of the negative impact this rapid urbanization had, including the destruction of fertile agricultural land in the delta area of Shanghai, with highlighting at the same time the government's response intended to limit and mitigate the negative developments. Marton and McGee apply the idea of "synergetic capital" proposed by Boshier (2001) in the context of rapid urbanization in China. The article discusses what each of the various types of capital (that are sub-categories of "synergetic capital") may imply for making and maintaining the mega urban agglomerations along the East Coast of China attractive places to live and work.

Maiciej Stasiowski's contribution is concerned with the role of cinematic as well as computer animated architectural and urban planning approaches for challenging the traditional architecture predominant at a specific point in time. Those means, like previously drawings on papers and models made by paper, enable the visualization of potential new and idealized buildings and other urban structure that may radically deviate from the existing architectural style. The various media permit, so Stasiowski, to contest the dominant architectural ideologies and ontology of an epoch by simulating the results of a new architecture and urban planning. It facilitates an alternative architectural discourse in the field. Linking those tools to literature on utopian thinking, like Thomas Moore and Campanella's visions of utopian cities, Stasiowski explores various cases of shorts and architectural urban movies in more detail. It includes Lynch's (1960) film *The Image of the City* and computer based digital rendering like Matsuda's *Augmented City 3D*. Stasiowski points out that in all those simulations, flow and dynamic elements have become more important features than stability and the static component of architecture. He concludes that those tools permit planners and builders to create better mental images of the spaces that are to be built in the future.

Daniel Pasciuti's contribution is also focusing on urban development while providing a critical discussion of Zipf's law that explains the development or growth patterns of cities. The author's main argument stresses that deviations from the size development of urban settlements as predicted by Zipf's law need not be seen as a sign of disorder or anomaly but may rather be interpreted as reflecting a normal alternative development pattern. Pasciuti highlights that, instead of exclusively focusing on strict hierarchical development patterns and structures, alternative development patterns also need to be considered normal development alternatives. Discussing hierarchical and heterarchical development structures in more detail, Pasciuti is contrasting the urban development in the UK with the development in the Netherlands. While urban development in the UK clearly follows the hierarchical development pattern as per Zipf's law, the latter stands for a more heterarchical pattern of urban growth. In other words: urban development is not only following the predicted distribution pattern of city size development according to Zipf's law. Empirical oddities that may not fit into the assumptions and conclusions of the growth model embedded in Zipf's law do not need to be explained away but they may constitute alternative urban growth patterns.

Nina Toleva's chapter is likewise concerned with the development of urban structures and growth and transformation of cities. In her article, however, she zooms into the microstructure of the city and identifies different types of cores and rings around those cores as well as different types of relationships between those cores and their spheres of influence. Next to the central-urban core, intra-urban cores and peri-urban cores exist that may resemble either areal, linear or circular structures. Each of those cores in poly-centric cities are impacting their surrounding areas either in a positive or negative or in a neutral manner. Therefore, they may either be a magnet of attraction or a place that needs to be avoided or a neutral territory. Based on a range of detailed assumptions and some observations from fieldwork, Toleva proposes a formula that can be employed in order to quantitatively specify the interactions between those different urban cores in any urban agglomeration. Even though that model may not yet have been completely refined, as Toleva points out, it is a useful tool to quantify interconnectivities and their changes over time as a city or metropolitan area develops.

Nuray Özaslan's contribution to this reader focuses on large shopping centers and highlights how these transform the experience of public space in large cities and, in fact, the whole urban experience for locals. Her article highlights, referring back to Lefebvre's book *The Production of Space*, that capitalism tends to transform space into a commodity and redefines it as a territory that has economic utility either as a space for the production, transportation or consumption of commercialized goods. Özaslan focuses specifically on the development of large shopping centers that become ubiquitous features of large cities around the world. Often, those shopping centers are located at the edge of the city and are surrounded by large parking lots or, better, manicured parks. These (post)modern shopping malls are not simply offering the opportunity to buy products that are necessary, but they create a whole new type of shopping experience. Shopping becomes redefined as a enjoyable event rather than being an unpleasant but necessary activity. Next to vacations and cultural activities, shopping in those malls have likewise an event character. Özaslan points out that while these large, modern shopping centers are private properties, they appear to be public space since they resemble or mimic public space. Yet, at the same time, they are closely monitored and staffed with security guards to ensure that the shopping event will not be disturbed or interrupted by unpleasant events. Özaslan's article does particularly look at four of such large modern shopping centers that have been recently built in Istanbul. Istanbul is by far Turkey's largest city with currently more than 14 Mio. inhabitants and arguably belongs to the network of "global cities" (Sassen 2001). Özaslan points out that inner cities may become, as a result of the proliferation of those large (post)modern shopping malls that offer a safe and clean experience at the edge of the city, less frequented by the local population for shopping.

Timothy Stanley discusses the topic of monitoring of space (that also Özaslan highlighted for shopping malls) while looking at the contemporary use of surveillance in the urban setting in what he coins the "Disneysized city". Stanley relates his essay to Bentham's and Foucault's theory of the panopticon that leads to self-discipline and self-control. In the past, as he argues, the principle of surveillance was only applied to monitor prison inmates, sick and infected, workers, or individuals send to concentration camps. The emergence of the urban Disney city however, exactly reversed the situation. Stanley's main argument is that today rather the affluent areas with its glittering high-rise towers and gated communities, occupied by the rich, wealthy, and healthy, are extensively monitored. Fear of terror, crime, diseases etc. that may threaten the urban and suburban paradises of the leisure class brings individuals to voluntarily submit themselves to permanent surveillance. But this has some hidden costs, as Stanley points out, since the sanitized and purified ghettos for the rich and wealthy are nothing but only a simulacrum of safety and normality and consumerism.

Stefan Litz's contribution at the end of the book also is related to the topic of fear and monitoring and zooms in on the development of modern types of urban fortifications that are prevalent in many countries but are rapidly proliferating in the USA. Many homeowners rely on private security services and many prefer to live in gated communities or fortified urban condominiums that are designed to provide enhanced security and safety to their inhabitants. This article provides an overview of the development of gated communities and other types of modern urban fortifications in the USA and argues that other countries may follow suit as their socio-economic conditions may eventually mirror the situation existing in the United States of America. Many traditional defense structures like town walls, towers etc. were razed in the late 19th century in many towns and cities in continental Europe. Such fortifications were thought to be no longer needed or practical and, in fact, increasing wealth and the emerging and eventually blossoming welfare state ensured that crime against property and life remained relatively low in Europe. In the USA, once colonialization and submission of the first nations was completed, and a relatively powerful federal state and government had emerged, forts and fortifications were also deemed to be no longer necessary. The desire to refortify space to assure the safety of property and physical integrity reemerged though with increasing fear of crime and violence especially in many urban areas in the US. Similar trends that focus on fortifications can be identified in other urban agglomerations around the globe as well. This is a very problematic and worrying development and as pointed out in the article. Walls are only the second-best option to ensure physical integrity. The best option is to ensure that all citizens have sufficient means to maintain a decent lifestyle and to make for the majority of the population access to weapons impossible or difficult.

Even though all the selected essays collected in this reader approach the metropolis from various perspectives and employ different theoretical frameworks and research methods, they all have one purpose in common: they intend to help the reader to better understand some of the many faces of the city. Far from being comprehensive or exhaustive, almost needless to say, the selected articles are intended to stimulate interest to further explore the *conditio urbana* by consulting additional literature that may adopt other conceptual and theoretical lenses and/or focus on other aspects of the urban experience. I am confident that all the articles in this book will be thought provocative and help readers to better understand what it means to live in an urbanized society.

REFERENCES

Boshier, S. 2001. "Territorial Development and the Contribution of Synergetic Capital: A Contribution to the Discussion on the Intangibility of Development." In *New Forms of Regional Development Paradigms*, edited by Asfaw Kumssa, and Terry G. McGee, 17–32. London: Greenwood Press.

Duneier, Mitchell, Philip Kasinitz, and Alexandra Murphy (eds.). 2014. *The Urban Ethnography Reader.* Oxford: Oxford University Press.

Goethe, Johann Wolfgang. Ed. 1992. *Italian Journey: 1786–1788.* Translated by W. H. Auden and Elizabeth Mayer. London et al.: Penguin.

Kasinitz, Philip (ed.). 1994. *Metropolis. Center and Symbol of Our Times.* New York: New York University Press.

LeGuts, Richard T. and Frederic Stout (eds.). 2015. *The City Reader.* London et al: Routledge

Lin, Jan and Christopher Mele (eds). 2012. *The Urban Sociology Reader.* London et al.: Routledge.

Ranciere, Jacques. 1999. *Disagreement.* Minneapolis: University of Minnesota Press.

Sassen, Saskia. 2001. *The Global City: New York, London, Tokyo.* Princeton: Princeton University Press.

Sorkin, Michael. Ed. 1992. *Variations on a Theme Park: The New American City and the End of Public Space.* New York: Hill and Wang.

Chapter 2

Walking in Kafka's Space Boots: Questions of Mobility and Stability in a Modern Landscape[1]

Marcella Livi

> "Our period demands a type of man who can restore the lost equilibrium between inner and outer reality. This equilibrium, never static but, like reality itself, involved in continuous change, is like that of a tightrope dancer who, by small adjustments, keeps a continuous balance between his being and empty space."

Sigfried Giedion[2]

Introduction

In the above quote Sigfried Giedion's words reflect the spatial complications that are pertinent to our present inquest into Kafkaesque spaces as related to our everyday perception and usage of space. As the word Kafkaesque has been greatly used, overused, and to a certain degree abused, I will use this expression sparingly as I try to connect it most of all to space and its importance within our world through a literary Kafkan lens.

Franz Kafka's vertiginous universe tells us about the haunting struggles with which ordinary men are confronted. In their existential framework, these battles are frequently bound up with spatial inadequacies and spatialized problem formations in the characters' paths. Persecuted by an invisible and to a certain degree unknown authority, the protagonists are chased through public and private landscapes, which are interwoven with the omnipresence and omnipotence of a greater structure of surveillance. Here, we are reminded of Foucault and his everyday places that fall

---

[1] This chapter is an edited version of the essay "Walking in Kafka's Space Boots: Questions of Mobility and Stability in a Modern Landscape" first published in *Spaces and Flows: An International Journal of Urban and Extra Urban Studies* 2 (4): 93-100.

[2] Qtd. In Vidler,alking in Kaf Anthony. *Warped Space.* (Cambridge Massachusetts: The MIT Press, 2001), 50/51.

under this type of observation; schools, jails, and today perhaps even offices with their cubicle structure designed to instill a sense of self-observation. In this paper, I will investigate the ways in which Kafka's unlikely heroes, specifically from the novel *The Trial,* and from his fragmentary novella *Wedding Preparations in the Country* process space throughout their search for something beyond their surface existence. It is during this process that the characters appear to alter the original spatial coordinates according to their movements and travels. Thanks to Stanley Corngold we know that in Kafka it is experience that catches fire, ice, and everything in between (Corngold 2011, 10). It is experience in itself that takes precedence over the individual. In fact, Kafka's characters are most frequently found to be *blank* in their identities and in their presumed agency. What never remains unelaborated are the trajectories embarked upon by the women and men that populate Kafka's literary landscapes; the experience, though seemingly disconnected from the characters is what carries not only the characters but also the reader on a wave of multiple realities that are forced to co-exist. We can detect Kafka's deep skepticism about modernity and perhaps its claim to a type of reconciliation of varying truths. "Mitmenschen"[3] in Kafka often turn out to be "Gegenmenschen". Interplays between exterior and interior properties often take place and they lead to all kinds of difficulties for the characters that are caught up in Kafka's dizzying universe. Many exceptional critics have written extensively on the struggle brought about by the dissonance between the internal and the external in Kafka's fiction. Stanley Corngold, Mark Anderson, Walter Benjamin, and Theodor Adorno are amongst the authors that I will refer to. Mark Anderson's *Kafka's Clothes*, for example, brilliantly focuses on the link between the characters' clothes and the connection the clothes provide to reality as well as to the historical and cultural perception thereof. Benjamin examines the existential fragmentation of the modern city-dweller brought about the modern city's architecture and distribution of space. This paper will then attempt to highlight not only the physical realms of Kafka's characters and their significance but it will also shift attention from the characters to the perceived existence of the characters' journeys. Throughout this essay I will provide links between Kafka's portrayals of spatial dilemmas and our own functioning in space. Franz Kafka's spatial imageries, in many ways, anticipated the psychological and physical structures that make up our world today.

At the core of my analysis is the assumption that the inconsistent relation between the characters and their spatial connections unequivocally manifests existential complications; this very notion is something that has persisted throughout modernity and even today, perhaps on a grander scale. Looking at Kafka's works may enable us to uncover present-day glitches in our spatial interactions. The conflicts of his protagonists may bring us closer to a smoother understanding of our mobility and stability in today's ever changing technological and geographical environment.

---

[3] "Mitmenschen" are people with whom we co-exist while the definition of "Gegenmenschen" comes close to the meaning of antagonists.

Travelling Through Surfaces

When analyzing Kafka's texts, it is important to pay attention to the texture of his literature. Unlike authors such as Thomas Mann, Kafka's literary style is space- rather than word-oriented. This can be seen not only in the very language he uses, but especially in the filmic portrayals of his characters' dire circumstances. We find a narrative that is spatially aggressive towards the reader and the characters. The storylines of Kafka's works shift the reader's attention from the internal dealings of the characters to their travels and paths. Kafka nudges his reader's interest towards a spatial legibility that ranges from the smallest of spaces to entire cities. The spatial depictions on which I will concentrate in the next few pages underline the *surfaces* and the surface encounters that they produce. But in his characteristic habit of perverting commonly accepted norms Kafka flips standard readings of what space should be and pushes not only his characters but also the reader over the border of generally believed spatial readabilities. As Mark Anderson remarks, Kafka's work portrays the world as a mere surface apparition without any irrevocable truth that "would ground it as a permanent reality" (Anderson 1991, 43). Hence, by infusing a superficial understanding of the modern space in his stories Kafka highlights the forcedly superficial aspect of the artfulness, or *fakeness,* that dominates the places that his characters cross. In connection to artfulness and our own saturation with movies and films we should consider Herman G. Scheffauer's claims:

> Space hitherto considered and treated as something dead and static, a mere inert screen or frame, often of no more significance than the painted balustrade-background at the village photographer's has been smitten into life, into movement and conscious expression (Vidler 2001, 102p).

And so, though what is referred to here is film, the argument still pertains to Kafka's texts as the influence of filmic elements dominate his writing. In fact, what we find in the connection between film and Kafka's representations is something quite contemporary; we discover another link to our movie-dominated and spatially determined societal structure that in many ways shapes the way in which we exist. What I mean by 'movie-dominated' is this: we are frequently subjected to images and spatial set-ups through the visual media. As a result, we are influenced by filmic elements and perhaps internalize various features that are then propagated in our every-day existence. Considering the visual, and to some degree, the inherently superficial aspects of art we can easily loop back to the notion of surfaces and the connected surface encounters that prevail in a modern and contemporary reality. Such encounters are beautifully depicted in the chosen selections of Kafka's stories. Further, we must consider movement and the strain involved in traversing Kafka's interpretatively skewed landscapes. As challenging and difficult as these spaces may be we may come to recognize much of our own trials in the paths taken by the displaced bodies of Kafkan characters who in turn de-territorialize other bodies. Let us then explore the notion of *Raumgefühl*[4] as linked to movement and existence. We shall begin with *The Trial* and *Wedding Preparations in the Country.*

Pierced Space

Perhaps one of Kafka's best-known novels, *The Trial* is a beautiful example of distorted space. The spatial configuration that plays a central role in *The Trial* is the very concept of the *room.* By this, I do not intend one very specific room but rather the notion that life-changing and defining things happen in partitioned, confined places. These confined places are however also part of a grander architectural framework that signifies much more than plainly visible walls and ceilings. In K.'s situation, for example, it implies much more than the scope of a mere trial. Space is all enveloping and may not have his personal scopes in mind when it is shaped and in turn shapes. When Henri Lefebvre writes that, "Architecture produces living bodies, each with its own distinctive traits, " (Lefebvre 1991, 137) we must wonder not only about the characters that Kafka's protagonists encounter, but also how their relationships transform or change the space around them. In K.'s example, we may wonder about how those relationships make him an outsider once he is positioned face to face with the law. Along those very lines, we can see how our daily spatial meetings and battles come to potentially position us inside as much as outside of our own fate. Lefebvre's question of whether space occupied by a specific group of people can be treated as a message resonates as focal for our present inquiry into Kafka's works and today's space. The bodies that are within occupied space also make up that space and shape it according to their experience. What message do our daily ventures seek to transmit through a selected architecture? For K., we must look into the dark chambers of the court to further pursue this question. Yet again, we must remember that bodies create space and govern motion at the same time (Lefebvre 1991, 171). They are spatial messengers whose roles are tightly linked to the functionality of the places that K. crosses. The presence of the characters in relation to K. serves as a representative tie for the opaque communicative pipelines that the law utilizes to impose its will. In this mental frame of reference, bodies and space can be said to be vital to each other's existence.

Within this context, let us look at the Occupy Wall Street example. The demonstrators used their bodies not to complement the space they were in; quite the contrary. They used their bodies for space-shaping purposes, for the determination of being visible in a specific location. The demonstrators intended to lend their cause purpose by changing the original meaning of the street. They did not need to speak, they had *space.* In fact, their location evolved into a city-like venue saturated with meaning. We find occasions of this type throughout *The Trial*, beginning in K.'s

---

[4] *Raumgefühl* can be described as the ability to properly find one's bearings in space.

bedroom that is transformed into a prison through the mere presence of the unwanted wardens. The Occupy Wall Street example also points to something which does not always seep through in Kafka's stories: Space is promiscuous, which means that the victim or perpetrator of a system may gain the upper hand by properly maneuvering through it. The importance of the body or bodies in the novel and for our present objective cannot be overestimated; they produce and are produced by the dire architectural structures, which they inhabit. We may even claim that space is really an extension of the body, constructing its walls and ceilings in accordance to the bodies they fill. Again, we are reminded of K.'s intimate quarters that are invaded and taken over by the wardens, who do not hesitate to occupy the room and impose new physical regulations on K. K. is appalled by the penetration of his private space and he equates this infraction to violence on his own body. What we frequently find in Kafka's texts is precisely this: a violation of personal space.

Let us now consider Kafka's fragmentary novella *Wedding Preparations in the Country* where the looming act of travelling provokes angst and discomfort for the protagonist, Eduard Raban. In addressing travelling, we will quite evidently tackle spatial movement and Kafka's feared speed with which transportation methods work. Speed, being one of our most important themes for Kafka's characters, is a chronic subject in other works and one that deserves to be looked at for our current purposes. Franz Kafka himself once stated that human beings are caught between different types of influential technological systems: one that is 'natural', and the other that is 'ghostly' (Zilosky 2011, 179). By 'natural' methods he refers to trains, and automobiles; machines that would allow significant others to see each other within a few hours. By 'ghostly' means he refers to telegraphs and telephoning. Kafka himself dreaded trains and stuck to writing letters. This brief biographical piece of information should resonate well when examining the current novella in the context of how Kafkan space-traversing approaches echo our own. In connection to this, scholars such as Aby Warburg have claimed that space-conquering methods brought about through technological progress may actually efface any chance of having a stable distance for reflection, for the treasured *Denkraum* (Vidler 2001, 48p). By space eroding techniques, Warburg specifically thinks of cars, planes, telephones, etc. The speed of the train seemed excessive to many living during Franz Kafka's time. Raban, for example, despises the noises caused by the train's rapidity and the effects that the violent vibrations have on his body. In fact, psychiatrists of Kafka's time frequently reported 'train-diseases' which meant that the train's motions on individuals were felt so deeply by travelers that people would continue to shake and tremble in their sleep even after their trip had ended (Zilosky 2011, 181). Looking at the natural methods of movement further reveals the communicative fragmentation experienced by modern means of travelling. Much like our protagonist Raban, we may find it difficult to establish meaningful connections in our fast-paced environments. In Raban's experience the passengers on the train come and go depending on their stops. This makes it tremendously difficult for Raban to satisfy his need for interpersonal communication. Thus, we can say that the method of travelling by train offers a distinct personal exit or entrance to individuals seeking to change their location. This passage also exemplifies surfaces of a personal kind. What I mean by this is that Raban's prepared opening to a potential conversation is nothing more than small talk, the most superficial form of interpersonal communication, and one that we engage in quite frequently. The surface encounters throughout the novel are not simply spatial but also reflect the psychological fabric woven through the collective consciousness of the time. If we think of our own travels on airplanes or trains, we can find similar struggles as Raban. We may converse for a few hours with our seat neighbor, but our conversations are forcedly kept superficial.

In Kafka's works we find a preoccupation with a reality that subtracts human agency and places a focus on the malleability of physical arrangements. The people in Raban's city, for example, are described as "Blendscheiben", they are reflective discs mirroring the lights from the stores. In this account we can envision people as blank objects that exist in order to reflect the spatial clues thrown at them by their environment. In fact, throughout the story we are offered words portraying surfaces to explain the world in which Raban lives (examples would be Gate, Wall, 'Blendscheiben', Mosaik, to only name a few). The representation of Raban's world is one of surfaces and surface encounters. Kafka's description of Raban's city offers a link to our world of appearances, to the usage of our advanced 'ghostly' means. And so, though Kafka may have feared physical means of connecting more than the cited 'ghostly' methods, we should zoom in on the forms that those 'ghostly' measures have taken on today. Social Media and the Internet in general come to mind. In these virtual worlds space is penetrated in an oftentimes-involuntary manner, and the thinking process is also abbreviated and distorted, allowing for almost no direct communication but plenty of indirect contact. This unfortunate product of online interaction gives its users entry into an unsettling sort of space, a place where no one truly has control over the information that is propagated, a place where pictures become the property of an invisible force. K.'s dilemma is quite similar to this situation; not only does he not understand where the accusations against him come from, he also lives in an architectural environment that provokes general unease and a feeling of uncanniness. We are reminded of the attempt Eduard Raban makes when he ponders sending his fiancée a telegram instead of physically travelling to her. We can thus assume that 'ghostly' means cuts away not only the obvious physical meeting of two persons but also the responsibility one feels towards another human being. In fact, the unavoidable encounter and direct communication he would have to face causes Raban to feel uneasy. In the end, Raban travels to his fiancée only to experience physical unease on the train.

Critical thinkers such as Freud, Todorov, and others have explored uncanny encounters and spatial structures. Freud in particular pointed to the spatial structuring of our mental lives, therewith facilitating the translation and interpretation of visual stimuli. Thus, we may ask: Does architecture establish not only physical but also mental boundaries, and should its goal be to help overcome them?

Uncanny Architecture

In his influential and literarily inspired essay, Sigmund Freud writes that the advantage of the writer over real life is that of intensification of emotions and sensations, this applying in particular to the Uncanny.

Nothing could be truer of Kafka's texts. While presenting us with familiar ideas and structures that are undoubtedly easily recognizable, he infuses his characters' environments with trickery attached to spatial disorientation. Intellectual uncertainty in connection to outside orientation can bring about a number of spatial fears and anxieties. It can also arouse more internal struggles when it comes to dealing with the ability to properly negotiate one's surroundings. The Uncanny is such a feeling of spatial unease. Tvetan Todorov also critically engages the Uncanny in his examination of the Fantastic. He describes it as something, which creates supernatural fear, but it is something that can be explained away with the help of scientific knowledge. In other words, the Uncanny is the Supernatural *explained* (Todorov 1975, 42). Freud's and Todorov's definitions of the Uncanny may not be mutually exclusive; actually, they both point to one of our main issues at hand: they both point towards a similar struggle with outside components that simply do not match one's intuitive and psychological compass. Disorientation and anything associated with spatial inadequacy also threads a direct line to the sensation felt when the Uncanny presents itself. In Franz Kafka's *The Trial* the Uncanny is everywhere. The sites of action are also the sites of fear and discomfort; they are places where communication breaks down and the Uncanny is diffused. When thinking of the Uncanny, I believe that Social Media Sites also have the effect of spatial disorientation.

Another spatial structure that we should address within the context of the Uncanny is *the house*. Let us remember Edgar Allen Poe's "The Fall of the House of Usher", and the dread that the author imbued into the home, a person's alleged safe haven. Anthony Vidler describes it as having a "veritable absence of overt terror" which creates the effect of "disturbing unfamiliarity with the evidently familiar" (Vidler 1992, 18). The description of Poe's work strikes a chord in relation to Kafka's novel. The settings and constructions should all be well familiar to K. at least on a cognitive level. But against all reason, he finds himself disoriented and ill at ease. A vivid example of this is the 'court-town', which may be construed as more of a ghost town. Once K. is at the hall where his trial is to be conducted, he finds himself in a Lewis Carroll-like world; the ceilings are unbearably low so that whoever is in the room bumps his head and has to curve his back along the ceiling. The place where K.'s fate is to be decided is terribly uncomfortable, a place intent on clouding judgment it would seem. Thus, the very thing so crucial to K. to win the trial is denied him. Not only that; through the obstructive rooms yet open doors through which K. walks, the communication to his fellow humans is rendered complicated and indirect. If we think of some current structure that many of us deal with every day we may think of the stunting cubicles that many working people are confined to; the walls are too short to grant us privacy, yet too tall to allow for a communal sense of being.

What happens to K. is then not only a modern dilemma but also a contemporary one. "The ordinary man is trapped in the common fate" (Certeau 1988, 2) of lies and deceit, and misery. In fact, according to Freud the ordinary man's fate is indeed to be duped, frustrated, and forced into labor, thus finding himself subject to the laws of dishonesty and despair (Freud 2010). Few are the intellectual open escape routes and this representative everyday man yields to the misapprehension that he should be able to solve all mysteries in life under the protective wing of providence. The everyday positioning of the modern man sets the stage for our arena, the arena through which Kafka brilliantly enacts spatial unease as tied to existential obstacles. It is only through the ordinary staging of man that uncanny effects can be successfully produced.

Conclusion

To conclude this paper, I would like to point to the various levels of discourse that we have covered in the previous pages. I have illustrated various types of space that all interact with one another and are crucial to our perception of the world. Our discussion on Social Media can show the creation of entirely new spaces that are not physical yet just as present. To further investigate virtual spaces and add onto this present analysis it would be interesting to consider more virtual worlds, such as Second Life. The example of the Occupy Wall Street Movement may exemplify how spatial elements can lead to the politicized reception of space. Renowned scholars such as Walter Benjamin (2002) and Theodor Adorno have rightly interwoven Marxist readings into Kafka's fiction, focusing in particular on the position of the bourgeoisie within changing forms of space.[5] And though is it easy to see how Kafka's texts lend themselves well for this purpose, I intended to also place special emphasis on the spatial positioning of the internal/external existence against a modern and contemporary backdrop.

---

[5] As elaborated by Walter Benjamin in *The Arcades Project.*

REFERENCES

Anderson, Mark. 1992. *Kafka's Clothes: Ornament and Aestheticism in the Habsburg Fin de Siècle.* Oxford: Clarendon Press.

Anthony Vidler. 1992. *The Architectural Uncanny.* Cambridge Massachusetts: The MIT Press.

Benjamin, Walter 2002. *The Arcades Project.* Belknap Press, Mass.

Corngold, Stanley. 2011. "Special Views on Kafka's Cages." In: *Freedom and Confinement in Modernity: Kafka's Cages*, 10, edited by. Kiarina Kordela and Dimitris Vardoulakis. New York: Palgrave Macmillan.

Lefebvre, Henri. 1991. *The Production of Space.* trans. Donald Nicholson-Smith Oxford: Blackwell.

Michel De Certeau. 1988. *The Practice of Everyday Life.* Berkeley and Los Angeles: The California University Press.

Sigmund Freud. 2010. *Civilization and its Discontents.* New York: W.W. Norton & Company.

Tvetan Todorov. 1975. *The Fantastic.* Ithaca: Cornell University Press.

Vidler, Anthony. 2000. *Warped Space: Art, Architecture, and Anxiety in Modern Culture.* Cambridge, Mass.: MIT Press.

Vidler, Anthony. 2001. *Warped Space.* Cambridge, Mass.: The MIT Press.

Zilkosky, John. 2011. "Samsa war Reisender: Trains, Trauma, and the Unreadable." In *Kafka for the Twenty-First Century*, 179- 206, edited by Stanley Corngold and Ruth Gross. New York: Camden House.

Chapter 3

'Maximum City[1]': Bombay, Spatial Politics, and Representation[2]

Kalpana Bora Barman & Rohini Mokashi-Punekar

> *If you want to live in the city you have to think ahead three turns and look behind a lie to see the truth and then behind the truth see the lie[3].*

Introduction

In the current era of global truths, postcolonial geographies are often in conflict with the global history of the city. Bombay[4], the *locus classicus* of Indian modernity and the Indian equivalent of the global city, is defined by spatial and temporal ambivalence owing to multiple and visible disparities in the socio-cultural and economic fabric of the city. Such fragmentation of the city is further heightened by the recent surge of identity politics, communal riots and urban economic inequalities. Contemporary Bombay enjoys the status of being the most advanced and developed city of India, but the city's 'modernity' contains within itself many contrasts and contradictions. Yet, despite all, the many spaces of this vibrant city are united by their existence in a single space—Bombay/Mumbai[5].

This paper is concerned with the examination and understanding of urban space in contemporary Bombay and the representation of the same in contemporary Indian Fiction in English. Among the many existing narratives on Bombay, Vikram Chandra's colossal saga of crime, *Sacred Games* (2006) and Murzbaan Shroff's

---

[1] The term has been borrowed from Suketu Mehta's book of the same name published in 2004.
[2] This chapter is an edited version of the essay "'Maximum City: Bombay, Spatial Politics, and Representations" first published in *Spaces and Flows: An International Journal of Urban and Extra Urban Studies* 1 (3): 151-166.
[3] p. 32. Chandra, Vikram. 2006. Sacred Games. New Delhi: Penguin. Henceforth, all references are from this edition unless indicated otherwise.
[4] The paper uses the name 'Bombay' over 'Mumbai' to maintain continuity besides attempting to showcase the trajectory of the city growth.
[5] 'Bombay/Mumbai' has been obligated to indicate the inherent conflicts and contradictions that are contained within the city.

collection of urban tales titled *Breathless in Bombay* (2008) are two texts that locate Bombay in its contemporary moment of globalized realities. Both texts are layered accounts of this vivacious yet visceral city, narrated through a comprehensive selection of characters and incidents that exemplify the diversities inherent in this multi-ethnic, hybrid city. Using Henri Lefebvre's theory of the 'production of space' and supported by sociological readings of the city, the paper will attempt to understand Chandra and Shroff's narration of the city as alternatives to the overwhelming tale of globalization. The first section of the paper focuses on the history of Bombay, while the second section attempts to negotiate a framework of analysis by highlighting the idea of the city in India, its conflicts and contradictions. It also focuses on the Lefebvrian theory of space that provides the theoretical framework to examine the spatial representations of Bombay. The third and fourth sections discuss the selected texts within the negotiated framework, and the final section sums up the paper and its arguments.

Production of Social Space in Bombay

The last decade of the twentieth century witnessed Bombay experience a tremendous socio-political upheaval in the wake of the communal riots in 1992-93[6] which resulted in the dissolution of the city's iconic status as the cosmopolitan hub of India[7]. Consequently, Bombay then emerged as the locus for much urban and literary scholarship, a trend reiterated by the very recent episode of 26/11[8]. The multiplicitious temperament of Bombay is an interesting point of departure to discuss the ways in which this South Asian city differs from the otherwise established readings of the city at large. In their Introduction to the book *Theorizing the South Asian City: Urban Landscapes, Cultural Documents and Interpretive Experiences* (2003, 3) Robbie Goh and Brenda Yeoh argue that "micropolitical and historical factors create urbanisms that are finely inflected and nuanced" so that the South Asian city is a "rich terrain of complexities produced in the cities of the region where culture and history intersect with power, politics and policy in myriad and often dialectical ways". In the context of India, the idea of the city was largely the outcome of anti-colonial nationalist thought[9]. In his essay "Are Indian Cities Becoming Bourgeois at

---

[6] On 12th March 1993 Bombay witnessed a series of explosions that enveloped the city in terror and destruction. Prior to this that city was one of the key centres of communal riots of 1992, which were offshoots of the Ram Janambhoomi-Babri Masjid episode in Ayodhya. The riots and blasts remain a bloody chapter in the history of the Bombay, the memories of which continue to affect the city even today.
[7] S. Hussain Zaidi's *Black Friday* is another pioneering book that chronicles the exhaustive police investigation of the March 12, 1993, bombings in Bombay. Interestingly, Vikram Chandra dedicates *Sacred Games* to Zaidi.
[8] Bombay was once again attacked by terrorists on 26th November 2008. In popular imagination this was the city's very own 9/11.
[9] The struggle for Indian independence was pivoted on the city. While the village was seen as a counter to the city where traditional ideals were upheld, the city itself became the site for the enactment of nationalist

Last?" Partha Chatterjee claims that the modern Indian city was bereft of normative specificities primarily because of the "perceived lack of agency by the Indian elite in thinking about the city" so that the industrial city of the colonizers was "unquestionably a creation of western modernity" (John et al. 119). He claims that there has never been any organic imagination of the desired, modern Indian city, thus leaving it bereft of normative specificities. In *The Idea of India* Sunil Khilnani argues that post-independence Indian cities have become "bloated receptacles for every hope and frustration reared by half a century of free politics and exceedingly constrained and unequal economic progress" (Khilnani 1997, 109). Objectified as the edifice of modernity via television and cinema, cities are now "places where the idea of India is being disputed and defined anew" (Khilnani 1997, 109) and Bombay exemplified this universal desire for modernity with explicit sophistication (Khilnani 1997, 136). The centrality of this city thus prompts a series of questions about the ways in which the dominant discourses of this particular city were made possible. For Vyjayanthi Rao the answer lies in the fact that Bombay defines the terminal conditions of modernity in India[10]. Yet, the history of Bombay does not fit into the institutional depictions of the city. Constructed by colonial ideology, reshaped by nationalist thought, and pulled in opposing directions by the global economy, Bombay has been both a site of imperialist imposition as well as a source of indigenous power. This city, Sujata Patel[11] points out, "symbolized the paradigm associated with achievements of colonial and post-colonial India both in the economic and cultural spheres" (Patel 1995, 3).

Urban life, experience and culture have always been irreducibly multiple. Contemporary theories on postmodern geography[12] have continued to contest the established models of the city to ascertain the multiplicitous nature of urban space. This critical trajectory has proven to be of prime importance in comprehending specific subject responses to the urban as in the case of feminist and post-colonial responses. Urban space evolves and changes constantly resulting in the recognition of new descriptive models and metaphors. Christine Boyer, in her book *The City of Collective Memory* argues that as urban space continues to change and evolve, the city becomes knowable through fresh metaphors and spatial paradigms:

> [T]he city has been re-presented in different ways: that is, different structural logics—call them aesthetic conventions—have been imposed for various

---

politics. Colonial power was rooted in the city, and Gandhi believed that colonial rule would meet its end if the cities could be brought to a standstill.

[10] Rao, Vyjayanthi. 2006. "Risk and the City: Bombay, Mumbai and other Theoretical Departures." India Review. 5 (2). Accessed August 7, 2009 https://www.files.ethz.ch/isn/19242/Rao_2005-08.pdf

[11] In her essay "Bombay and Mumbai: Identities, Politics and Populism" (1995) Sujata Patel traces the history of Bombay as well as its many avatars. She identifies the city as one of promise and possibilities despite its obvious and overwhelming problems.

[12] Postmodern geographers like Edward Soja, David Harvey and Michael Dear argue for the examination of the newly emerging urban spatialities that are inherent in the postmodern city of centrelessness.

reasons and at separate times upon the city's imagined (imaged) form. Every discourse sets up a spatial order, a frozen image that captures the manner in which the transitory present is perceived. Momentarily arresting disruptive and energetic forces, representational forms become succinct records of what we consider to be the present reality. These aesthetic models transform our sense of the real, for the image of the city is an abstracted concept, an imaginary, constructed form. (Boyer 1996, 32)

The city, Boyer suggests, has moved through three aesthetic models, which correspond to the city's response to the stages of capitalism: the city as work of art, framed and presented as a 'closed and unified spatial order', as panorama, a 'bird's eye perspective that request deciphering and reordering' and finally, the centreless postmodern city of spectacle, which has no subject and motive force behind its accepted fragmentation (Boyer 1996, 32-5). Such formulations of the contemporary cityscape are complementary to disorientating experience of postmodern spatiality. The overwhelming material reality of the city, the quality which James Joyce described as 'cityful' in *Ulysses* (1968) leads to the familiar image of the restless, changing, unknowable city. In the work of the writers that this paper discusses, the city of Bombay appears in many guises: some familiar from the historical images of the city and some newly generated in response to the specific challenges of the postmodern city. The megapolis, with its constantly changing and shifting population, multifaceted appearance and plural temporality embedded in the built environment, is unknowable. Terms such as 'flux', illegibility and chaos have become a commonplace way of describing what is essentially a new 'sense of place', even if this is paradoxically a sense of a *loss* of place.

Urban space can be comprehended and contested by different forms of its representation. For Henri Lefebvre, the analysis of space has been divided by philosophical concepts of spatiality that insist on the distinction between abstract and metaphysical space and 'real' or lived space. Lefebvre's *The Production of Space* reflects on the production of such spaces. Spatial imaginary is premised on hybrid spatialities, i.e. spaces emerging from different orders of experience and representation. This space is both material and imagined. It is signifying and non-signifying, perceived and directly experienced, practical and theoretical. Social space is a social reality that corresponds to different social and productive arrangements. For Lefebvre the *process* of producing space and the *product*—that is, the produced space itself—are two inseparable aspects. This complex interplay is explained by a conceptual triad that incorporates three moments as identified by Lefebvre: representations of space, representational space, and spatial practices (Lefebvre 1974, 33). *Representations of space* refer to the conceptualized space, the discursively-constructed space of objectified representations. As the space of capital, conceived space has a substantial influence in the production of space and finds expression in monuments, towers, factories, as well ideological, linguistic, symbolic relations between lived space and the conceptual framework. *Representational space* is the directly lived space of everyday life experienced through complex symbols and images of its inhabitant and users. This space "overlays physical space, making symbolic use of its objects," and can be linked to the underside of social life (Lefebvre 1974, 39). It is also an elusive space that the imagination must seek to change and appropriate. *Representational space* functions at the intersection of the lived experience of perceived and conceived. *Spatial practices* are the practices that 'secrete' society's space. It is a production of relations between objects and products. The spatial practices of any society can be revealed by 'deciphering' the space of that society (Lefebvre 1974, 38). Spatial practices structure daily life and a broader urban reality and, in doing so, ensure social cohesion, continuity and spatial competence (Lefebvre 1974, 33). Lefebvre's spatial triad provides the interpretive grid though which to examine the spatial imaginaries of Bombay to reveal the identities of the various cities that exist within the city.

Literary scholarship on Bombay began with Salman Rushdie's much-celebrated *Midnight's Children* (1980), a novel that located the city in its moment of post-independence and post-colonial predicament. In more recent times Suketu Mehta's *Maximum City: Bombay Lost and Found* (2004) captures the city in its global avatar as the now-renamed city of Mumbai. As Mehta chronicles his journey back to the city of his childhood by mapping, in true Bollywood flashback mode, the 'urban catastrophe' of Bombay, he finds "the cities within me" (Mehta 2004, 3). Mehta claims, "There are many Bombays; through the writing of a book, I wanted to find mine" (Mehta 2004, 13). The episode of the renaming of the city from 'Bombay' to 'Mumbai' in 1995 is particularly interesting for this leads to the question of the ownership of the city, its spaces and, by extension, a claim to its history. Thomas Blom Hansen articulates that for the inhabitants of the city the renaming of Bombay is pivoted on questions of "which space, and whose, should the name fix and territorialize as its object; which, and whose, history should it refer to and demarcate; and in which in which language should the name properly be enunciated" (2005, 3). For Arjun Appadurai, Bombay has always been identified with the ideals of cosmopolitanism[13] which, of late, has been violently compromised (Appadurai 2000, 630). The renaming of the city was one such act, a culmination of the Shiv Sena's[14] xenophobic agenda of ethnic exclusivity and cleansing which dented the city's reputation of cosmopolitanism and multiculturalism. Bombay's transformation from its status as a center of trade, commerce and bourgeoisie nationalism to a postcolonial dream-city full of promise, possibilities and failures is mapped in the ethno-political ideology of the Sena.

---

[13] Arjun Appadurai. 2000. "Spectral Housing and Urban Cleansing: Notes on Millennial Mumbai." Public Culture, Special Issue on Cosmopolitanism, edited by C. Breckenridge, H. Bhabha, D. Chakrabarty and S. Pollock. 12(3) 627-651.

[14] Founded on 19th June 1966 by Balasaheb Thackeray, the Shiv Sena is responsible for the re-naming of 'Bombay' as 'Mumbai'as part of its attempts to claim the city as belonging to the Marathi *manus.*

Contemporary Bombay now is what Dilip Padgaonkar calls a permanently altered city," "a deeply divided city," and a "city at war with itself," (Guha 2007, 643). Sociological studies reveal the existence of parallel, and often multiple, equivalents of the various systems of the city. This result in the creation of multiple worlds existing in a single geographical space, but this space is shared, understood, used and appropriated differently. In addition, the relations of economic interdependency and exploitation mark the city as a space containing global wealth as well as local poverty. The cultural interchange between individuals and communities result in a new global cultural economy which Arjun Appadurai reads as a "complex, overlapping, disjunctive order"[15]. In this context, the city is replete with competing narratives of power, exploitation, violence and indigenous attempts at redemption and justice. The drastic change in the city-ethic is highlighted by Rushdie when he reads the Bombay of *Maximum City* as a 'ruined metropolis' which has almost been destroyed by the "corruption, gangsterism, and neo-fascist politics."[16] Vikram Chandra and Murzbaan Shroff capture this essence of the global city as they narrate the city's underbelly in their respective works.

Chandra's and Shroff's Narration of Life in Bombay

Vikram Chandra's *Sacred Games*, now popular as a web-series in on Netflix, documents the city of Bombay as the seat of crime, corruption and the politics of the underworld, with all the ramifications of a Bollywood[17] potboiler. *Sacred Games* originates in Chandra's earlier short-story collection *Love and Longing in Bombay* (1997) where the many conflicts and contradictions of post-liberalization Bombay were mirrored by employing humour, passion, subtle irony and romance. In one heady episode titled "Kama" Sartaj Singh, a world-weary cop who was "past forty, a divorced police inspector with middling professional prospects" (Chandra 2006, 10) investigates a murder and soon find himself drawn into the vortex of corruption and deceit. In *Sacred Games* Sartaj pursues the charming, ruthless and larger-than-life gangster, Ganesh Gaitonde, and this forms the premise for the action in the novel. The novel begins at the end. Almost immediately at the beginning of the novel the reader is shocked into the death of Gaitonde, "the boss of G-Company and wily and eternal survivor" (Chandra 2006, 29), who kills himself rather than being caught by the police. The death of Gaitonde and his moll in a nuclear bunker stacked with loads of

---

[15] In his widely cited paper "Disjuncture and Difference in the Global Cultural Economy," Arjun Appadurai argues that the globalized world is highly interactive so that the present world system is an 'imaginary landscape.' As identity-markers become slippery the "search for certainties is regularly frustrated by the fluidities of transitional communication" (Appadurai 1990, 5).

[16] Rushdie, Salman. 2004. Accessed 20 July 2007. http://www.suketumehta.com

[17] Bollywood, formerly known as Bombay cinema, is the Indian Hindi-language film industry, based in Mumbai (formerly Bombay). It is the largest film industry in the world. The term 'Bollywood' is a portmanteau of 'Bombay' and 'Hollywood.'

newly counterfeited rupees in a swampy area of Kailashpada sets off the action in the narrative. Chance, and not deduction, leads Sartaj to the sinister Guruji who has been plotting a nuclear holocaust in Bombay that was to be subsequently blamed on Indian Muslims and Pakistan, resulting in inevitable consequences. Dickensian in scope, *Sacred Games* mirrors the depthless postmodern city[18]. The story is set in the newly-renamed Mumbai—here the city is not just a background but also a major character in the novel. The author himself says, "There's an energy about the place that is unmistakable and very, very seductive,"[19]. In the novel Katekar echoes this sentiment, "Once the air of this place touches you, you are useless for anywhere else" (Chandra 2006, 946). In its review of the novel *The Hindustan Times* hails *Sacred Games* as "a landmark in the history of Indian English literature," "the greatest book on Bombay ever written.[20]" Chandra's representation of Bombay provides fertile territory to explore the various ramifications of the city vis-à-vis its position as a symbol of India's global modernity.

Sacred Games takes off from where Salman Rushdie's *The Moor's Last Sigh* leaves and produces the idea of a residual city through the infernal narrative of crime. The narrative locates Bombay in a moment of crisis when the city becomes home to global terror especially after the infamous blasts and riots. The lords of the Bombay underworld are divided in the machinations of the city, and the city too is a victim to the intrigues of the gangland. The divided loyalties of the mafia and the subsequent proxy wars structure the theme of many cinematic narratives, with Ram Gopal Verma's *Satya* and *Company* being fitting examples[21]. Extensive and exhaustive research lends Chandra's narrative a gripping hold on the grim murkiness of the city. The detailed depiction of the police and crime nexus function as the alternative narrative of the city caught in the throes of globalization. Corrupt police practices, gang rivalry concerning their areas of operation expose the networked city that is linked by violence, terror, claustrophobia, the uncanny and the mysterious. Bombay thus becomes a disenchanted city troubled by darkness, death and ruin. The dark side of Bombay's underworld is powerful parallel of the global narrative of the city. The world of cops and gangsters in *Sacred Games* provides the counter-narrative to the narrative of globalization that unfolds in the city as the author negotiates the urban labyrinth to expose the city haunted by ruin, fear, catastrophe and crisis.

---

[18] In *the Condition of Postmodernity: An Enquiry into the Origins of Cultural Change* (Harvey 2004), David Harvey defines the postmodern city with the rise of historical eclecticism, multiculturalism, and spectacle.

[19] Vikram Chandra. 2007. Interview. "*Sacred Games*: An Epic of Mumbai's Underworld." *npr.org*. Accessed September 21, 2007. https://www.npr.org/templates/story/story.php?storyId=6768039

[20] Ashok Banker. Review of *Sacred Games* by Vikram Chandra. *Vikramchandra.com*. Accessed 4 January 2020. https://www.vikramchandra.com/publications/sacred-games/

[21] Released in 1998, *Satya* is a landmark Bollywood film that changed the course of Bombay gangland movies forever. *Company*, released in 2002, continued to tell the tale of the Bombay underworld unapologetically.

In *Sacred Games* Bombay reflects the glamour and wealth that has attracted millions from the villages to migrate to this city of dreams. The city has witnessed rapid transformation towards the last decades of the twentieth century when religious and political conflicts finally caught up with the city's commercial and cosmopolitan communities, a fact that was evident in the riots of 1992-93. Although the liberalization of India's state-controlled economy in the 1990s pushed the city into prosperity, it also became home to various forms of capitalist endeavors. More recently, a series of scams and scandals have exposed the convoluted web of greed and power that has spread its tentacles to include politicians, business tycoons, professionals, mafia dons, Bollywood stars and slumlords. Bombay is now the idiom of what Arjun Appadurai calls 'scapes' [22] of global cultural flows by which the growing disjunctures among the multiple worlds within the city can be imagined. Such rich material provide the backdrop for the twin narratives of Sartaj and Gaitonde as they pursue their destinies across Bombay, India's most hectic, frenzied and chaotic metropolis. The spaces of the city are captured through the wider lens of hopes and dreams. Bombay is the big city of big dreams endorsed on billboards, beautiful and unreal, and millions swarm into this city chasing these dreams. In this sense the city becomes Lefebvre's representational space in its symbolization of a magnificent dream of promise and possibilities for all. For many the city becomes the site for the enactment of exploits, escapades and the exercise of power. In the novel Ganesh Gaitonde's journey in the city is symbolic of the lives of the many people who come to Bombay to find their fortunes but are, sooner or later, lured into its dark and grim underworld.

The figure of Sartaj Singh, who "could hold the whole city in his heart, from Colaba to Bandra" (Chandra 2006, 23), and his aide Katekar are the key strands through which the narrative traverses the many streets, bye-lanes and *gullies* of the city which now "was too vast, escaped from [them]" (Chandra 2006, 23). Through Sartaj the narrative traverses into the city's streets and slums, his solitude and romanticized idealism are challenged by the trickster city and its overwhelming wickedness, ferocity, scandals and breakdowns. The gruffness of his character is described and achieved through his forays into the city's streets and shantytowns, his melancholy solitude, his muted romanticism, and his "senseless, embarrassing idealism", which is often challenged by "the aged-and-cured wickedness of the city, its piquant scandals, its bitter breakdowns, its ferociously musty unfairness" (Chandra 2006, 87). Katekar, on the other hand, loved the everyday life in the city evident in of the "enormous bustle of millions on the move, the hurtling local trains with thick clusters of bodies hanging precariously from the doors, the sonorous tramp and hum

---

[22] Arjun Appadurai outlines the international cultural flows in terms of *ethnoscape*, *technoscape*, *financescape*, *mediascape*, and *ideoscapes* which contribute to the "imagined worlds" constituted by the historically situated imaginations of persons and groups spread around the globe (Appadurai, Arjun. 1996. "Disjuncture and Difference in the Global Cultural Economy." In Modernity at Large: Cultural Dimensions of Globalization, 27-47, Minnesota, University of Minnesota Press.

of the crowd inside the tall hall of Churchgate Station" (Chandra 2006, 72). The daily hustle and bustle of the city made Katekar "feel alive" (Chandra 2006, 72). His city signifies the represented space of urban pandemonium, chaos and confusion wherein paradoxically exists order and cohesion. This bohemian city is a crawling behemoth that, Sartaj fears, may one day fall apart and be gone. This sense of loss is intrinsic to the experience of urban modernity. Thomas Blom Hansen posits that, "the narrative of an ideal Bombay is a historical fantasy that conceals the fact that Bombay always was fundamentally divided by class, caste and religion" (Hansen 2001, 5). Urban violence, repression, corruption and crime, as Rajnarayan Chandavarkar has shown in his studies on colonial Bombay[23], have always been a part of the city's life. Hansen further argues that Bombay is Janus-faced, where the city's survival is dependent on the underworld, on sectarian violence, and exploitation (Hansen 1998, 5). The city of opportunities is also the city of abuse as corruption and exploitation govern almost all spheres of life.

Sacred Games is a literary map of Bombay, the city that contains and is claimed by all but belongs to none. As he makes his way through the narrow lanes of Navnagar's slums, Sartaj Singh observes, "In this city, the rich had some room, the middle class had less, and the poor had none" (Chandra 2006, 544). Gaitonde, who serves as Sartaj's foil, is also deeply rooted in the geography of the city. His personal claim of the city's spaces is reflective of his desire to own it:

> I took the land between NC Road and the hill which overlooks it. You know Gopalmath basti, from NC Road all the way up the hill and four miles wide, from Sindh Chowk to G.T. Junction? All that was empty land then, nothing but a wasteland of weeds and bushes—it was municipal land. The government owned it, and so nobody owned it. I took it. (Chandra 2006, 398)

Since *Sacred Games* is centered on the underworld, Chandra situates his action in the slums and shanties of the city to expose the underbelly of Bombay. The description of the Navnagar slum in the early pages of the book is reflective of the lives of the migrant community where "everything was smaller, closer, the pathways narrow between the uneven walls of cardboard and cloth and wood, the tumbling roofs covered with plastic" (Chandra 2006, 20). Katekar's "furious contempt" for these jhopadpatti-dwellers who let "dirt and filth and garbage pile up not two feet from their own door" (Chandra 2006, 20) reflects the attitude of the privileged towards those surviving at the periphery. Katekar, whose caste certificate reads as OBC (Other

---

[23] Rajnarayan Chandavarkar's *Imperial Power and Popular Politics: Class Resistance and the State in India 1850-1950* (1998) offers a revisionist view of the relationship between class and politics in India between the period of the Sepoy Mutiny of 1857 and Independence, and asserts the significance of the role of the working classes in shaping the pattern of India's capitalist development.

Backward Caste), is disapproving of the residents of Navnagar primarily because they are encroaching on his city, his home—a space he is seemingly reluctant to share. The reasons for such hostility can be traced to the catastrophe of 1992-93 and the politics of the Shiv Sena when every man began to feel secure only in his part of Bombay. In her paper on the aftermath of the riots of the city Jyoti Punwani examines the ways in which "Bombay came to be divided into 'safe' and 'unsafe' areas in January 1993, the balance being skewed in favour of the majority community" (Punwani 2003, 239). Katekar's attitude is reflective of these ideas of safety and belongingness which, he feels, is threatened by the visible but unwanted migrant (in this case the Bangladeshi migrants), thus leading him to relegate them further beyond the boundaries of the periphery. Interestingly, Katekar himself lived in a small *kholi*[24] amidst "a crowded huddle of kholis, mostly pucca, with electrical wire strung over the roofs and through doorways" (Chandra 2006, 25). His small dwelling is representative of Lefebvrian spatial practices which his wife, Shalini, appropriates with "a clean efficiency that lived very functionally in the very small space that was her" (Chandra 2006, 24). This space is informed by Shalini's awareness and enactment of her role as the homemaker. The appropriation of this little space to create the ambience of a happy family translates into the representational essence of the ways in which the inhabitants of Bombay negotiate and internalize the city. As each family (and individual) adds to the next, the city is enveloped in a "cool and endless glow, impossible to know, or escape" (Chandra 2006, 23). The migrants create and thus produce a space within the city, claim it for their own, but live in constant fear of its loss; Shalini is assured and proud of her ownership of the space of the kholi, which she confidently transforms into her home. The city thus symbolizes the representational space of home that is invoked and claimed by all but is used very differently. Katekar's kholi is also symbolic of the spatial crisis of Bombay. The small space that housed his family was divided by a sheet, the other side of which acted as a small room for his two sons. The small but clean kholi also contained their kitchen. This neatly divided space symbolizes of the gradual destruction of privacy and the rapidly disappearing possibility of creating a world that is personal. Katekar's life in the kholi is representative of the spatial disillusionment that has gripped the city.

Bombay is further captured through the profane street language so unique to the city. Chandra's narrative is generously and unapologetically peppered with untranslated vocabulary as the truisms of the "bitter secret of life in the metropolis" (Chandra 2006, 11) are spelt out. The street language becomes the identity marker for many characters including Gaitonde. He describes his gang in the following manner:

> They learned the language, and then the walk, and they pretended to be something, and then they became it. And so for American dollars, we said

---

[24] Kholi literally means a room in Marathi. It also represents an apartment in a chawl/chaal.

choklete, not *dalda* like the rest of our world; for British pounds, *lalten*, not *peetal*; for heroin and brown sugar, *gulal*, not *atta*; for police, *iftekar*, not *nau-number*; a job gone wrong was *ghanta*, not *fachchad*; and a girl so impossibly ripe and round and tight that it hurt to look at her was not a *chabbis*, but a *churi*". (Chandra 2006, 119)

The use of such language, as Gaitonde points out, "set us apart from the rest, made us belong to each other more because we spoke a private tongue, and to become one of us you had to learn it, and in learning it you were changed." (Chandra 2006, 119). The need to highlight the uniqueness of the gang is fuelled by a desire to mark it as different from those existing elsewhere. The significance of different speech variants lies in the fact that they act as unique identity-markers of not only the many different criminal communities but also of the different crime pockets in the city. In the context of Lefebvrian spatial theory, the speech variants of the gangs, once again, signify Bombay as a representational space, a space that is invoked, imagined and appropriated by the overarching mantle of criminal vocabulary.

The Bombay of *Sacred Games* is claimed by all but belongs to none. As he makes his way through the narrow lanes of Navnagar's slums, Sartaj Singh observes, "In this city, the rich had some room, the middle class had less, and the poor had none" (Chandra 2006, 79). Within the spatial geography of the city emerge new identities that are asserted through spatial behavior. Chandra's Bombay signifies the larger transformation of post-colonial urban space. In the context of the city, the gang-world acts as an alternative community to the existing urban milieu. As the city of crime, Bombay becomes the site for the politics of urban space. The action of the narrative is situated primarily in the streets, nightclubs, bars, shantytowns and slums—spaces that have otherwise been identified as crime areas. The street symbolizes freedom from the constraints of home and enables liberation from the claustrophobic restriction of prohibited urban spaces. The street empowers the gangs that control it so that the control of space transgresses spatial boundaries and social hierarchies. The contemporary social topography of Bombay is an essential mix of heterogenic elements laced with coercive homogenization. In this context, the space of crime translates into an alternative space to such socio-political coercions. The depictions of Bombay's anarchy and disorder as an urban legend in the grand unfolding drama of corruption, conflicts and political intrigues—the city as fascinatingly dark, crowded, murky, ruthless and violent—in *Sacred Games* translates into a powerful experience and a allegory for the contemporary cityscape.

Such allegorical representation of Bombay continues in Murzbaan Shroff's vibrant collection of short stories. *Breathless in Bombay* is a collection of snippets from the lives of those struggling to survive in the ruthless city. In his Introduction Shroff narrates the incident his friend's outburst at the migrants stocking their belongings at the police *chowky* in Kemp's Corner (the friend, incidentally, lived at Kemp's Corner, South Bombay, one of the richest areas of the city). He resented the use of this official space by people who are not recognized as citizens of the city (or 'encroachers' as he called them): "why they were permitting *these* people to use our roads as their home, cooking, eating, washing, and defecating there?" (Shroff 2008, ix). To this the cops replied, "*Kai, sahib,* let them be, no? They also deserve to live. Where they will go if we throw them out? How do they affect our lives in any way by being here?" (Shroff 2008, ix). While the friend's attitude is reflective of the larger outlook of the legal citizens of Bombay towards migrants, Shroff's stories give voice to the desires, hopes, dreams and complexities of the marginalized actors within the stratified society. Using a wide range of characters, the author focuses on the everyday problems of those eking out a living at the periphery. Beginning with the water crisis of the *laundrywallas* in "Dhobi Ghat", the doomed relationship Vicki and Nandkumar in "Traffic", the *maalishwalla* Bheem Singh's reminiscences of the life in the village—each story narrates the lives of characters waiting for the realization of their hopes and dreams. The ugly and monstrous city of Bombay is "oblivious to [the] piquant little communities holding its own, frozen, by its own choice, in time" (Shroff 2008, 6) as they are caught in the throes of intrigues for survival tactics and globalization.

Breathless in Bombay captures the city's commercial flurry. The overwhelming narrative of global city is de-centered as the author arranges his tales around the otherwise invisible urban characters. The negotiation of the city's invisible spaces by these characters highlights the fact that for them spatial continuity, cohesion and order are possible only if they seek it in the indiscernible pockets of the city. This brings to attention the essence of postmodern urban life that is structured by difference and disparity. Globalization and commercialization has resulted in the homogenization of the city's marginalized spaces. Sandeep Pendse[25] shows how the 'toilers of the city' are "relegated to the periphery of existence in the city, both literally and figuratively; actually and ideologically" (Pendse 1995, 9). Ironically, the city itself depends on their services for its existence. Urban life is desperately dependent on the sweat, toil of the otherwise unrecognized, and unacknowledged population, a fact Shroff attempts to highlight in his stories. The city is structured by vicious contrasts, and it is a space of both temptation and betrayal. The lives of those on the fringes of urban life narrate a different existence, one that is distinctly marked by its own class-bound forms of struggle. While the city makes possible encounters and relationships among those struggling to survive, this is not easily achieved: the new centres of power obliterate the invisibility of certain social groups so that the urban narrative is centered not on the workforce but on the city.

Urban space in Bombay thus becomes splintered and fragmented by the technological forces of global capitalism as is evident in the stories. Mataprasad

---

[25] In his paper titled "Toil, Sweat, and the City" Sandeep Pendse explores the "organization of space; importance, relevance and precision of time; and reordering of rhythms of existence" in the lives of the toilers that result in deprivation, but subsequently lead to formation of new identities based on solidarity of the workforce.

Mahadev's account in the opening story "Dhobi Ghat" reveals the ruthless underside of globalization and commoditization. His profession is threatened by the simple washing machine, and Mataprasad is bemused as to how he could "fight a machine that never strikes back, that just takes over man's life quietly, with new, new promises everyday" (Shroff 2008, 3). He is baffled that "people were happy to bury their prejudices just so they could be seen as modern" (Shroff 2008, 2). Shroff devotes entire pages to the description of the *dhobi ghat,* the washing area, and the process of washing to draw attention to the workings of the lives of the *laundrywallas*. Life in the *dhobi ghat* had its own pace "its own space, its own serenity" (Shroff 2008, 6). This serenity and sense of community is threatened by the city's attempts at beautification so that the *ghat* risked being dotted with skyscrapers once the authorities had their way. The open-ended story reiterates the fact that people at the fringes of the city continue to bear the brunt of modernization and the imminent invasion of new technologies and temptations, just as the city "weighed its gloomy pallor of the people, reminding them of the baggage they carried: another day of abstract non-achievement, simply the mediocrity they'd inherited or the luxury they'd not" (Shroff 2008, 23). For the migrant masseur Bheem Singh, in "The Maalishwalla," Bombay is the "city of cold transactions" (Shroff 2008, 61), a "city of bastards" (Shroff 2008, 60). As he pursues his profession in Chowpatty, he realizes that Bombay is a "city of dark realism, of lonely, self-preserving nights and hot, oppressive days" (Shroff 2008, 71). The spatial practices of these marginalized people does allow the possibilities of survival in a space that they cannot claim for their own, but survival is constantly threatened as they are subjected to constant demographic dislocation. Such spatial displacement results in the segmentation of the city and the larger concentration of slum pockets. As a representation of space Bombay exists as a geographical space for all the inhabitants of the city, but as a representational space it continues to elude those millions of migrants who arrive at the city to seek their intangible fortunes.

The title story "Breathless in Bombay" captures the vagaries and facade of the Bombay elite in Aringdham Bannerjee and Ritika's Trilok's wedding. Aringdham's meticulous planning of the wedding, its theme, dress-code, a pan-Indian cuisine—Punjabi, Goan, Hyderabadi, Continental—are attempts to "camouflage the reality; it threw a deft security blanket over his past, the shame of being born poor, of having led a life of grim, unyielding misery" (Shroff 2008, 274). The narrative captures the social realities of the upper echelons of Bombay society and exposes their farcical attempts at civilized and dignified living. Very early in life Aringdham learnt about a "world where relationships did not survive, nor niceness, nor dignity, where all that was good was forgotten in a daze of myopic blindness and where limits were crossed with unpardonable ease" (Shroff 2008, 275). These spatial inequities represented in the text are founded on the social and economic stratification of the people. The desired exclusivity of the upper class too rests on unpleasant social realities. People like Aringdham seek escape by "build[ing] a wall high and solid till he could no longer see the squalor, no longer hear the shouts, the curses, and the screams of denial" (Shroff 2008, 275). Seen in Lefebvrian terms, such spatial practices inform the acceptance or denial of the spaces of the city. The city itself becomes a representational space that is internalized to obliterate unpleasant truths. The city thus offers the possibility of negotiation so that it is informed by subjective responses to the urban. Economic prosperity and exclusivity are significantly distinct from the condition of the marginalized, and the disproportionate economic distribution is glaringly visible in the simultaneous existence of extremities and spatial disparities. Bombay contains spaces of brilliance and perfection "where achievement had no limit, beauty no boundaries, and poverty and coarseness no place whatsoever" (Shroff 2008, 278). Yet, for those residing in the city's underbelly Bombay offers a space of contentment despite its challenges:

> for theirs was not the vice of music, or of fine food, or of dance, or of clever conversation. Theirs was the voice of deep abysmal sleep, the will of fate and the stars above theirs was the voice of a single dream, an unchanging dream; to prepare for another day of labor, another day of toil, another day of survival, which would allow them to sleep on a half-empty stomach, or half-full, if they were that lucky, that is. (Shroff 2008, 306)

Shroff's representation of Bombay is premised on the urban predicament of the inhabitants. As a represented space the city is a spatial arrangement of a multilayered society existing on a single geographical space. The spatial practices of the inhabitants of the city inform the ways in which the many spaces of the city are used, appropriated and contested. Shroff's Bombay is thus a representation of the human and humane aspects of the city, a re-imagining of the bitter-sweet realities of his beloved city.

Conclusion

Both *Sacred Games* and *Breathless In Bombay* present alternative perspectives to the otherwise established readings of the city, and in this sense depart from conventional city literature that uses the urban landscape primarily as a backdrop for narratives of upper-middle class agony and angst. The increasing sensitivity to the trials and tribulation of ordinary individuals is evident in the recent works by contemporary writers of Indian English Fiction, particularly Rohinton Mistry, Manil Suri, and Kiran Nagarkar among others. The local and cultural tensions, the chaotic city life juxtaposed against a nefarious underworld based on the gullies and gutters of Bombay offer an overarching glimpse of the city besides endorsing a strong sense of community among the displaced and dispossessed.

The new strategies of urban development have given rise to new forms of spatial politics. In Bombay urbanization's marginalizing tendency has led to the contestation of public spaces among the urban poor and the middle classes. In his study of gated residential enclaves in Bombay, Mark Anthony Falzon argues that urban lifestyles of the middle classes, influenced by a global consumerist culture, shape people's perceptions of space and its organization:

> [T]he middle and upper classes tend to perceive the homeless, slum dwellers, beggars, "urchins," and hawkers as undesirables who "encroach" on the city's public spaces and make it difficult for the former to lead what they see as a decent, healthy, and safe life. For the elites, life in the city is a constant siege. [it is] against this siege that one must fortify. (Falzon 2004, 159-60)

On this same note Leela Fernandes argues for the growing visibility of the new middle classes whose identity is defined by their roles as consumers. This apparently results in the "politics of forgetting" where certain marginalized social groups are rendered invisible (the underworld) and forgotten (the workforce), and processes of exclusion are naturalized by the elite and the upper-class through subjective definition of citizenship. Arjun Appadurai reads the newly emerging forms of citizenship as "deep democracy" or "globalization from below" (Appadurai 2002, 38) where the inhabitants of the periphery engage with urban governmentality by using "legitimate precedents (Appadurai 2002, 33) to legalize their cause[26].

The process of spatial production and spatial reorganization in Bombay needs to be understood in its unique historical, social and cultural context. The state is an active agent in globalizing the city, but there exists agencies whose roles are equally decisive. Even though marginalized communities expose the failures of globalization, the process of spatial reorganization and approximation of the city has engendered numerous forms of grassroots politics among the urban poor. Literary mapping of the city's spaces is but one of the many interventions that can aid in the understanding and negotiation of urban space. Much of the recent literature on Bombay encourages the association and exposition of the multiple realities of the city. The interest generated by a combination of fiction and reportage while describing the city, and the information revealed in these narratives locate Bombay as a thriving commercial city, an impending urban catastrophe, and, as Suketu Mehta fittingly calls it, a "maximum city." Chandra opines, "The citizens of Bombay love to complain about the city endlessly, but [they] also will defend it fearlessly against outsiders making the same complaints."[27] Towards the end of *Sacred Games*, Sartaj puts it succinctly, "When you're away from it, you can miss it, physically you can ache for it—even for the stink of it" (Chandra 2006, 924).

Contemporary Bombay is experiencing a contradictory process where global advancement contributes to the marginalization of the lesser known communities and

---

[26] Arjun Appadurai. "Deep Democracy: Urban Governmentality and the Horizion of Politics." Public Culture 14 (1), Winter 2002: 21-47.

[27] Vikram Chandra. 2007. Interview. "*Sacred Games*: An Epic of Mumbai's Underworld." *npr.org*. Accessed September 21, 2007. https://www.npr.org/templates/story/story.php?storyId=6768039

spaces in the city—a fact reiterated in Shroff's fiction. While globalization had introduced the city to new ways of urban development, it has also promoted exclusion and marginalization. Critics like Saskia Sassen argue that globalization underestimates the agency and contingency of the local. In this context, the imaginary city of literature contests and complements the institutionalized narratives of the city. Postcolonial cities like Bombay are endowed with multiple legacies that render them as sites of Lefebvre's representational spaces. The interactions and exchanges between the multiple spatialities of the city, as well as the transactions between the local and the global mark it as a vastly complex and widely contested site. Vikram Chandra and Murzbaan Shroff's representation of the spaces of Bombay only explicate the ways in which this city carries different significations and offer different realties for its vastly diverse population.

REFERENCES

Appadurai, Arjun. 2002. "Deep Democracy: Urban Governmentality and the Horizon of Politics." *Public Culture* 14 (1): 21–47.

———. 2000. "Spectral Housing and Urban Cleansing: Notes on Millennial Mumbai." *Public Culture* 12 (3): 627–651.

———. 1996. *Modernity at Large: Cultural Dimensions of Globalization.* Minnesota: University of Minnesota Press.

Boyer, Christine M. 1996. *The City of Collective Memory: Its Historical Imagery and Architectural Entertainments.* Cambridge, MA. and London: MIT Press.

Chandra, Vikram. 2006. *Sacred Games.* New Delhi: Penguin.

Chatterjee, Partha. 2006. "Are Indian Cities Becoming Bourgeois at Last?" In *Contested Transformations: Changing Economies and Identities in Contemporary India,* edited by Mary E. John, Praveen Kumar Jha and Surinder S. Jodhka, 113–124. New Delhi: Tulika

Falzon, Mark-Anthony. 2004. "Paragons of Lifestyle: Gated Communities and the Politics of Space in Bombay." *City and Society* 6 (2): 145–167.

Fernandes, Leela. 2000. *"Restructuring the New Middle Class in Liberalizing India."* *Comparative Studies of South Asia, Africa, and the Middle East.* http://citeseerx.ist.psu.edu. Accessed on 11 November 2009

http://citeseerx.ist.psu.edu/viewdoc/download?doi=10.1.1.504.6182&rep=rep1&type=pdf

Guha, Ramchandra. 2007. *India After Gandhi: The History of the World's Largest Democracy.* London: Picador.

Hansen, Thomas Blom. 2001. *Violence in Urban India: Identity Politics, 'Mumbai', and the Postcolonial City.* New Delhi: Permanent Black.

Khilnani, Sunil. 1997. *The Idea of India.* New Delhi: Penguin.

Lefebvre, Henri. 1974. *The Production of Space.* Translated by Donald Nicholson-Smith. Cambridge, Mass.: Blackwell. 1991

Mehta, Suketu. 2004. *Maximum City: Bombay Lost and Found.* New Delhi: Penguin.

Patel, Sujata. 2003. "Bombay and Mumbai: Identities, Politics and Populism." In *Bombay and Mumbai: The City in Transition,* edited by Sujata Patel and Jim Masselos. 3–30. New Delhi: Oxford University Press.

Pendse, Sandeep. 2007. "Toil, sweat and the city." In *Bombay: Metaphor for Modern India.* 1995, edited by Sujata Patel and Alice Thorner, 3–25. New Delhi: Oxford University Press.

Punwani, Jyoti. 2003. "'My Area, Your Area': How Riots Changed the City." In *Bombay and Mumbai: The City in Transition,* edited by Sujata Patel and Alice Thorner, 235–264. New Delhi: Oxford University Press.

Sassen, Saskia. 1991. *The Global City: New York, London, Tokyo.* Princeton: Princeton University Press.

Shroff, Murzbaan. 2008. *Breathless in Bombay.* London: Picador.

Chapter 4

The Jugaad of Urban Planning in India: Recognizing Gender in Innovation, Risk and Active Citizenship[1]

Adishree Panda

Introduction

Understanding what it means to be a citizen of a dynamic country, such as India, is as difficult to figure out as it is to solve a jigsaw puzzle that has thousands of different pieces that fit together to become one comprehensive picture. Each piece of the puzzle (or each city in India) is unique and when they all are assembled, they belong to an overarching entity (country). Due to an established high-density population and the corresponding scarcity of resources, citizens from different strata of the country tend to adopt various survival strategies—sometimes within the purview of the state and sometimes outside of it. Most of the population resorts to what is colloquially known as *jugaad* or managing to get things done with any means available using elements of innovation and risk in their execution. Consequently, one of the various ways of perceiving what it is to be Indian is to have the inherent ability of knowing that any puzzle or problem can be solved with just a little bit of ingenuity.

The Oxford Learner's Dictionaries (2020) defines *jugaad* as "the use of skill and imagination to find an easy solution to a problem or to fix or make something using cheap, basic items". It is in the urban context that the resourcefulness in daily activities is witnessed at a higher frequency due to reasons ranging from the impact of the higher density of populations in cities and their surrounding areas to a lack of recognition of the basic rights of citizens who do not have a registered identity in the city. Hence, *jugaad* can be viewed as a survival strategy adopted by individuals to function in situations when their citizenship rights are not being acknowledged and the implementation of their substantive citizenship, or their power to actually enjoy their rights, is contested. Even though *jugaad* is adopted in different forms by various individuals, it is more evident amongst lower income groups due to the limited

[1] This chapter is an edited version of the essay "The Jugaad of Urban Planning in India: Recognizing Gender in Innovation, Risk, and Active Citizenship" first published in *The Global Studies Journal* 11 (1): 25-42.

recognition of their citizenship rights and the difficulties they face to cope with daily challenges.

Even amidst the strict legal frameworks of recent urban planning and development missions and schemes by the Government of India, such as the Smart Cities Mission (SCM), Atal Mission for Rejuvenation and Urban Transformation (AMRUT), and *Swachh Bharat* Mission (SBM) or Clean Indian Mission, the informal sector has a tendency to flourish via innovative strategies that mostly go unrecognized by the government. Sometimes such strategies also slip under the radar due to the difficulty in defining them as "legal" activities, as laid down by government regulations. Moreover, every individual who wants to engage with entrepreneurial activities in the informal sectors must accept specific risks involved in conducting innovative strategies. There is also a distinction between the type of risks and challenges that women and men face in implementing their entrepreneurial ideas. Therefore, exploring which section of society has a higher ability to conduct such activities provides an insight into the functioning of the informal sectors in cities.

It is thus significant to understand the functioning of current urban planning systems as well as the gaps in these systems that lead to individuals resorting to *jugaad* activities. In order to achieve a better understanding of the term and its importance in the everyday language of Indian society, especially in the informal sectors, there is a need to delve into the aspects of risk in conducting such activities on a daily basis. A theoretical analysis of existing 'gender-aware' frameworks will also give us insight into who has a higher likelihood of taking on these risks (Brush, de Bruin, and Welter 2009; Nicholson et al. 2005), and the factors leading to engagement in these activities (Orhan and Scott 2011; Brindley 2005). Further, by deconstructing the notion of *jugaad* through a gendered lens, the possible implications of these practices can be examined for developing a planning framework that would support the creativity and resourcefulness of the individuals.

The research has been conducted primarily through the methodology of literature review of secondary source materials by analysing the current planning systems of India and their efficacy in allowing for participation amongst communities. Through an understanding of risk, gender, and risk-taking in the informal sector, the author aims to present theoretical concepts that need to be considered for inclusive urban planning. Few case studies have also been selected to illustrate elements of innovation and risk amongst grassroots initiatives and movements.

The objective is, thus, to delve into the underpinnings of *jugaad* in relation to the threefold dimensions of citizenship, risk, and planning in urban India, and the implications that each of these dimensions have on each other. *Jugaad* activities may be observed as being born out of the need to bridge the gap between the formal and substantive citizenship rights of individuals, which calls attention to the development of a planning framework that should inherently reduce such a gap. However, once implemented, such activities also demonstrate the innovative potential of individuals that should be supported by the same framework. Therefore, by re-framing an everyday term of the Hindi-language vocabulary and interrogating it through the theoretical perspective of a gendered lens, it opens up an avenue for developing an inclusive planning framework that should be incorporated into existing urban missions and schemes of India. Moreover, it would contribute towards tapping into the creativity of people to think of solutions for the problems of their city.

Positioning Jugaad: Theoretical Reframing of an Everyday Concept

Any activity that individuals engage in to have a livelihood stems from the need to achieve an end goal—be it to provide food for their families, to sustain a business, or to build a house. However, the ways in which they conduct such activities may be viewed differently based on norms and legal frameworks and on their adherence to the formal planning systems. Compliance to such societal norms and the legal sanctions set out by the government may not always be achievable by individuals who lack the means to acquire resources via formal methods. This leads to resorting to alternative and creative methods of survival.

The meaning of the colloquial Hindi term *jugaad* is usually to have "an innovative fix" or "improvised solution born from ingenuity and cleverness" for a problem (Radjou, Prabhu, and Ahuja 2012, 4). It is a term used casually by many residents of India but reflects an inherent characteristic of Indian society of looking for solutions that are not always deemed as formal methods. Such activities have various actors involved who can be from any part of society and does not have a fixed duration of completion.

The activities are often based on a novel idea and their execution is dependent on factors that may appear random initially—but require every element to work in tandem with each other for successful task completion. For instance, re-utilizing a used plastic bottle as a shower head (figure 1) is considered as much of a *jugaad* activity as is the conversion of similar plastic bottles into light bulbs by various households in the Philippines[2] (figure 2) through chlorine and water to harness solar energy. Such ideas can range between different scales of functioning—for instance, Figures 1 and 2 demonstrate the multiple uses of plastic bottles—and are not only limited to Indian cities, but are present in any place where everyday items are converted into products with alternative uses.

---

[2] Since 2006, the *Liter of Light* Foundation run by social entrepreneur Illac Diaz specializes in building light bulbs from used plastic bottles that use solar power as the energy source. This innovation is now available in fifteen countries, including the Philippines. More information at: Maria Scarzella Thorpe, "Interview: Philippines Social Entrepreneur Illac Diaz Listens to, and Learns from, Local Talent," Asia Society Northern California, 2014. https://asiasociety.org/blog/asia/interview-philippines-social-entrepreneur-illac-diaz-listens-and-learns-local-talent.

Image 1: Converting Bottle into Shower Head and into Light Bulbs
Image 2: Steps to convert a plastic bottle into a shower head.
Children holding plastic bottles made into light bulbs by the Liter of Light Foundation in the Philippines.

Radjou, Prabhu, and Ahuja (2012, 4) elaborate that: "Jugaad is, quite simply, a unique way of thinking and acting in response to challenges; it is the gutsy art of spotting opportunities in the most adverse circumstances and resourcefully improvising solutions using simple means. Jugaad is about doing more with less". So, an important characteristic of a *jugaad* activity is its novel approach towards existing, traditional, and conventional ways of doing things—the element of innovation. When an individual uses a uniquely different permutation and combination of resources to complete a task that significantly reduces the effort and resources being used, it becomes a *jugaad* way of doing things.

The act of *jugaad* involves an element of risk too, which brings forward the extensive discussion on how risk is defined in different sectors and which sections of a society engage in such activities (Nicholson et al. 2005; Orhan and Scott 2001). Nicholson et al. (2005) have stated that risk propensity is dependent on different factors such as age, sex, and even personality of an individual, and varies across sectors. Hence, individuals in informal sectors may expose themselves to specific risks, such as failure and uncertainty, monetary loss, closure of businesses for bypassing the law, or even risks of violence or being convicted when doing *jugaad*. Since *jugaad* involves unconventional approaches, the legality of the task varies depending on the scale at which it is being performed. A person who does *jugaad* activities is usually referred to as a *jugaadu* individual. A jugaadu person can be from any section of a society—from being a lone entrepreneur to being a minister in a government department, and from being a women's initiative member to being an industry owner with a male-dominant task force. This means that it is an activity that is cross-sectional and is sometimes even viewed as a subversion of the normal state of affairs, especially when it is adopted as a survival strategy by lower income groups to circumvent acts of exclusion in existing urban missions and schemes.

According to Mahadevia and Joshi (2009, 7): "There are three types of subversions observed in urban space; one where the poor subvert as an outcome of exclusions, two where the non-poor subvert to push their own interests and in reaction to overregulation under the Master Plan and current land legislation regimes, and three where the state subverts in favour of the vested interests, causing the capture of urban resources". Subsequently, such activities frequently branch into either having a negative connotation wherein it is a method of rebellion by people against the system, or having a positive connotation of them accepting their surroundings and developing innovative solutions from scarce resources when there is a failure of formal procedures. Alternatively, it is also implemented in the situation of advancing one's own interests, which may even be at the expense of others.

The exploration of the framework within which an individual functions and adapts leads us to various questions regarding different dimensions of a *jugaadu* person that can take us one step closer to understanding what determines an activity to be a jugaad activity. For instance—who undertakes such risks to innovate and what are the challenges faced by those who take these risks? What are the characteristics of a risk-taker? And where and under which conditions do the individuals take these risks? Such questions bring forth into the social, economic, and political implications of doing *jugaad*, and the extent to which individuals get involved in such activities is a reflection of their context.

Conceptual Framework

In urban areas, the concepts of citizenship, risk, and planning are inextricably interlinked and with changes in the functioning of each, there are implications for the other aspects. As depicted in figure 3, there is a gap between the formal and substantive citizenship of individuals that needs to be closed for both women and men so that urban practice and implementation of missions and schemes match the theoretical rights provided to citizens. The dichotomy between the public and private spheres of citizens and the level of (non)interference between the two categories are important points of consideration, as it intercedes the decision-making processes of the state for the citizens. Furthermore, the achievement of substantive citizenship can be made more feasible if it is viewed through a lens of social justice wherein the appreciation of rights of citizens and the (re)distribution of benefits and resources would be addressed equitably. This would enable involvement of all stakeholders in the different legal processes and a mutual recognition of the state and citizens to collectively engage in actively shaping the city at different levels of policymaking.

Due to the gap between practice and theory, the road to fulfilling an individual's substantive citizenship is replete with various types of risks and vulnerabilities. There is a further hierarchy of these vulnerabilities depending on the social and economic categories of caste, class, religion, and gender, that the individual belongs to. Gendered risks and inequalities are obstacles that are present at different stages of accessing resources and opportunities, which are often perpetuated by the formal institutions themselves. So, for lower income groups in cities, the hierarchy of vulnerability mediates the risk-taking and decision-making processes that they undertake for their daily survival. There is a subsequent need for a planning framework that would deal with the intersectional character of the risks involved in closing this gap and would cut across both formal and informal methods of functioning to mainstream gender issues and provide protection from these different types of risks. Moreover, it should have a dynamic character with "room for manoeuvre" to mould itself according to the changing requirements of the citizens (Levy 2015).

Figure 3: Relationship between formal and substantive citizenship, risks, and planning in the context of *jugaad* activities in cities.

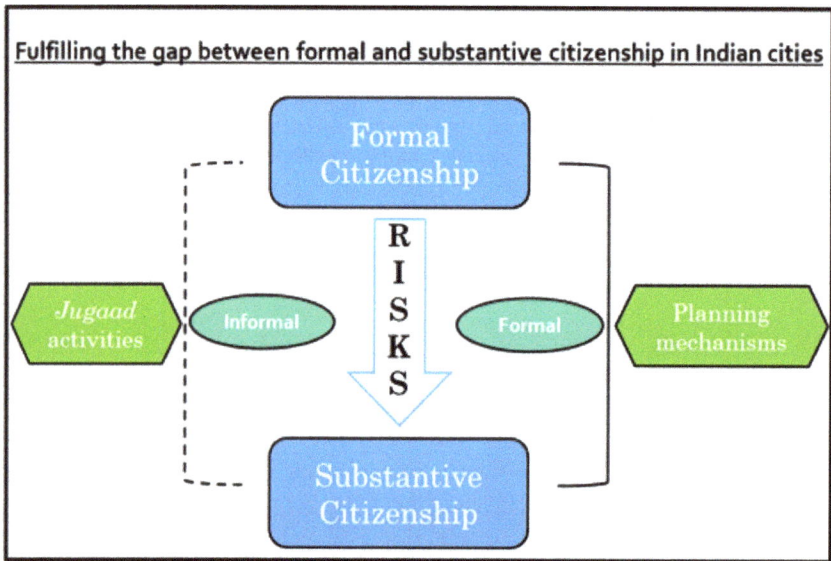

Source: Figure by the Author

The state has incorporated few formal planning mechanisms to close this gap to provide requisite services through various policies and institutions. The Sustainable Development Goal (SDG) 11 by the United Nations highlights the importance of having resilient, sustainable, and inclusive cities; and India's urban schemes have been working towards achieving this goal. But these mechanisms, when applied at the local level, are not always efficient in the recognition of rights and the equitable distribution of resources in a participatory or socially just manner. At this juncture, individuals adopt alternative survival strategies and ways of gaining access to resources through conducting *jugaad* activities, which are sometimes deemed as informal methods of operating. The limitations of planning mechanisms exacerbate the risks of individuals and tend to increase the rate of these activities. However, these activities alternatively can have a positive connotation of being creative approaches towards problem-solving. A possible terminology for this aspect can be *upyogi* jugaad—the definition of '*upyogi*' approximately translates to 'useful' in Hindi. Consequently, the ideal planning framework incorporated within urban missions and schemes should be able to support the participation and inclusion of citizens and accept their innovative approaches.

Reframing Jugaad in Urban Practice in India

Even though the scope of understanding of *jugaad* is quite broad, its recognition in the urban policy and planning frameworks of India can be narrowed down to a few specific aspects. Because *jugaad* is a characteristic inherently present in most citizens of India, the acceptance of its innovation as an important factor that has transformative power for communities also needs to be formally validated within urban missions and schemes. Furthermore, the gendered challenges in policy and planning frameworks need to be reflected upon so that their implementation in cities have higher efficacy. An exploration of these concepts, in the context of Indian society within which *jugaad* takes root and flourishes, follows.

Promoting Active Citizenship and Innovation

The acquisition of political citizenship for social groups, such as women or ethnic minorities, has occurred at different times for each group in various countries. The lack of uniformity in acquiring citizenship has been dependent on a country's historical and social context and its views on what rights should be available to different social groups. For instance, women were not allowed to exercise their right to vote in most countries until the twentieth century for various reasons. They were not allowed to enter the public domain or engage in political debates and women's education was not considered an important concern, which had a significant bearing on their exclusion from politics. They were also not allowed to own property[3] in many countries, which implied that they were dependent on the men in their family to make any major economic decisions for all members; this also led to female voices being considered insignificant for political matters. In effect, the granting of political citizenship to individuals is an important matter of the state, which determines the level of recognition of individuals' daily rights in society.

---

[3] For instance, before the Hindu Succession Act 1956 was enacted in India which granted property rights to women, Hindu women did not have rights to ownership of property as per customary and *Shastric* laws that were being followed at the time. Further, women were not allowed to inherit property from their fathers until the 2005 amendment to this act.

The involvement of governments and their politics was usually kept separate from so-called 'women's issues', such as housework or childcare, which implied a non-interference of the (male-dominated) public spheres in the (female-dominated) private spheres. However, beginning in the 1960s in the background of the second wave of feminism, a dominant ideology that came to the forefront was that the "personal is political". It sparked various debates about the dichotomy of the public and private realms in political theorizing and policymaking (Grant 1993). Such an interrelationship between the two realms stressed as significant that the government was either choosing to ignore 'apolitical' issues of the private realm or underestimating the actual extent of their involvement in determining who has the reins in this realm. It also provided the backdrop to raise the importance of rights of women to engage in social and political matters in the public sphere—and the arduous tasks that women undergo for fighting for those rights.

As India is a democracy, the representatives who are elected make the major legal decisions on behalf of citizens and, depending on their political agendas, devise urban planning schemes that have to be strictly followed by the members of urban areas. According to the Right to Fair Compensation and Transparency in Land Acquisition, Rehabilitation, and Resettlement Act of 2013[4], the state has the right to eminent domain when there are disputes over land or it is the ultimate owner of public land. The exercising of this develops out of the right of the state to decide the percentage of private sector involvement in public services and infrastructure development, and the state's power to determine the prioritization of socio-economic elements in the policies they make based on their current urban development focus. In other words, the constitution lays down the formal citizenship roles of individuals, and the accomplishment of their substantive citizenship is dependent on the conditions and facilities provided by the state.

In this scenario, however, societal conditions play an equally relevant role in determining the fulfilment of the substantive citizenship of individuals, as low-income families are often not even considered to be formal citizens of particular states due to their inability to register their identities. A unique identification number with fixed address proof is usually a compulsory requirement for exercising legal rights in India and for acquiring basic necessities, such as access to water and electricity—and this requirement is difficult to execute for poor families or migrants who dwell in slums in cities with no fixed addresses. Such dwellers try to circumvent the situation by finding alternative solutions—or doing *jugaad*—to acquire facilities or switching to private service provision when public services are not accessible to them, which only adds to their costs. The collusion of state and society, thus, sometimes makes it difficult for individuals from lower income backgrounds and informal settlements to have the

---

[4] This Land Act 2013 has replaced the earlier version of the Land Acquisition Act of 1894 which has now been repealed. More information about the 2013 Act can be accessed at: https://indiacode.nic.in/bitstream/123456789/2121/1/201330.pdf.

power to perform their substantive citizenship, which increases their frequency of opting for alternative strategies for survival.

Walby (1994) has suggested that the achievement of social citizenship has gendered implications due to different societal pressures on individuals. She states that "access to citizenship is a highly gendered and ethnically structured process" (Walby 1994, 391). This implies that in order to move towards a modern and democratic citizenship, it is important to have a universal approach towards the concept so that all citizens are granted power to exercise their rights regardless of their age, sex, or socio-economic backgrounds. This highlights the importance of the distinction between the public and private realms in determining citizenship and that there is often a thin line separating the two, as the state only gets involved in the private domain depending on the situation at hand. Thus, the type of social relations in a society determines the kinds of power granted to individuals for conducting their substantive citizenship, which points to a relevant relationship between gender and citizenship. As different groups of women and men face multi-pronged vulnerabilities, they cannot be considered a homogenous category for the solving of problems.

Even though innovation plays an important role in the recognition of *jugaad* as a substantial activity, it is also an activity that is limited to only those who have the resources available to them to innovate in the first place. Implementing innovation involves a level of decision-making and influence within the household itself to engage in the activity. At the grassroots level, women are often recruited to participate as members in such activities from within communities, but women-led initiatives face higher hindrances in establishing their ideas due to the dominance of males at the entry points of procedural institutions. Hence, there is a need for the understanding of a 'gender-aware' framework of innovation that recognizes the creative potential of all members of the community instead of solely focusing on conventionally established approaches which only consider the voice of the conventional 'leaders' of the household.

An instance of *jugaad* demonstrated in India's urban areas is the inequalities faced by low-income families when accessing resources during disasters and their consequent survival strategies that become a requisite in such a situation. According to a UNDP and GROOTS International 2011 Report, access to secure housing and the loss of livelihoods are often considered to be the major issues for the urban poor, and a lack of such infrastructural support by the state forces them to seek shelter in disaster-prone areas due to the lower affordability rates. However, in a post-disaster situation, since most of the mainstream support of state bodies is focused on these infrastructural issues, there are other equally important problems that are overlooked—such as the health and sanitation concerns of women. Due to the discomfort felt by women to talk about their health problems in public or to men outside their families, it becomes an issue that needs delicate handling, which can be dealt with by transforming such taboo topics into mainstream discussions. Since the lack of inclusion in policy formation processes and marginalization of some groups or communities further compounds the vulnerability faced due to environmental risks or physical factors, consultative processes are extremely relevant to ensure that all individuals have the opportunities to which they are entitled.

Swayam Shikshan Prayog (SSP) is an organization that supports grassroots women's groups in the tsunami-hit districts of Tamil Nadu to participate in local governance processes and reconstruction methods employed in disaster and risk areas (UNDP and GROOTS International Report 2011), which has contributed to bringing health concerns to the foreground. The organization helps by ensuring that the voice of the communities is heard through facilitating community-led problem-solving processes when the support provided by the government bodies is not adequate to address the needs of the community. In the Nagapattinam and Cuddalore districts of Tamil Nadu, the mobilization of women in the recovery processes allowed for "creating spaces for women to organize and share ideas, and facilitating networking, peer-to-peer learning exchanges, and awareness-raising campaigns" (UNDP and GROOTS International Report 2011, 37). Through these alternative, and sometimes informal methods of communication, women felt more comfortable about raising their concerns and participating in the cause to spread their training and knowledge. This enabled a sustainable access to health services even after the termination of emergency services provided by the government in the disaster areas.

The Swachh Bharat Mission—Urban (SBM-U) is an urban mission that is being advocated for by the central government of India to address health and sanitation issues in urban areas. According to the guidelines provided by the Ministry of Housing and Urban Affairs (MoHUA) (2017, 12), the mission "aims to ensure that— No households engage in the practice of open defecation; No new insanitary toilets are constructed during the mission period, and Pit latrines are converted to sanitary latrines". As women's sanitation is a sensitive issue in urban India and is not openly discussed in many households, the mission has encouraged innovative women-driven initiatives for higher participation and involvement. For instance, in Bihar, women self-help groups (SHGs) are being looked at as the "harbingers of social change" by pooling resources to construct toilets to end open defecation (Khan 2017). Jeevika, a poverty-alleviation initiative of the government of Bihar, has highlighted the importance of creating women SHGs and community organizations, and recognizing them as social service providers at the central government-level for facilitating their economic viability.

Without proper health and sanitation plans and state strategies in place in many cities, such innovative and *jugaad* strategies must be currently relied upon for dissemination of health and sanitation knowledge. However, it is important to ensure that these initiatives are provided with long-term institutional and financial support so that they are self-sustaining and continue to impact urban areas even beyond the mission duration.

Addressing Gendered Urban Risks and Inequalities

Kumar and Bhaduri (2014) shed light on how the two terms of *jugaad* and "grassroots innovation" are increasingly being identified with the informal sectors due to their potential for growth along with other industries in the economy. The informal sector forms an important contributor to the economy, especially in developing countries, as it is closely interlinked with the operations of the formal sectors. Due to factors, such as the optimal usage of resources, availability of relatively cheap labour, and alternative job opportunities, the contribution of informal sectors cannot be neglected. However, the availability of alternative jobs comes at an opportunity cost of increased risks and vulnerabilities. The conditions under which the labourers have to work are not always optimal due to the cost-cutting methods opted by the business owners, and they are sometimes severely exploited.

Socio-economic and political conditions usually act as the push factors for individuals who resort to *jugaad* activities in the informal sectors. As these activities include certain entrepreneurial risks, individuals who get involved have varying degrees of involvement based on the risks they are willing to take. It is vital to examine the concept of *jugaad* through a gendered lens, as women and men face different risks and challenges for entering the informal sector. The existing literature on women and risk-taking in innovative entrepreneurial activities elaborates on the 'gender-aware' framework (Brush, de Bruin, and Welter 2009), through which the entry of women in risk activities can be analysed as well as the challenges faced by women in unlocking their innovation potential. Women particularly face issues of recognition of their innovation potential and often face barriers in leading entrepreneurial activities, especially at the small-scale level.

Orhan and Scott (2011) have elucidated on the 'push' and 'pull' factors that showcases gender-based motivations for women and men to enter into public economic activities as well as the intensity of the risks that they would face. Some 'push' factors are 'elements of necessity', which includes aspects such as low-income levels or inability to fulfil personal responsibilities due to strict work schedules; 'pull' factors usually involve factors such as the wish for satisfaction derived from job or the need for having a flexible work schedule. There are different combinations of these factors that determine entry into entrepreneurship depending on the negotiation between the necessities that are unavoidable and the choices that are available to an individual because the decisions that are made depend on their socio-economic context. For instance, due to the socially conditioned role of women as family caregivers, a flexible work schedule becomes an important aspect for them to enter any public activities. Furthermore, when women with families enter the public arena, the risk of the activities tends to rise in relation to the private domain because, in addition to professional responsibilities at the workplace, the expectations of taking care of the family do not reduce.

Brush, de Bruin, and Welter (2009) elucidate in their framework that both individual and societal factors play an equally important role in determining entry into businesses. Structural and infrastructural limitations as well as family pressures and expectations restrict women's entry into entrepreneurship at the grassroots level because their decision-making abilities are often influenced by both 'internal' and 'external' forces (Brindley 2005). Elaborating on the public-private dichotomy mentioned previously, women moving into a public realm face higher risks in many societies, which is why they are restricted from moving out of the private realm by decisions made within the household. Armstrong and Squires (2002) emphasize that such 'spatial divisions' further reproduce sexual inequalities in societies and need to be addressed for mainstreaming gender issues. The 'relative disadvantages' that women face often lead to their businesses incurring lesser income than their male counterparts, as Loscocco et al. (1991) have noted in their work. They further mention that such disadvantages are structurally perpetuated due to the characteristics of the business itself.

In the case of *jugaad* and its elements of innovation and risk, the leadership of such activities has been primarily recognized as the domain of males due to their seemingly higher propensity towards doing risky activities; in consequence, they get higher infrastructural support to conduct such activities. However, it has been observed that the actual workers are mostly women due to their higher inclination towards such tasks. Namely, flexible working hours and low-key operations allow them to work without any need for a lengthy official registration. But the same factors that restrict them from working in formal sectors also put them at risk in the informal sectors due to exploitation of their labour, with no fixed working hours in strenuous conditions and a lower pay scale. Recently, women-owned small-scale businesses and enterprises are steadily rising, but structural changes in the planning systems need to be effected for any ground-breaking involvement of women in leadership in the foreseeable future.

Like other inequalities, Razavi and Silke (2010, 107) have stated that "gender inequalities are complex". Even though employment levels of women in informal sectors have grown, leadership positions are not often accorded to women themselves and their labour is often utilized in an exploitative manner. The differences in wages and income levels, leadership opportunities, and their representation in legal and political matters have led to disparities in the conditions of women and men in the workplace. Planning frameworks thus need to recognize the efforts of women at the grassroots level and work towards diminishing the structural and organizational disparities that are unable to accord women a similar level of opportunities to enhance and stimulate their innovation potential. The recognition of their efforts would enable higher participation of women in entrepreneurial activities and instead of just being members of the informal sector, they would also be a part of the upper echelon.

To break such barriers and achieve empowerment of women, various possibilities and factors can be examined to convert *jugaad* into a more open and accessible activity. These include providing micro-financing to grassroots movements (Mayoux 2000), which could help enhance the self-sufficiency of women-run enterprises and reduce the risks of involvement in *jugaad* or creative activities. Furthermore, partnerships between local and global actors could also lead to the 'economic empowerment' of women on a larger scale and enable them to become more effective participants in their communities instead of being limited to a donor-recipient relationship with private corporations (Wesely and Dublon 2015). In their urban missions and schemes, the government can thus act as a business incubator in such a scenario by ensuring that financing methods and partnerships are provided within an open and supportive environment instead of being bogged down by regulations. Even though each of these possibilities has their own gendered and structural challenges that need to be overcome before any progress is made, there is growing recognition of the innovative potential at the grassroots level in Indian cities, which can be tapped into with proper planning frameworks in place.

A case study that illustrates the constant gendered challenges and obstacles faced by some women—and a *jugaad* method to overcome them—is the creation of an "alternative banking" system by the cooperative Self-Employed Women's Association (SEWA) for the financial needs of its members. In her work, Abbott (1997) describes how the women of the Association faced daily struggles to establish themselves and were constrained by the registration process set by higher authorities. Their legitimacy was constantly under scrutiny due to the illiterate status of some of the impoverished women involved in the Association. To gain entry into a world of finance that was usually considered a domain of the elite, they challenged the powerful structure of the banking system by requesting to create an 'alternative banking' system by pooling their resources to suit their needs. Initially, their request to establish this system, and for funding their initiatives, accordingly, were not taken seriously. However, they continued to persist and forged ahead with their own banking system, ultimately initiating radical modifications in the monetary system of the entire country, such as a shift from private to nationalised banking (Abbott 1997).

Such cooperatives and community organizations can be utilized to support the comprehensive rejuvenation of cities. The Atal Mission for Rejuvenation and Urban Transformation (AMRUT) is an urban mission of the central government that focuses on largescale infrastructural improvement in urban areas. The main purpose of AMRUT is to improve the quality of life of the citizens of cities, especially those who are poor and disadvantaged, through provision of basic services to households, building amenities, and upgrading public transport. Since the coverage of 500 cities and towns of the urban mission is very wide, its reach can be limited and excludes some people who either do not have legal access to these urban services or are unable to afford it. Municipal governments have been entrusted with the responsibility of preparing the Service Level Improvement Plans (SLIPs) that are incorporated by state governments into their State Annual Action Plans (SAAPs), which are then approved by the central government. In effect, the onus lies on the municipal governments of cities to reform the institutional structure to improve delivery of urban services to citizens, especially the urban poor, by seeking the involvement of community organizations, such as cooperatives and SHGs. The latter's participation and input will contribute towards a better understanding of the issues on the ground and improving capacities of the governments for effective mission implementation.

Facilitating Inclusive Urban Planning and Entrepreneurialism

Cities in India are hoping to align their planning visions to attain the United Nation's SDG 11 of "making cities inclusive, safe, resilient and sustainable by 2030"[5]. To achieve this, the central government is currently implementing various urban missions and schemes focused on sustainable urban development with emphasis on projects spread across different parts of the city. Such missions are being developed in the hopes of attracting the interest of private corporations and collaborations with international investors. Development in sites of informal settlements, specifically areas with slums, is part of such ongoing projects aimed at converting the city into a space of beautification and entrepreneurialism. According to McFarlane (2012, 2795), "The informal settlement emerges not simply as a space excluded from or resistant to entrepreneurial strategies, but as a key frontier in the production of contemporary urban entrepreneurialism." In this context, the co-production of such entrepreneurialism involves a co-operative effort between varied actors ranging from the local population, to civil society organisations, to state government bodies and international institutions.

Although urban entrepreneurialism has shifted focus towards informal settlements and civil society organisations, there is still the presence of *jugaad* activities in such settlements that have not yet been recognized formally. These activities are conducted out of the need to adapt to planning frameworks that do not fully support the resource needs of the settlements, as the capacity of the urban missions and schemes is not wholly efficient in dealing with their comprehensive issues. These missions and schemes themselves reproduce various inequalities in the distribution of resources among the population because an equitable public distribution system is either not in place or not implemented effectively due to issues, such as corruption or elite capture of resources. This failure of equitable distribution ultimately results in intersectional implications across social categories, as different caste, community, religious, and gender groups are affected differently and have to resort to varied coping mechanisms. A failure in the planning framework, thus, is also represented by an inadequacy in the recognition of the rights of different groups to access to resources.

There are occasions when even the state does some jugaad of its own to serve its interests, meaning that such activities are not limited to the lower income groups. Roy (2009, 80) argues that "urban planning in India has to be understood as the

---

[5] In 2015, many member countries of the United Nations adopted the 2030 Agenda for Sustainable Development and its seventeen Sustainable Development Goals (SDGs), which includes SDG 11 as one of its dedicated goals for cities. For more information: https://sdgs.un.org/goals

management of resources, particularly land, through dynamic processes of informality". Informality here represents a 'state of deregulation', and she elaborates that the law becomes open to interpretation when there is a situation wherein the state has to reap benefits from any situation and has an avenue of profit in partnership with private collaborators (Roy 2009). For instance, in order to acquire land that is occupied by slum dwellers, it undergoes a process of 'unmapping', or a process of not recognizing the rights of the current residents to occupy the area because their residency is considered illegal. The development of the land is categorized under 'public purpose', which would require an evacuation of all the current residents, and usually an established resettlement plan is not in place that can compensate for the losses incurred by the displaced individuals.

The individuals and collectives that engage in *jugaad* activities enter such activities due to several reasons, including 'coping behaviour', when there are limited economic opportunities and 'rational behaviour', when some individuals seek to sidestep regulations set by the state (Kumar and Bhaduri 2014). The implications for some of these activities is that individuals often find it difficult to follow the strict rules of entering businesses due to low capital and financial support by formal institutions, as they do not have the collateral for acquiring resources to execute their ideas. Similarly, due to the existence of 'legal pluralism' in cities, legal mechanisms have various interpretations based on the vested interests of powerful groups, which have a tendency to exclude many individuals from the formal regulatory mechanisms of the state (Fernandes and Varley 1998). Since inefficient urban planning can have a tendency of reproducing inequalities, resorting to jugaad and innovative strategies is an alternative for independent and collective entrepreneurs who wish to find survival solutions for the occasional perpetuating exclusionary actions of state bodies.

Although the urban poor face disadvantages in terms of urban planning frameworks that structurally exclude them, they sometimes do hold a collective political leverage that helps in overcoming their vulnerabilities. In situations known as 'votebank politics', if a particular poor community is the majority vote holders during elections in their constituencies, they often adapt a survival strategy of supporting political leaders who have the power to improve their conditions. Mahadevia and Joshi (2009, 3) elaborate that "the poor in the cities subvert the Planning through political patronage", which enables them to engage in 'coping strategies' that can diminish the negative effects of developmental planning.

The case study of an area called Nandigram on the outskirts of the Calcutta metropolitan region in West Bengal showcases the power of the community with political backing (Roy 2009). The residents resisted a planned development by the ruling party of converting the region into a Special Economic Zone (SEZ) because it deeply affected their agricultural livelihood. The state government made the decision to collaborate with private enterprises to transform the area into an international economic hub and incur profit under the pretext of 'public purpose', but without consulting the residents first because the government is the ultimate owner of public land in India. Instead of quietly resigning to the situation, the residents, along with the support of the opposition political party, fought to stop the detrimental development from occurring. Despite facing a lot of violence, they ultimately succeeded, and the SEZ operations had to be shifted. This demonstrates the strength of communities when they come together for the common purpose of recognition of their rights and striving for a planning framework that strengthens their coping capacities instead of exacerbating the risks that they face.

Another extensive urban mission by the central government that aims to make 100 cities of India 'smarter' is the Smart Cities Mission (SCM), which promotes innovative practices and solutions for achieving sustainable urban development. According to the Government of India: "The purpose of the Smart Cities Mission is to drive economic growth and improve the quality of life of people by enabling local area development and harnessing technology, especially technology that leads to Smart outcomes" (SCM 2015, 3). This area-based approach is to be adopted by cities for improvement of existing areas, renewal or redevelopment, extension or green-field developments, and pan-city smart solutions, like e-governance and citizen engagement (Shakti Sustainable Energy Foundation 2015). However, in terms of both area-based development and pan-city 'smart' solutions that can be replicated in other areas and cities, existing resources must be used judiciously and innovatively. Notably, as part of this initiative, the central government has encouraged cities to send their development proposals to this mission to compete, out of which the most effective proposals are selected.

A Special Purpose Vehicle (SPV), which comprises of membership from state and city governments as well as the private sector, have been set up in the selected cities to implement the Smart City Proposals (SCPs) that were developed by the city governments in collaboration with external entities, such as consultancies and policy think tanks. Cities' SPVs are responsible for the implementation of the SCPs—herein is the opportunity for them to involve and include different stakeholders to achieve sustainable urban practice. The *jugaad* practices of communities that demonstrate innovative resource management can be showcased as best practice examples under the SCM, which then have the possibility of being adapted in other areas and cities. Thus, to achieve inclusivity as per SDG 11, a participatory approach to planning that can promote coordination within governments as well as between the governments, private sector agencies, and communities involved in urban development of cities is required.

The Jugaad of Urban Planning

From being ruled by the Mughal emperors, to being colonised by the British, to currently being an independent and democratic modern state, ideas of (and about) India have historically transformed in often contradictory ways due to contestations between religious ideologies, political struggles, and economic development. As Khilnani (2004, 149) expresses: "India's cities are hinged between its vast population spread across the countryside and the hectic tides of the global economy, with its ruthlessly shifting tastes and its ceaseless murmur of the pleasures and hazards of modernity". Along with the constant reinvention of India's cities, the definition of the "Indianness" of its people has also transformed over the decades. One thing that remains unchanged, however, is peoples' ability to persist and improvise survival strategies irrespective of difficulties in their socio-environmental conditions.

The role of the state in India is paramount in developing policies for the welfare of its citizens, and so it is also their responsibility to facilitate the accomplishment of these policies for the benefit of all citizens. However, there are some structural limitations in achieving this goal that have gendered connotations, as there is unequal availability of opportunities for women and men. Basu (1998, 7) elucidates: "State intervention often complements, upholds, and reinforces the interests of patriarchal communities by disregarding or denigrating women's attempts to free themselves from community sanctions". In this scenario of restricting the abilities of a few sections of society, fulfilling substantive citizenship becomes difficult, which leads to citizens opting for alternative solutions or means to an end that may not be the formal route laid down by the state. Such alternative strategies, or *jugaad* activities, turn into a lifestyle choice for those excluded from decision-making processes and those who wish to make the best of their current situation.

Chen and Raveendran (2011, 1) have stated that the urban workforce of India is "becoming increasingly informal", with a notable percentage of the workforce self-employed and either working from home or in "open public spaces". With such a trend in the employment patterns of the country, the labour force seems to be opting for alternative job markets instead of being absorbed into 'formal wage employment' sectors. Due to a high population density in cities for reasons, such as migration from rural areas in search of better living or economic opportunities, there usually remains a higher demand for jobs in relation to the supply by the formal labour markets. This leads to individuals opting for alternative strategies to acquire resources for their survival. The informal economy, then, presents itself as a solution to the problems of unemployment even though it is not often acknowledged as a legitimate form of wage labour. Hence, alternative job markets are equally significant and need to be included in the planning frameworks initiated to improve the poverty and employment issues of the country.

If transformative power must be given to the citizens themselves by tapping into the creativity potential found in such informal sectors, then a pre-requisite for improving planning frameworks is to mainstream gender issues in order to increase participation of all communities and recognition of their potential. This research study aims to supplement the existing literature on the understanding of citizenship rights of the urban poor in cities and the survival strategies they adopt when these rights are not acknowledged by formal institutions. By understanding these survival strategies through a gendered lens, this study hopes to contribute to creating an inclusive planning framework that would act as a supportive mechanism to reduce the risks and vulnerabilities faced by different communities.

Based on works by Rawls (1971) and Young (1990), developing a planning framework with a social justice lens would be extremely helpful in ensuring that gendered challenges are being addressed. Such a lens would entail participation of all stakeholders in shaping the urban development of the city, recognition of their citizenship rights and a fulfilment of their duties in a responsible manner, and a redistribution of resources conducted judiciously amongst citizens (figure 5). A framework of social justice that promotes citizen participation might even eliminate the need for negative *jugaad* entirely by recognizing the framing of jugaad from a gendered perspective and allowing the possibility of closing the gap between the fulfilment of formal and substantive citizenship for both women and men. It would enable individuals to secure justice and ensure that their social circumstances, environmental risks, economic conditions, and political lifestyles are all filled with opportunities and choices to improve their surroundings, rather than limiting them.

As *jugaad* is a dynamic process with citizens constantly adapting to their ever-changing environs and demands of society, the planning framework consequently needs to have a 'room for manoeuvre' clause so that it is a resilient framework that can respond to changes without extreme ramifications (Levy 2015). Indian urban planning has a tendency to have a strategic spatial planning bent, implying a focus on entrepreneurialism on a short-term and profit-based project basis with different spaces of the city being worked on separately, which is not akin to an integrated approach to planning wherein different components of the city are developed together. Moving beyond this project-based approach with a possible shift towards strategic action planning would be useful in accommodating the innovation and risks that are a part of *jugaad* activities. In addition to expanding the 'room for manoeuvre', the strategic action planning approach would also engage in a reciprocal recognition method to fulfil the urban missions in a manner that aligns with SDG 11. This entails individuals and the state working as collaborative partners along with recognition of mutual efforts to be agents of change in cities.

Figure 5: Tenets of social justice.

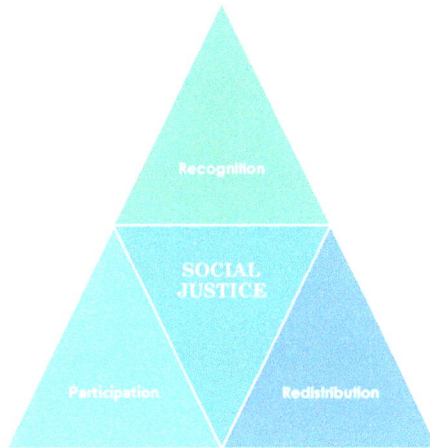

Source: Adapted by Author from Rawls 1971; Young 1990

Before looking into the adaptive strategies of citizens, it is also relevant to ensure that they are living in a situation that facilitates convenient access to all entitled opportunities and optimal utilization of allocated resources. The onus for this facilitation lies firstly with the state, which has a legal responsibility to support its citizens; secondly with the society, which has a moral obligation to not allow discrimination or exclusion amongst its members; and finally, with the citizens themselves, who should be aware of their accountability and actively fulfil the duties required of them. Beyond these minimally expected roles, any additional actions performed by the citizens to reduce their burdens should be encouraged, as it would inculcate participation and convert them from being a passive member of society into being an active agent of change. For instance, the ideology of co-operatives having various services that induce collective mobilization of citizens to work in partnership with government organizations is a pragmatic approach in overcoming the heterogeneous risks faced by the citizens.

As stated in a WIEGO paper (2014, 2) on co-operatives and the informal economy: "Cooperatives can provide income and enhance livelihoods, help workers gain control of and improve their employment conditions, and enhance workers' access to resources, facilities, public institutions, and markets". And, due to their frequent inclusion and mobilization of poor women and men to influence policy-making decisions at the local and national levels, they also "promote a wider model of socially inclusive development" (WIEGO 2014, 2). Co-operatives can thus play an important role in incorporating the innovation of *jugaad* activities and absorbing some of the unavoidable risks for conducting these activities in the informal economy. With financial support provided by international organizations, legal groundwork laid by the government, and a system of accountable governance arranged amongst its membership, the flexibility provided by a co-operative institution would be useful in the self-organization of workers in a sustainable manner.

Attempting to develop an ideal planning system that can adapt to an idea of *jugaad* should thus have the tenets of social justice as well as strategic action planning to have equal participation of all individuals concerned, recognition of their rights, and a just redistribution of resources. In such a scenario, it is significant to understand that even though *jugaad* could have been avoided if there was a functional and inclusive planning framework, once it has occurred; it is relevant to focus on the positive aspects of innovation and creativity of *jugaad* to ensure at least an avenue for inclusive participation. Emphasizing the idea of *upyogi jugaad*, or useful *jugaad*, can serve as a possible suffix for the extended *jugaad* vocabulary. Such recognition of the potential of a positive *jugaad* can enable all citizens of cities to have an equitably granted power to shape their lives as well as transform their city.

REFERENCES

Abbott, Dina. 1997. "Who Else Will Support Us? How Poor Women Organise the Unorganisable in India". *Community Development Journal* 32 (3): 1 99–209.

Ahluwalia, Isher Judge. 2014. *Planning for Urban Development in India*. Indian Council for Research on International Economic Relations.
http://icrier.org/Urbanisation/pdf/Ahluwalia_Planning_for_Urban_%20Development.pdf

Armstrong, Chris, and Judith Squires. 2002. "Beyond the Public/Private Dichotomy: Relational Space and Sexual Inequalities". *Contemporary Political Theory* 1 (3): 261–283.

Basu, Amrita. 1998. "Appropriating Gender". In *Appropriating Gender: Women's Activism and Politicized Religion in South Asia*, edited by Patricia Jefferey, and Amrita Basu, 3–14. New York, London: Routledge.
https://books.google.co.in/books/about/Appropriating_Gender.html?id=rlTTLckmR88C&redir_esc=y

Batliwala, Srilatha. 2007. "Taking the Power out of Empowerment: An Experiential Account". *Development in Practice* 17 (4/5): 557–565.

Bhatia, Anisha. 2017. *Women at The Forefront of Swachh Bharat Abhiyan: Inspiring Stories of Sanitation Revolution from Across India*. NDTV. Accessed from: http://swachhindia.ndtv.com/women-forefront-swachh-bharat-abhiyan-inspiring-stories-sanitation-revolution-across-india-14173/

Brindley, Clare. 2005. "Barriers to Women Achieving Their Entrepreneurial Potential: Women and Risk". *International Journal of Entrepreneurial Behaviour & Research* 11 (2): 144–161.

Brush, Candida G., Anne de Bruin, and Friederike Welter. 2009. "A Gender-aware Framework for Women's Entrepreneurship". *International Journal of Gender and Entrepreneurship* 1 (1): 8–24.

Chen, Martha Alter, and G. Raveendran. 2011. "Urban Employment in India: Recent Trends and Patterns". WIEGO Working papers, Working Paper No. 7.
http://www.wiego.org/sites/default/files/publications/files/Chen-Urban-Employment-India-WIEGO-WP7.pdf

Co-operative College. 2014. *Co-operatives and Workers in the Informal Economy: Possibilities and Challenges*. Women in Informal Employment Globalizing and Organizing (WIEGO).
http://www.wiego.org/sites/default/files/publications/files/Co-operative_College-Cooperatives_Informal_Workers_2014.pdf

Edesio, Fernandes, and Ann Varley, eds. 1998. *Illegal Cities: Law and Urban Change in Developing Countries*. London, New York: Zed Books.

Fordham, Maureen, Suranjana Gupta, Supriya Akerkar, and Manuela Scharf. 2011. *Leading Resilient Development: Grassroots Women's Priorities, Practices and Innovations*. Report by UNDP, GROOTS International & Northumbria University School of the Built and Natural Environment.
http://www.undp.org/content/undp/en/home/librarypage/womens-empowerment/leading-resilient-development---grassroots-women-priorities-practices-and-innovations.html

Grant, Judith. 1993. "Review Essay: Is the Personal Still Political?". *NWSA Journal* 5 (3): 404–411.

Khan, Mohd Imran. 2017. "14,000 Rural Women are Changing Bihar, One Toilet at a Time." YourStory. Accessed from: https://yourstory.com/2017/10/open-defecation-bihar/

Khilnani, Sunil. 2004. "Cities". In *the Idea of India*, 107–149. India: Penguin Books.

Kumar, Hemant and Saradindu Bhaduri. 2014. "Jugaad to Grassroot Innovations: Understanding the Landscape of the Informal Sector Innovations in India". *African Journal of Science, Technology, Innovation and Development* 6 (1): X-XX.

Levy, Caren. 2015. "Expanding the "Room for Manoeuvre": Community-led Finance in Mumbai, India". In *the City in Urban Poverty*, edited by Charlotte Lemanski, and Colin Marx, 158–182. Houndmills, Basingstoke: Palgrave/MacMillan.

Loscocco, Karyn A., Joyce Robinson, Richard H. Hall, and John K. Allen. 1991. "Gender and Small Business Success: An Inquiry into Women's Relative Disadvantage". *Social Forces* 70 (1): 65–85.

Mahadevia, Darshini, and Rutul Joshi. 2009. *Subversive Urban Development in India: Implications on Planning Education*. Working Paper 1, Centre for Urban Equity. CEPT University, Ahmedabad,

India.
http://cept.ac.in/UserFiles/File/CUE/Working%20Papers/01CUEWP1_Subversive_%20Urban_
%20Development_%20in_%20India_%20Implications_%20on_%20Planning_%20Education.p
df

Mayoux, Linda. 2000. "Micro-finance and the Empowerment of Women: A Review of the Key Issues".
Social Finance, Working Paper No. 23, ILO. http://www.ilo.org/wcmsp5/groups/public/---
ed_emp/documents/publication/wcms_117993.pdf

McFarlane, Colin. 2012. "The Entrepreneurial Slum: Civil Society, Mobility and the Co-production of
Urban Development". *Urban Studies* 49(13): 2795–2816.

McLeod, Ruth. 2000. "Bridging the Financing Gap in Housing and Infrastructure the Mumbai Case Study".
India: SPARC. http://www.ucl.ac.uk/dpu-
projects/drivers_urb_change/urb_infrastructure/pdf_shelter_settlements/HI_McLeod_Bridging_
Gap_India.pdf

Ministry of Housing and Urban Affairs. 2017. "Guidelines for Swachh Bharat Mission – Urban".
Government of India.
http://www.swachhbharaturban.in:8080/sbm/content/writereaddata/SBM_Guideline.pdf

Nicholson, Nigel, Emma Soane, Mark Fenton-O'Creevy, and Paul Willman. 2005. "Personality and
Domain-specific Risk Taking". *Journal of Risk Research* 8 (2): 157–176.

Orhan, Muriel, and Don Scott. 2001. "Why Women Enter into Entrepreneurship: An Explanatory Model".
Women in Management Review 16 (5): 232–247.

Radjou, Navi, Jaideep Prabhu, and Simone Ahuja. 2012. "Jugaad: A Breakthrough Growth Strategy". In
Jugaad Innovation: Think Flexible, Be Frugal, Generate Breakthrough Growth, 1–28. San
Francisco, CA: Jossey Bass.

Rajavi, Shahra, and Silke Staab. 2010. "Gender Inequalities at Home and in the Market". In UNRISD
Report, *Combating Poverty and Inequality: Structural Change, Social Policy and Politics*, 107–
131. France: UNRISD Publications.
http://www.unrisd.org/80256B3C005BCCF9/(httpAuxPages)/8BACF1B0908D70E1C12577890
0323600/$file/PovRepCh4.pdf

Rawls, John. 1971. *Justice as Fairness. A Theory of Justice"*. Cambridge, Massachusetts: The Belknap
Press of Harvard University Press.

Right to Fair Compensation and Transparency in Land Acquisition, Rehabilitation and Resettlement Act
2013. Accessed from: http://indiacode.nic.in/acts-in-pdf/302013.pdf.

Roy, Ananya. 2009. "Why India Cannot Plan Its Cities: Informality, Insurgence and the Idiom of
Urbanization". *Planning Theory* 8(1), 76–87.

Shakti Sustainable Energy Foundation. 2015. "India's Flagship Urban Missions – Smart Cities and
AMRUT". Accessed from: http://shaktifoundation.in/indias-flagship-urban-missions-smart-
cities-and-amrut/

Singh, Apula. 2016. "Let's Talk About AMRUT Before We Get to Smart Cities". Huffpost. Accessed from:
https://www.huffingtonpost.in/apula-singh/lets-talk-about-amrut-before-we-get-to-smart-
cities_a_21476982/

Smart Cities Mission. 2015. "What is Smart City". Ministry of Housing and Urban Affairs, Government of
India. Accessed from: http://smartcities.gov.in/content/innerpage/what-is-smart-city.php

Thorpe, Maria Scarzella. 2014. "Interview: Philippines Social Entrepreneur Illac Diaz Listens to, and
Learns from, Local Talent." Asia Society Northern California. Accessed from:
https://asiasociety.org/blog/asia/interview-philippines-social-entrepreneur-illac-diaz-listens-and-
learns-local-talent

Walby, Sylvia. 1994. "Is Citizenship Gendered?" *Sociology* 28 (2): 379–395.

Wesely, Marissa and Dina Dublon. 2015. "Empowering Women at the Grassroots". *Stanford Social
Innovation Review* Spring 2015: 27–33.

Women in Informal Employment: Globalizing and Organizing (WIEGO). 2014. "Co-operatives and
Workers in the Informal Economy: Possibilities and Challenges". WIEGO: Cambridge, USA.

Young, Iris Marion. 1990. "Displacing the Distributive Paradigm". In *Justice and Politics of Difference*, 37.
New Jersey: Princeton University Press.

Chapter 5

Visual Ideology and Social Imaginary: A New Approach to the Aesthetics of Globalization[38]

Tommaso Durante

Introduction

This article attempts to develop an alternative theoretical framework that approaches contemporary globalization through its visual-ideological dimension. This is achieved by looking at the phenomenon as a complex material and ideational process, ideologically articulated. In this perspective this study looks at particular types of symbolic forms working as complex, rhetorical, and powerful devices depicting a recurrent theme, a motif, a "pictorial trope" (see also Wilson 2008) that helps to frame and mobilize people's perception of the "world as a whole" (Robertson 1992, 8). In this perspective, such practice-based research approaches "the social world objectively, as a symbolic system" (Bourdieu 1989, 132) and is carried out by means of photographic fieldwork in selected global and fast globalizing cities across the planet. Theoretically informed and methodologically articulated, this investigation seeks to sketch the visual ideology of globalization through the identification of particular class of images and their categorization as "condensation symbols and other visual ideological markers of globality" (Durante 2016, 54–56). The study is not about "political symbols" (Edelman 1985) rather it explores the different ways in which the symbols themselves can be understood in order to demonstrate the utility and, indeed, the necessity of these different new figures of knowledge to grasp the complex phenomenon of globalization. While existing studies on the ideological dimension of globalization as such have been so far mainly focused on the discursive-ideological dimension of the multidimensional process (Steger 2009), in a world dominated by images, this study highlights the dynamic tension between the local and the global by means of visual constructs to better understand the impact of globalization on local-national meanings, cultural identities, and nation-state (see also

---

[38] This chapter is an edited version of the essay "Visual Ideology and Social Imaginary: A New Approach to the Aesthetics of Globalization" first published in *Spaces and Flow: An International Journal of Urban and Extra Urban Studies* 9 (1): 15-34.

Albrow 1996). It also attempts to grasp and encode new visual-discursive understandings of the interaction among spaces, people, and media representations, including the different materiality of the web. The theoretical issues related to "condensation symbols and other visual ideological markers of globality" (Durante 2016, 54–56) are at the core of this research contribution, which aims to advance methodological knowledge in the "new" field of Global Studies as well as to expand the range of studies in socio-political theory where these "new" categories can be employed (Juergensmeyer 2014; Darian-Smith and McCarty 2017; Mittelman 2004; Pieterse 2013; Steger and Wahlrab 2017).

This article is meant as a contribution to fill the gap in the knowledge of the visual-ideological dimension of globalization. This is achieved through a broad and improved understanding of how the "global imaginary," the rise of a new public consciousness (Steger 2008) as an "organised field of social practices" (Appadurai 1996, 31), is turned at a certain point in time into the visual ideology of globalization. The global imaginary can be defined as the perception—the sense—of the world as a whole that frames the epochal change we are witnessing shaped by the forces of globalization. In this respect, this study also makes use of complementary constructs articulated by Jacques Lacan (1956), Charles Taylor (2007), and John B. Thompson (1982).

More specifically, this investigation aims to grasp and visualize how "pre-reflexive self-consciousness"[39] is translated through media representations into the visual ideology of globalization. Thus, it is argued that these particular classes of images constitute the tangible, visual-ideological dimension of the global. In that sense, they contribute to constructing the ideological shift from the national to the global. In this respect, this study acknowledges a continuum [40]between scientific understanding and subjective experience (see also Merleau-Ponty 2002), arguing that, at any given point in time, subjectivity represents the condition for every objective understanding of the world. Thus, by giving to the objective and subjective aspects of globalization phenomenon equal consideration, it can be argued that the ongoing process of change and transformation "does not merely happen in the world 'out there' but also operates through our consciousness, 'in here'" (Steger and Wahlrab 2017, 2).

---

[39] A pre-reflective self-consciousness is pre-reflective in the sense that it is not an explicit form of self-consciousness. However, a reflective self-consciousness is possible only because of a pre-reflective self-awareness that is an ongoing and primary self-consciousness (Callagher 2006).

[40] This study embraces continuity between scientific understanding and qualitative research (experience) and recognises the value of this continuum. As Maurice Merleau-Ponty observes, "the perceived world is the always presupposed foundation of all rationality, all values and all existence. This thesis does not destroy either rationality or the absolute. It only tries to bring them down to earth" (Merlau-Ponty 2002, 13). Thus, it can be said that the subjective experience and its scientific re- description are part of the same order of signification (see also Durante 2013, 35–38; Jay 1994, 303).

I deem it useful to clarify that in this article I use ideology as a "neutral" tool for critical investigation and not as a squarely political concept.[41] However, it has socio-political and cultural implications that I will further unfold through the case-study in the dedicated section (Condensation Symbols and Other Visual Ideological Marker of Globality: Globe-Trotter Case study). In social studies, "political ideology" is generally defined as a certain set of ideals, principles, doctrines, myths, or symbols of a social movement, institution, or group that defines and explains how society should work (see also Freeden 2013; Steger 2008, 2013b). Therefore, political ideologies are necessary constructive elements in a democratic society (Schwarzmantel 2008). Indeed, a political ideology largely concerns itself with how to allocate power and to what ends it should be used. In that sense, these visual global constructs under investigation do not suggest how power should be used. Nevertheless, it can be argued that, by mediating and re- arranging local-national meanings around the global, these new cultural objects give more and more symbolic power to the "global." According to Roland Barthes (2013), visual images have both a literal (direct) denotative meaning and a connotative one, which is essentially an ideological one. For this reason, images must be understood in their defined socio -historical and cultural context (see also Berger 1972). Therefore, these complex new figures of knowledge need to be further investigated and deeper understood through a process of critical analysis and interpretation. By applying this process to the selected visual evidence (Figure 1), it will be possible to grasp how, beyond the detection of the ideologies and systems of values embedded in the identified new cultural object, the global is precisely injected into the local-national and vice versa.

Due to the complexity of the globalization and aiming to account of its visual-ideological dimension, this investigation calls for a transdisciplinary approach by looking at the link between the material (aesthetic) and ideological (ideational) dimensions of the process. It is undeniable that the pictures featured in this article represent some of the concrete tracks and keys to access the social (global) imaginary; however, such access and the related interpretation still remain quite problematic. Deeply aware that globalization also works through visual images, the identification and categorization of this new class of cultural objects constitute the methodological original contribution to the literature on the phenomenon with respect to previous scholarship. Indeed, in acknowledging the intimate relationship among aesthetics, imaginary, and ideology, this study attempts to grasp the point in time at which the pre-reflexive imaginary dimension is turned into the visual-ideology of globalization. This study does not deny the value of the current approaches to globalization dynamics, but it strongly asserts that they can be better understood if we also

---

[41] Deeply aware that ideology is a slippery term and evokes strong emotional responses, it is necessary to clarify that with the term "neutral", this study refers to Michael Freeden's use of ideology as a "neutral" tool for investigation (2003)

investigate the way in which the abstract notion of the phenomenon is turned into concrete real-world experience through practice-based research.

In this respect, it can be observed that, from the dawn of history, human beings have been creating objects to symbolize, to represent, and to convey message. The symbol[42] is a cultural construct (Arnheim 2004); it is not the thing itself but a representation—something that stands for something else. In that sense, the symbols of the global, such as in Figures 5 and 7, can refer to the idea of the world as a whole, a concept related to something that is absent or impossible to perceive without the mediation of representation, something whose perception or feeling depends in some way on the symbol itself. Accordingly, this study argues that these images of the global not only reflect but, even more, construct ideology. Thus, in investigating the relationship between the social imaginary and the ideologies of globalization, a new interesting aspect emerges. It is a process that sees the transformation of people's imaginary dimension into the visual ideology of globalization. Therefore, the originality of this investigation is that it is carried out through practice-based research.

While one can easily agree on the importance of globalization as an economic and political process, it would be a mistake not to consider its cultural visual-ideological dimension of equal importance. Thus, located at the crossroad of global, urban, and media studies, this investigation looks at the entanglements between social imaginaries and global ideologies by making use of a new class of images "as historical evidence" (Burke 2001, 7), and it combines photographic fieldwork with visual methodology (Banks 2001; Barthes 1964; Collier and Collier 1986; Faccioli and Gibbons 2007; Grady 2007; Pink 2004, 2008; Pink, Laszlo, and Afonso 2004; Rose 2011) and methods of critical analysis and interpretation (Fairclough 2001, 2003, 2010) in order to gain new knowledge.

As previously acknowledged, there is no objectivity without subjectivity because object and subject are understood as part of the same order of signification. Although this new regime of representation and signification—this new aesthetic aspect of contemporary globalization—does not represent a particular cultural or political entity, it does have socio-political and cultural implications that require to be further investigated. Indeed, limitations can be identified in regard to the very nature of the empirical evidence and the entity of the sampled material. These aspects and the way in which they support my arguments will be better developed in the last section of this article specifically dedicated to this important feature.

---

[42] Rudolf Arnheim's visual thinking theory, and in particular his reflection on "Pictures, Symbols, and Signs" (2004, 135- 152), helps to structure the symbolic dimension of the phenomenon of globalization and the important role images play in suggesting, supporting, and sustaining the shift from the national to the global. In so doing, this study pays particular attention to logo brands, logotypes, and media representations in general in relation to their spatial settings. Accordingly, and by following Rudolph Arnheim's argument (2004, 140–148), there is an "Image Scale" and an "Experience Scale," both of which work together to determine the function and value associated with images. This suggests that images can be simultaneously representations and abstractions, while symbols evoke emotions associated with situations (Edelman 1985

My arguments are based on the hypothesis that these new figures of knowledge are more than new thinking tools, more than new categories to frame the undergoing process of globalization. "Condensation symbols" and "visual ideological markers of globality" (Durante 2016, 54–56) are new cultural objects that embody a new aesthetic form of global imagination, a new visual regime of representation and signification that captures the present historical moment. Thus, to construct my argument, I begin with an understanding of globalization as a material and ideational process; then I deal with the visual-ideological aspect of globalization—the production, circulation, and consumption of increasing particular symbolic forms; and finally, I explain why this particular type of visual images works as the visual ideological apparatus of globalization by also suggesting related implications. Therefore, this chapter, in investigating the visual-ideological articulation of the phenomenon by locating it within the social imaginary, attempts to open a new space of discussion (aesthetics) [43] on globalization. In doing so, it aims to answer the following question: "What role do 'condensation symbols and other visual ideological markers of globality' play in the construction of the visual-ideological dimension of globalization especially in cities?"

Globalization as a Material and Ideational Process

Although globalization, as a concept and as a process, is highly contested and sometimes has very different meanings in different places, in the academic world as well as in popular media discourses, the phenomenon is largely investigated and understood as the global rise of market capitalism (Arrighi 2005; Beck 2000; Centeno and Cohen 2010; Friedman 1999, 2005; Gilpin 2000; Hart-Landsberg 2013; Mittelman 2000; Sklair 2000; Steger 2009). However, in the last two decades, the digital revolution changed the ways in which we communicate, share, and consume ideas and, above all, the ways in which we imagine fitting together, what is generally defined as the social imaginary. Indeed, the development of new media technologies with the spread of satellite communication, transportation technology, and logistic advancements has given people, goods, services, and capital unprecedented mobility and ubiquity. While we are witnessing an increasingly globalizing world that encompasses a range of political, economic, and cultural changes affecting the whole social world (Harvey 1991), we are also witnessing the re-configuration of the urban and extra-urban spaces across the planet. Even though people's common perception and understanding of space is that it is simply there, intangible and given, transnational cultural flows (Castells 1994, 1996) that are globally spread twenty-

---

[43] With the term aesthetics, this study refers to the original meaning of the ancient Greek world, aisthēsis, the whole sensorial experience, a modality of "distribution of the sensible" (Rancière 2013). It means that rather than reducing the aesthetic practice to the visual perception and to the limited philosophy of art, it is concerned with the whole sensorial fabric of human experience.

four-hours-a- day, seven-days-a-week are filling "the social fabrics of cities" (Netto 2016)[44] with symbolic forms of representational, ideological intensity. As a result, transnational flows are destabilizing the ideological geopolitical boundaries of the modern nation-state and, at the deepest individual level, re-shaping people's social imaginary, and ideologies. The particular class of images identified as "condensation symbols and other visual ideological markers of globality" are part of the global spread of transnational cultural flows and carry embedded values, norms, and culture that mostly facilitate and promote the Western ideals of a free-market ideology—an economic system based on supply and demand with little or no government control.

This study, by linking the social imaginary with global ideologies, is also committed to demystifying both the conception of space as "natural" (see also Bourdieu 2009; Durante 2013; Harvey 1991; Lefebvre 1991, Soja 1989) and an understanding of commercial images as transparent windows—media representations (see also Barthes 1964, 1972; Durante 2013; Hall 2003; Nichols 1981; Rose 2011).

Drawing from Manfred B. Steger's notion of the "global imaginary" as the "people's growing consciousness of belonging to a global community" (2010, 11), with the term "global imaginary" this study refers to a way of seeing and feeling who we are and how we fit together. This is the result of an ongoing process of symbolic construction of the social world happening through the production of a discursive-visual narrative that constitutes our *common sense*[45] of the global in our everyday life. In this respect, "condensation symbols" and "visual ideological markers of globality," although apparently different in their structure, are both visual constructs (cultural objects) able to affect local and national meanings with the same strength. Indeed, both of these "new" thinking tools/figures of knowledge condense many levels of meaning, s y m b o l i c a l l y denoting different geographic scales at local, national, and global levels. The difference between a visual ideological marker of globality and a condensation symbol is that the first one denotes the symbolic collapse of the global over the local and the national while the second one condenses different hybrid layers of meanings. In that sense these visual constructs are able to create the global imaginary in a single place, event, or image. Indeed, I argue that at a certain point in time, the ideational dimension of the global, through media representations, is turned into the "visual ideology" of globalization.

---

[44] In bringing together urban analysis and social science, Vinicius M. Netto (2016) puts forward an innovative conceptual framework, the social fabrics of cities, to reconsider some fundamental features of city-making as a social process. Netto sees the cities as the place of encounters and communication where the causality of events and the repetition of activities are what characterise societies.

[45] By drawing on Antonio Gramsci's (1971) notion of sēnsus commūnis—common sense, this article understands this term as a cultural context where the dominant ideology is practiced and spread, and political power does not maintain control just through violence and economic coercion but also through ideology. This happens through a dominant neoliberal culture in which the system of values of one particular group is turned into common sense for the majority of people by means of media production and re-production.

Here, ideology is understood as related to "discourse" rather than language (Benveniste 1971; Fairclough 2003; Foucault 1994) and as working to suggest to people how to act, or not to act, within the constraints of a given social project, such as the global integration of economic, political, and cultural networks. In that sense, in this article the notion of free-market ideology is seen as the dominant framework that helps to translate the underlying social imaginary into concrete political agendas at the local-global scale. It also works to legitimate a dominant power by promoting beliefs and a system of values linked to neoliberalism and its economic consumeristic and individualistic worldview (Bauman 2006; Harvey 2007; Steger and Roy 2010). This happens by means of the shaping forces of globalization that are transforming the world into a global mall as a result of the geographical borderless project of economic markets' integration. Accordingly, in today's highly-mediatized and increasingly globalizing societies, the systems of representations, of which visual images are the most dominant expression, work as ideological tools that suggest, support, and sustain the shift from the national to the global.

Image, Ideology, and the Social Imaginary

We live in a context in which visual images dominate the world. As a result, they are powerful strategic devices in the meaning-making process of globalization, and for this reason they are also crucial to understand the phenomenon itself. The cultural objects considered in this study are complex visual constructs that represent us in this process (see also Barthes 1964; Cassirer 2008; Nichols 1981; Worth and Gross 1974). In that sense, visual images are ideological tools participating in the construct of the global society and, as a result, into the construction of the global citizen. This approach to globalization draws on Walter Benjamin's aesthetic perspective on change (Benjamin 2002) that mainly relies on visuality rather than on textuality, and on W. J. T. Mitchell's theory of "the surplus value of images" (Mitchell 2005, 94), capable of changing societies' values, creating revolutions, moving people across the globe, and generating wars. In the attempt to sketch a global visual ideology or a visual ideology of globalization, this study considers visual-discursive formations made by text and images that can be produced by an institution, an organization, a significant group, or an individual with the aim to suggest, justify, contest, or change the social, political, cultural arrangements and processes of the modern nation-state by suggesting, supporting, and sustaining global change. On this basis, this study attempts to challenge textual-philosophical approaches to the social imaginary (Appadurai 1996; Castoriadis 1997; Steger 2008; Taylor 2007, Thompson 1982). This happens through a practice-based research and an aesthetic perspective that traces the production of the visual-ideological dimension of globalization by also contributing to overcome the traditional political-philosophical distinction between theory and practice.

In exploring the role that the new global consciousness plays in the construction of the global society, this study understands the "social imaginary" as something more liquid and less structured than an ideology (see also Steger 2008 and Taylor 2007). Drawing on Paul Ricoeur's (1986) identification of the historical elements and functions of ideology in mediating the gap between "belief" and "claim," and according to Max Lerner's (1943) statement that "ideas are weapons," while avoiding the long-lasting discussion on ideology as "false consciousness" (Engels 1972) I understand ideologies as effectively participating in the material and ideational construction of the social world. This happens because ideologies are capable of drawing us into an imaginary relation with the social order, which persuades us and helps to translate the pre-reflexive, imaginary dimension underlying our everyday life into concrete political agendas at any scale of the global. As a result, to grasp the relationship among images, aesthetics, and ideologies, this study makes use of ideology as a framework for critical analysis.

With the term ideology, this study understands the various systems of beliefs, values, life-styles, and strategies underlying and articulating the largely pre-reflexive social (global) imaginary, which endow it with meanings and values such as the idea of a global economic integration of local economies. This implies that, according to Steger's (2009, 217) observation, "it would be a mistake to reduce ideologies to an understanding of mere class claims or metaphysical speculations". It can also be observed that, while much has been said about language and ideology (Fairclough 2001, 2003, 2010), or images and ideology (Argan 1975; Mitchell 1984, 1986, 2005; Nichols 1981), the relationship between global images, social imaginary, and ideologies of globalization is still almost unexplored. For this reason, this article addresses the function and historically contingent ideological status of this new class of images identified as "condensation symbols and other visual ideological markers of globality" (Durante 2013, 2014, 2016). They include images, symbols, metaphors, visual stereotypes, catchphrases, and collective practices, the order of representation that provides the visible frameworks and narratives that, consciously or unconsciously, guide people in their everyday life.

It is worth noting that the term social imaginary refers to the way in which imagination, not simply reason, works in the construction of social institutions, representations, and practices. Thus, dealing with the social imaginary means dealing with the central terms in debates over the role of imagination in the construction of subjective and collective identities. More precisely, with the term "social imaginary" or "imaginary," this study understands the creative and symbolic dimension of the social world, the dimension through which human beings imagine their ways of living together and their ways of representing their collective life. In other words, the social imaginary can be defined as the set of values, institutions, norms, images, and symbols common to a particular social group and corresponding to defined societies. Concurring with Charles Taylor (2007), the term social imaginary can be understood as a state of our collective mind that, while not constituting an established reality, nevertheless is the historical consciousness of society and represents the system of meanings that underlies and drives a given social structure, community or a nation.

A New Aesthetic Approach to Globalization

Given that there are as many modes of globalization as there are globalizing agents, dynamics, and social imaginaries, this research is grounded in a given body of new figures of knowledge understood as visual ideological constructs. These images of the global were mainly collected during photographic fieldwork in some of the global and fast globalizing cities across the planet, and on the internet. To be categorized as "condensation symbols and other visual ideological markers of globality", they can be any type of media representation depicting the globe or the planet earth; however, my attention is mainly focused on symbolic forms combining texts and images (Figures 4, 7, 8 10, and 12). Actually, this study also takes into consideration catchphrases or statements such as "global forever" or the use of words such as "world," "worldly," "global," "globalize," "globality," and so forth (Figures 1, 2, 3, 4, 5, 6, 8, 9, and 11). Deeply aware that these symbolic forms are isolated fragments of the aesthetics of globalization, this study considers them as constitutive of the visual ideological apparatus of the complex, multifaceted and sometimes contradictory phenomenon of change and transformation. The symbolic power of this new class of images relies on the fact that at the meta-ideological level they represent the simplification of the abstract notion of globalization. This is due to the fact that they are able to turn a piece of ideology into the symbolic key elements of globalization discourse. However, it can be observed that each of these fragments does not represent an ideology in itself because, if so, it would have to morphologically highlight and reproduce the form and structure—the set of ideas—that constitute it (see also Freeden 1996). In this respect, let me observe that these symbols of the global are weak and challenging at the same time. They are weak because they may not necessarily represent structured concepts, discourses, nor be considered statements about globalization. At the same time, they are challenging because they are very sophisticated and emotionally charged cultural objects, condensing many layers of meanings and able to affect people's perception and understanding of the world.

Furthermore, because these global images have the power to synthesize and communicate complex and abstract messages, similarly to what happens with the symbols of national identity, they are capable to orient and guide people to navigate the complex socio-historical context in which we live by suggesting, supporting, and sustaining the shift from the national to the global. As a result, it can be argued that the socializing nature of these images of the global, such as any other nationalistic or religious symbol, relies on their very generic nature, while their symbolic power relies on their capacity to be emotionally embedded, ideologically charged, and strongly evocative. An example is the Travelex logo (Figure 10) or the RMIT University's "Shaping the World" catchphrase, overlapping and reinforcing an evocative artistic representation of the globe (Figure 9). Indeed, it can be appreciated that the effectiveness of these images, although not representing a normative or scientific dimension of the global, nevertheless contributes to construct the grand narrative of globalization. This happens because of their capacity to mediate and reconfigure the local and the national around the global by giving, in turn, more and more symbolic power to the global.

In identifying, visualizing, and collecting these new figures of knowledge, this study looks at the conceptual construct represented by the nation-state tied to a geographical territory (Sassen 2006, 2007) and to a defined culture as the ideological expression of the national imaginary of the twentieth century against condensed symbolic forms of the Global Age. Indeed, as the multidimensional process of globalization continues to undermine the national imaginary and its embedded nationalistic ideology, globalization forces are not only reshaping the new world order, economic power, and structures, but they are also affecting the symbolic environment on a local scale and, more broadly, people's perception of the world. In this respect, this study observes that the relationship between particular types of media representations and globalization should, in fact, be understood as constitutive, rather than simply representative or reflective, of a proper global visual ideology.

This thesis is grounded on the fact that people have always been using symbols to explain cosmic phenomena, the dynamic structure of the universe, philosophical concepts, religious systems of belief, and political ideologies. The challenging aspect of these classes of images is the fact that they preserve an identical emotional power in different contexts because of their symbolic power of "ideological de-contextualization" (Freeden 2003, 54–55).

The given body of visual evidence accompanying this article is characterized in different ways by "the condensation of spatial-symbolic scales which used to be fixed on the national but are now increasingly reflecting multiple levels mediated by the global" (Durante 2013, 71). Thus, it can be said that what came up from this study is that the objective dynamics of globalization are complemented by a visual-ideological dimension and that the given body of visual images grounding this article can be considered as part of its visual ideological apparatus.

Accordingly, this I claim that what we are witnessing is a phenomenon similar to the one related to the visual ideology of the Holy Roman Empire or, more recently, to the symbolic construction of nationalistic and political ideologies of the nineteenth and twentieth century. These latter visual ideologies contributed to the creation and consolidation of the modern self- contained nation-state. Some examples are the symbols of national identity such as national flags, national emblems, coat of arms/seals, or national iconic landmarks (e.g., the Eiffel Tower in Paris, the Statue of Liberty in New York, the Pudong skyline in Shanghai, Buckingham and Westminster Palaces in London, Tiananmen Square in Beijing, the Colosseum in Rome). However, it is worth noting that in the flows of visual representations, only a limited number of images gain prominence in the collective consciousness. These iconic (popular) images allow individuals to identify themselves with a collective identity—the global imaginary.

Globalization as a Visual-Ideological Phenomenon

Given that no experience is ever purely visual and that, due to the development of new media technologies, we are generally dealing with mixed-media representations (images, text, and sound), a cultural approach to globalization dynamics requires a strategic, tailored methodology. Accordingly, by making use of a visual methodology combined with other methods of critical analysis and interpretation, this study consists of photographic fieldwork and knowledge, and it is structured by combining practice-based research and words to engage in the process through which knowledge about the ideological dimension of globalization is created. Actually, given that the production of symbolic forms, texts, and images is rooted in places and media representations and they constitute the tangible traces of historical change, this study investigates the production, circulation, and consumption of symbolic forms within the urban social fabrics of defined global and globalizing cities across the planet. This happens through photography as a research tool for collecting data, and *as* data. In this respect, this study acknowledges that, because of the camera limitations, photographs do not provide us with an unbiased, objective record of the social and material world. However, limitations are fundamentally the limitations of those who use them, and social scientists can easily agree on the fact that "there is little we can see that is truly free from bias or personal projection" (Collier and Collier 1986, 10). Indeed, photographs can be used to show characteristic attributes of people, objects, events, or cultural objects, such in the case of this study, that often elude even the most skilled wordsmiths (Prosser and Schwartz 1998).

Thus, this study considers photographs as a medium that provides a degree of tangible detail with a sense of being there in space-time that is difficult to convey through textuality. The use of photograph is therefore regarded as evidence, as representation of something that can be interpreted in different ways (Burke 2001). For these reasons, this investigation approaches globalization from an alternative, aesthetic standpoint and with a research strategy that combines different methods of analysis and interpretation, new thinking tools, and photographic fieldwork. This tailored approach attempts to grasp the subjective-objective aspects of globalization that are usually investigated separately from each other (see also Banks 2008; Steger and James, 2013). Thus, in dealing with globalization from an aesthetics-of-change perspective, this study also attempts to overcome the modern dichotomy between idealism and positivism that lacerated the political philosophy debate of last century, while taking into consideration the ways in which visual images have their own agency.

The study is structured in two main stages. The first stage, informed by theory, provides the identification and the development of a tailored methodology to approach globalization as visual-ideological phenomenon in defined socio-historical contexts, internet included, through new theoretical frameworks. The second stage consists of selecting the given body of empirical evidence taken from the author's visual archive project of the global imaginary (Durante 2007– ongoing).[46] The archive in itself, and therefore the collected images, of which only a limited number are displayed here, undoubtedly constitutes a socio-ontological example with respect to the globalization phenomenon. Therefore, to avoid misunderstandings, this study is not interested in discussing if the visual ideology of globalization represents the true essence of the process or in proving that the visual-ideological apparatus represents the core system of the phenomenon. Rather, this study focuses on naming parts (condensation symbols and ideological markers of globality) and linking them to a process (globalization) by identifying a new theme/category (the visual ideology of globalization). In doing so, it aims to penetrate and unfold the underlying structures (imaginaries and ideologies) that affect local meanings and cultural identities in socio-historically defined societies.

Image 1: The Visual Archive Project of the Global Imaginary

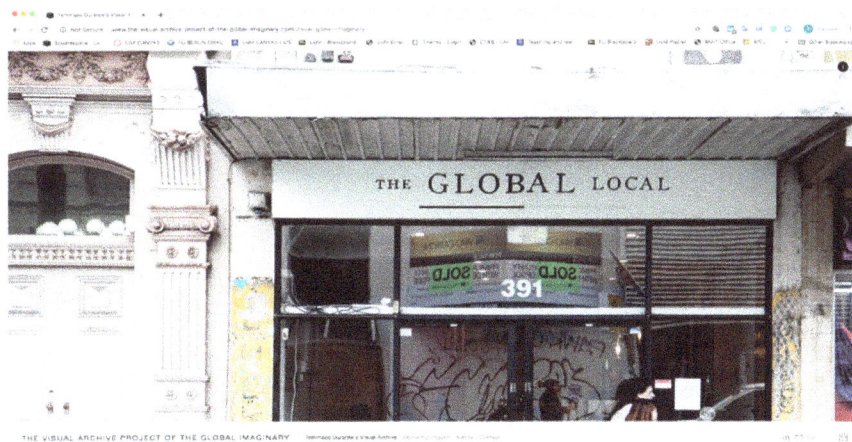

Source: Durante (2020)

The examples selected to support my arguments are images condensing a rich visual narrative of the global (Figures: 2, 3, 4, 6, 10, and 12), and ideological markers of globality (Figures: 1, 5, 7, 8, 10, and 11). In order to highlight how images affect the ideological landscape and people's consciousness in their everyday life, the given body of visual evidence is presented in its own right with the aim of providing the

---

[46] The archive collects visual data about globalization dynamics gathered during photographic fieldwork in selected global and fast globalizing cities across the globe. The main aim of this research project, which includes a dedicated web site, is to better understand globalization phenomenon and how the global imaginary is symbolically and socially produced (Durante 2007-).

reader with a "first hand" experience of these cultural constructs. Empirical evidence is displayed as they were available to the researcher during photographic fieldwork. These images are accompanied by captions to give the reader only the space-time coordinates of the discourse, while leaving the viewer free to make sense of their socio-historical ideologically charged nature. However, to better understand the importance of these new figures of knowledge, at the end of the next section, I carry out the analysis and interpretation of one selected piece of evidence. This will help to better understand, at a deeper level, how this new visual regime of representations and significations, which has already altered our way of perceiving and being in the world, is affecting local meaning while contributing to destabilize the modern self-contained nation-state.

Condensation Symbols and other Visual Ideological Markers of Globality

Figure 1: Globe-Trotter Suitcases, Heathrow International Airport, West London, UK

Source: Durante 2016

Figure 2: The Globe Tavern, Marylebone Road, Marylebone, London, UK

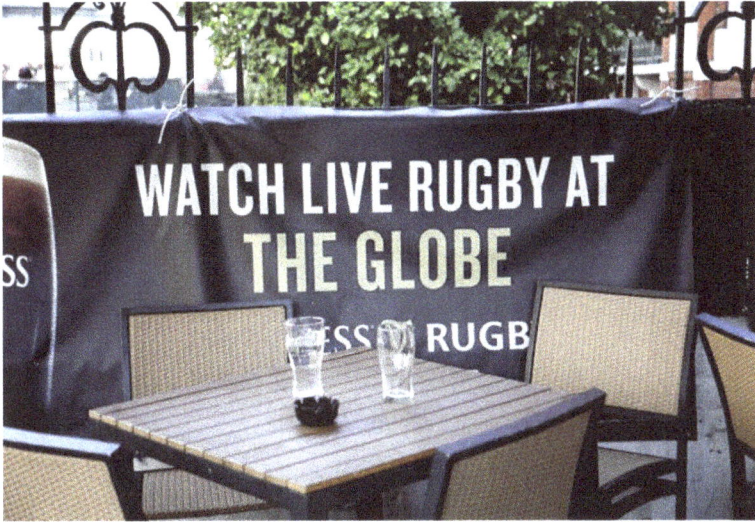

Source: Durante 2016

Figure 3: London Business School, Fifty Years Shaping Global Business, UK

Source: Durante 2016

Figure 4: Global Education, Australia, The Interne

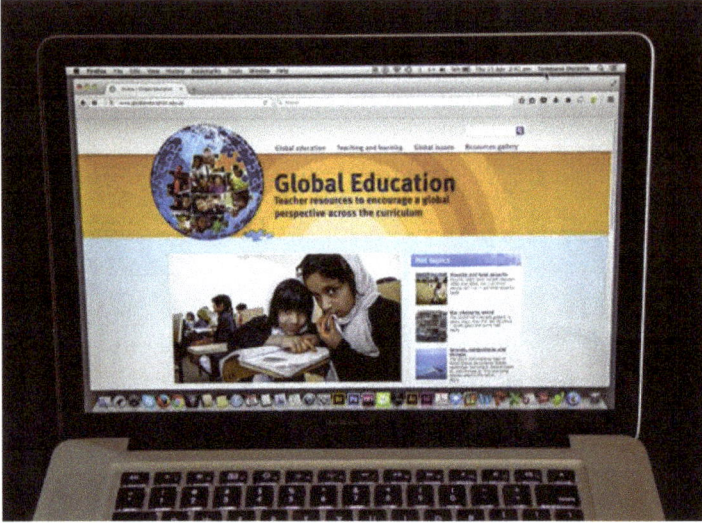

Source: Durante 2016

Figure 5: Global Airconditioning & Heating, Canberra, Australia

Source: Durante 2015

Figure 6: Max, The Globe Cans Pack, Summerhill Shopping Centre, Melbourne, Australia

Source: Durante 2016

Figure 7: Prosegur Logo, Alameda Santos, Jardim Paulista, São Paulo, Brazil

Source: Durante 2016

Figure 8: Globe Taxi Logo, Chicago, United States

Source: Durante 2015

Figure 9: Shaping the World, RMIT University Wall Advertisement, Melbourne, Australia

Source: Durante 2015

Figure 10: Aussie, Travelex Logo, Tullamarine Airport, Melbourne, Australia

Source: Durante 2015

Figure 11: Globalize, Bourke Street, Melbourne, Australia

Source: Durante 2014

Figure 12: Seoul Metro, Indoor Digital Advertising Screen, South Korea

Source: Durante 2013

Globe Trotter Suitcases

I took this picture (Figure 1) in February 2016 during a photographic fieldwork in London. Apparently, this image merely displays three suitcases and a sign with the logo brand Globe- Trotter. The suitcase brand was established almost 120 years ago, in 1897, by David Nelken in Saxony, Germany. Indeed, the company moved to the United Kingdom in 1932 where it has remained ever since, handcrafting their travel accessories in Hertfordshire. Having a history of artisanal production of travel accessories that dates back to the Victorian era, Globe-Trotter can be regarded as a particular case of glocalization. In this respect, it can be observed that while global forces push for an increasing standardization of the production processes and formats, a resistance happens that relies on linking a place to a particular handcrafted production, although made globally available. In this perspective, the Globe-Trotter brand pushes towards the production of sophisticated objects targeting a limited but wealthy category of consumers across the planet. Their products have been used by distinguished clients such as Sir Winston Churchill, HM Queen Elizabeth II, and in James Bond films (Globe-Trotter 2016).

What makes this visual evidence an interesting cultural object is the logo-catchphrase itself (Globe-Trotter) that works as ideological constraint in the meaning-making process at the site of reception (viewer/consumer). As a result, the act of buying Globe-Trotter products makes the consumer feel globally interconnected, a citizen of the world. However, by critically approaching this image, we understand how the global imaginary captures, adapts, and alters local-national meanings (Hertfordshire-United Kingdom) by re-configuring them around the global. Thus, while on the one hand this ideological marker can assist in understanding how the common sense of the global is symbolically and socially produced in our everyday life, on the other hand it also helps to grasp how it contributes to construct the visual ideological apparatus of globalization.

Towards a Visual Ideology of Globalization

On the basis of the given body of visual evidence and the analysis of the Globe-Trotter example, in order to start sketching a visual ideology of globalization without misunderstandings, it is worth clarifying that with the term "visual ideology" this study does not mean an "ideology of the image" (Hadjinicolaou 1978). Instead, it refers to a series of images understood as "visual paradigm" that, in their own right, both reflect and construct ideology. This latter term is defined visual in the sense of what is seen, not in the sense of the faculty of sight. Indeed, with the term "visual ideology" this investigation understands a system of symbolic forms—condensation symbols and other ideological markers of globality—covering a wide, comprehensive domain, that of the production and re-production of media representations with regard to globalization dynamics. Furthermore, the visual ideology of globalization is not the product made by an individual (i.e., an artist), but the result of the production and media-reproduction, circulation, and consumption of different cultural objects created by public institutions, private corporations, individuals, and groups. It transcends the subject-individual and is not constrained by geopolitical boundaries because it operates transnationally in an ideologically de-contextualized manner.

Therefore, this study does not understand the term visual ideology as an artistic style, an "ideology of the image" (Hadjinicolaou 1978), nor as the artist's ideology embedded within the work of art undergoing an iconological scrutiny (Argan 1975; Mitchell 1986; Panofsky 1972). Nicolas Hadjinicolaou defines a "visual ideology" as "the way in which the formal and thematic elements of a picture are combined on each specific occasion. This combination is a particular form of the overall ideology of a social class" (Hadjinicolaou 1978, 4). However, due to the very nature of the phenomenon, this study does not refer to any specific institutional apparatus, social class, or corporate production of media representations but to the different production, circulation, and consumption of media representations available in space-time-defined socio-historical contexts. Indeed, in an attempt to move towards a theory of a visual ideology of globalization, it is necessary to clarify that, with this term, this study understands the way in which the formal and thematic elements of particular media representations such as symbols, images, stereotypes, and metaphors condensing spatial-symbolic scales of the global are combined in a visual construct or single event that suggests, supports, and sustains the symbolic and social shift from the national to the global.

Conclusion

This research located globalization within the social imaginary by employing the concept of imagination to inform the study of particular media representations. In doing so, it looked at the subjective experience of being in an interconnected global world by means of a practice-based research that focused on the tension between subject and object, individual and world, by considering it as a continuum. Thus, it was argued that the visual-ideological apparatus of globalization, whose function is to suggest, support, and sustain the material and ideational process of globalization through the establishment of a new regime of visual representation and signification, has a political authority. Therefore, it can be said that the visual stereotype of the earth/globe/plane/sphere, or words such as global, globally, worldly, are among the most significant forms of symbolic expression that characterizes this new aesthetics of the global versus the most visible symbols of nationhood of the twentieth century. Indeed, this new class of images works as the visual-ideological apparatus of globalization in the symbolic and social construction of the imagined global society at the dawn of this new century.

It can be asserted that, globalization, beyond the economic forces it represents, the ideologies and systems of values it is linked to, has also a very structured and sophisticated visual ideological apparatus that produces frames of understanding and narratives that shape, orient, and guide people's lives, as it is pointed out in this study. This visual ideological apparatus emerging with the normative power of the factual reflects, constructs, and supports economic forces and power relations embedded in globalization dynamics by also affecting people's consciousness and ideology at the deepest, individual level. A focus on the changing visual-ideological landscape of the twenty-first century not only drives to a better understanding of globalization processes and how the global imaginary is symbolically and socially produced specifically in the urban context, but also allows to grasp its cultural visual-ideological dimension.

A visual ideology of globalization can be identified, analyzed, and interpreted only if we take the production of global visual imagery into serious account. Lastly, I am deeply aware that my attempt to define a visual ideology of globalization can be controversial and contested because it is not a theory in the scientific sense. Nevertheless, this study aimed to theoretically grasp and methodologically produce alternative knowledge about the complex phenomenon of globalization by means of condensation symbols and other visual ideological markers of globality understood as a new aesthetic form of global imagination within processes of social and cultural-ideological change in defined socio-historical contexts across the globe, at the dawn of this new century.

From a methodological perspective, the very subjective nature of both the gathering and the selection of empirical evidence of the global can provide ground for endless criticism of this study. Furthermore, the photographic media can be seen as a limitation in itself, being affected by the system of values, ideologies, and ethics of the photographer/researcher. However, because there is no other media like photography (the moving images excepted) capable to give back to the researcher the complexity of the social world, photographs still remain useful research tools. A further criticism could be the "reduction" of the aesthetic experience of globalization to its sensorial, subjective practice, but such criticism appears bland by comparison to the issue at stake—the identification and theorization of the visual-ideological dimension of globalization. It can also be contested that the sample provided in this article is made of selected and very limited empirical evidence. Even if it can be observed that displaying more data would not necessarily lead to more information, it is also true that sample sizes that are too small cannot adequately support claims of having achieved valid conclusions. However, this study relies on a large amount of visual data gathered in almost one decade. As a result, it was determined that the sample size was adequate also in the light of the fact that the visual data are qualitatively relevant and that such limitation, if this can be considered a limitation, could be overcome by accessing the online archive. Because this study relies on the visualization of pre-existing data gathered by the researcher, self-reported data can be seen as a limitation in themselves. Yet, the acknowledgement of the role played by the ideological frame of the researcher at the site of reception should not be seen as an objective limitation of the study.

Being of exploratory and interpretive nature, this study generates a number of opportunities for future research in terms of a more comprehensive understanding of the globalization and, more ambitiously, at a meta-ideological level with the theory of ideology. While this study has generated new conceptual categories, such as visual ideological markers of globality, it is to be noted its in-depth sampling strategy, focused on exploring, through the re-photography method, different cities and the Internet for almost a decade. Thus, the study could be extended not only through an analytical and interpretative approach, but also statistically. Indeed, due to the charged global-ideological nature of these cultural objects, they have socio-political and cultural implications that need to be further analyzed and interpreted. Therefore, more research will be necessary to refine and further elaborate these new findings from different perspectives.

The aim of this practice-based research was to address the dearth of specific scholarship about the visual-ideological dimension of globalization. Accordingly, the first major practical contribution of the present research is to participate in filling the gap in the literature about the phenomenon by also providing much empirical data on the contemporary process of change and transformation. These data could allow researchers in the broader field of social sciences and humanities to better understand globalization dynamics and help teachers in the transdisciplinary field of global studies. They can rely on visual evidence that will help the teaching-learning process through both an exemplification and problematization of the abstract notion of globalization and the visualization of the shift from the national to the global. This will allow to redesign lectures/seminars/tutorials accordingly. Also, researchers can make use of this visual evidence as case studies to achieve a deeper understanding of the phenomenon and its socio-political and cultural implications.

REFERENCES

Albrow, Martin. 1996. *The Global Age: State and Society beyond Modernity.* Cambridge, UK: Polity Press.

Arnheim, Rudolph. 2004. *Visual Thinking.* Berkeley, CA: The University of California Press. Arrighi, Giovanni. 2005. "Globalization in World-Systems Perspective". In *Critical Globalization Studies,* edited by Richard P. Appelbaum and William I. Robinson, 33–44. New York: Routledge.

Anderson, Benedict. 2011. *Imagined Communities: Reflections on the Origin and Spread of Nationalism.* London: Verso.

Appadurai, Arjun. 1996. *Modernity at Large: Cultural Dimensions of Globalization.* Minneapolis, MN: Minnesota University Press.

Argan, Giulio C. 1975. "Ideology and Iconology." *Critical Inquiry* 2 (2): 297–305. http://www.jstor.org/stable/1342905.

Banks, Markus. 2001. *Visual Methods in Social Research.* London: SAGE Publications Ltd.

———. 2008. "Visual Ideology: Problems of Subjectivity." *Visual Sociology* 4 (2): 127–40.

Barthes, Roland. 1964. "Rhétorique de l'image" [Rhetoric of the Image]. *Communications* 4 (1): 40–51. http://www.persee.fr/doc/comm_05888018_1964_num_4_1_1027.

———. 2013. *Mythologies.* New York: Hill and Wang.

Baumann, Zygmunt. 2006. *Liquid Times: Living in an Age of Uncertainty.* Cambridge, UK: Polity.

Beck, Ulrich. 2000. *What Is Globalization?* Cambridge, UK: Polity.

Benjamin, Walter. 2002. *The Arcades Project.* Cambridge, MA: Harvard University Press. Benveniste, Émile. 1971. *Problems in General Linguistics.* Coral Gables, FL: University of Miami Press.

Berger, John. 1972. *Ways of Seeing.* London: Penguin.

Bourdieu, Pierre. 1989. *Language and Symbolic Power.* Cambridge, UK: Polity Press.

———. 2009. *The Field of Cultural Production.* Cambridge, UK: Polity.

Burke, Peter. 2001. *Eye-witnessing: The Uses of Images as Historical Evidence.* Ithaca, NY: Cornell University Press.

Callagher, Shaun, and Dan Zahavi. 2014. "Phenomenological Approaches to Self- Consciousness." *The Stanford Encyclopedia of Philosophy.* https://plato.stanford.edu /entries/self-consciousness-phenomenological/notes.html.

Cassirer, Ernest. 2008. *The Symbolic Construction of Reality.* Edited by Jeffrey Andrew Barash. Chicago: The University of Chicago Press.

Castells, Manuel. 1994. *The Informational City: Economic Restructuring and Urban Development.* Oxford, UK: Blackwell.

———. 1996. *The Rise of Network Society: The Information Age.* Oxford, UK: Blackwell Publisher.

Castoriadis, Cornelius. 1997. *The Imaginary Institution of Society.* Cambridge, MA: The MIT Press.

Centeno, Miguel A., and Joseph N. Cohen. 2010. *Global Capitalism.* London: Polity.

Collier, John, and Malcolm Collier. 1986. *Visual Anthropology: Photography as a Research Method.* Albuquerque, NM: University of New Mexico Press.

Darian-Smith, Eve, and Philip C. McCarty. 2017. *The Global Turn: Theories, Research Designs, and Methods for Global Studies.* Oakland, CA: University of California Press.

Destutt de Tracy, Antoine Louis Claude. 2008. *Treatise on Political Economy.* Edited by Thomas Jefferson. Auburn, AL: Ludwig von Mises Institute.

Durante, Tommaso. 2007–. *The Visual Archive Project of the Global Imaginary,* Accessed January 20, 2017. http://www.the-visual-archive-project-of-the-global-imaginary.com/visual-global-imaginary

———. 2014. "Visual Culture and Globalization: The Visual Archive Project of the Global Imaginary." *Global-e,* June 1, Volume 8, Issue 4. Accessed January 20, 2017. https://www.21global.ucsb.edu/global-e/june-2014/visual-culture-and-globalization-visual-archive-project-global-imaginary

———. 2013. "The Symbolic Construction of the Global Imaginary in Sydney and Melbourne." PhD diss. RMIT University. Accessed January 20, 2017. http://researchbank.rmit.edu.au/view/rmit:160588

———. 2016. "The Global Images: On Globalization as Visual-Ideological Phenomenon." In *Narratives of Globalization: Reflections on the Global Condition*, edited by Julian C. H. Lee, 51–62. London: Rowman & Littlefield International.

Edelman, Murray. 1985. *The Symbolic Uses of Politics*. Champaign, IL: University of Illinois Press.

Engels, Friedrich. 1972. "Letter to Franz Mehring, London, July 14, 1893." In *Marx and Engels: Basic Writings on Politics and Philosophy*, edited by Lewis Feuer. London: Fontana Books.

Faccioli, Patrizia, and Jacqueline A. Gibbons, 2007. *Framing Globalization: Visual Perspectives*. Newcastle: Cambridge Scholars Publishing.

Fairclough, Norman. 2001. *Language and Power*. London: Routledge.

———. 2003. *Discourse and Social Change*. Cambridge, UK: Polity.

———. 2010. *Critical Discourse Analysis: The Critical Study of Language*. Harlow, UK: Longman.

Foucault, Michel. 1994. *The Order of Things: An Archaeology of the Human Sciences*. New York: Random House.

Freeden, Michael. 2003. *Ideology: A Very Short Introduction*. New York: Oxford University Press.

———. 2013. "The Morphological Analysis of Ideology." In *The Oxford Handbook of Political Ideologies*, edited by Michael Freeden and Marc Stears. Oxford: Oxford University Press.

Friedman, Thomas L. 2005. *The World is Flat*. New York: Farrar, Straus and Giroux.

———. 1999. *The Lexus and the Olive Tree: Understanding Globalization*. New York: Picador. Gilpin, Robert. 2000. *The Challenge of Global Capitalism: The World Economy in the 21ˢᵗ Century*. Princeton, NJ: Princeton University Press.

Globe-Trotter. 2016. *About*. https://www.globe-trotter.com/about/.

Gradi, John. 2007. "Visual Sociology." In *21st Century Sociology: A Reference Handbook*, edited by Clifton Bryant and Dennis Peck, 63–70. Thousand Oaks, CA: Sage Publications.

Gramsci, Antonio. 1971. *Selections from the Prison Notebooks*. New York: International Publishers.

Hadjinicolaou, Nicolas. 1978. *Art History and Class Struggle*. London: Pluto Press.

Hall, Stuart. 2003. "The Work of Representation." In *Representation: Cultural Representations and Signifying Practices (Culture, Media and Identities Series)*, edited by Stuart Hall, 13–74. London: SAGE Publications Ltd.

Hart-Landsberg, Martin. 2013. *Capitalist Globalization: Consequences, Resistance, and Alternatives*. New York: Monthly Review Press.

Harvey, David. 1991. *The Condition of Postmodernity: An Enquiry into the Origins of Cultural Change*. Oxford, UK: Blackwell.

———. 2007. *A Brief History of Neoliberalism*. Oxford, NY: Oxford University Press.

Jay, Martin. 1994. *Downcast Eyes. The Denigration of Vision in Twentieth-Century French Thought*. Berkeley, CA: University of California Press.

Juergensmeyer, Mark. 2014. "Preface: A Friendly Introduction to Global Studies." In *Thinking Globally: A Global Studies Reader*, edited by Mark Juergensmeyer, i–xiii. Berkeley, CA: University of California Press.

Lacan, Jacques. 1956. "Symbol and Language." In *the Language of the Self: The Function of Language in Psychoanalysis*, 29–52. Baltimore, MD: Johns Hopkins University Press.

Lefebvre, Henry. 1991. *The Production of Space*. Oxford: Blackwell.

Lerner, Max. 1943. *Ideas are Weapons: The History and Use of Ideas*. New York: Viking Press. Merleau-Ponty, Maurice. 2002. *Phenomenology of Perception*. London: Routledge.

Mirzoeff, Nicholas. 2015. *How to See the World*. London: Penguin.

Mitchell, W. J. T. 1984. "What Is an Image?" *New Literary History* 15 (3): 503–37.

———. 1986. *Iconology: Image, Text, Ideology*. Chicago: University of Chicago Press.

———. 2005. *What Do Pictures Want?* Chicago: University of Chicago Press.

———. 2007. "World Pictures: Globalization and Visual Culture." *Neohelicon* 2: 49–59.

Mittelman, James H. 2000. *The Globalization Syndrome: Transformation and Resistance*. Princeton: Princeton University Press.

———. 2004. "What Is Critical Globalization Studies?" *International Studies Perspective* 5 (3): 219–30.

Netto, Vinicius M. 2016. *The Social Fabric of Cities*. New York: Routledge.

Nichols, Bill. 1981. *Ideology and the Image*. Bloomington, IN: Indiana University Press. Panofsky, Erwin. 1972. *Studies in Iconology*. Boulder, CO: Westview Press.

Pieterse, Jan Nederveen. 2013. "What is Global Studies?" *Globalizations* 10 (4): 545–50. http://doi.org/:10.1080/14747731.2013.806746.

Pink, Sarah. 2008. "Analysing Visual Experience." In *Research Methods for Cultural Studies,* edited by Michael Pickering, 125–49. Edinburgh: Edinburgh University Press.

———. 2012. *Advances in Visual Methodology.* Los Angeles: SAGE Publications Ltd.

Pink, Sarah, Kurti Laszlo, and Ana Isabel Afonso. 2004. *Working Images: Visual Research and Representation in Ethnography.* London: Routledge.

Prosser, Jon, and Dona Schwartz. 1998. "Photographs within the Sociological Research Process." In *Images Based Research: A Sourcebook for Qualitative Researchers*, edited by Jon Prosser, 101-15. London: Falmer Press.

Rancière, Jacques. 2013. *Aisthesis: Scenes from the Aesthetic Regime of Art.* London: Verso. Ricouer, Paul. 1986. *Lectures on Ideology and Utopia.* New York: Columbia University Press. Robertson, Ronald. 1992. *Globalization: Social Theory and Global Culture.* London: SAGE Publications Ltd.

Rose, Gillian. 2011. *Visual Methodologies: An Introduction to Researching with Visual Materials.* London: SAGE Publications Ltd.

Sassen, Saskia. 2006. *Territory, Authority, Rights: From Medieval to Global Assemblages.* Princeton, NJ: Princeton University Press.

———. 2007. "Reading the City in a Global Digital Age: The Limits of Topographic Representation." In *Cities in Globalization: Practices, Policies and Theories,* edited by Peter Taylor, Ben Derudder, Pieter Saey, and Frank Witlox, 231–48. London: Routledge.

Schwarzmantel, John. 2008. *Ideology and Politics.* London: SAGE Publications Ltd.

Sklair, Leslie. 2000. "The Sociology of the Global System." In *Globalization: The Reader,* edited by Frank Lechner and John Boli. New York: Routledge.

Soja, Edward. 1989. *Postmodern Geographies: The Reassessment of Space in Critical Social Theory.* London: Verso.

Steger, Manfred B. 2009. *Globalisms: The Great Ideological Struggle of the Twenty-First Century.* Lanham, MD: Rowman & Littlefield Publishers.

———. 2008. *The Rise of the Global Imaginary: Political Ideologies from the French Revolution to the Global War on Terror.* New York: Oxford University Press.

———. 2010. *Globalization.* New York: Sterling Publishing Co., Inc.

———. 2013a. *Globalization: A Very Short Introduction.* Oxford: Oxford University Press.

———. 2013b. "Political Ideologies in the Age of Globalization." In *the Oxford Handbook of Political Ideologies,* edited by Michael Freeden, Lyman Tower Sargent, and Marc Stears, 214–231. Oxford: Oxford University Press.

Steger, Manfred B., and Ravi K. Roy. 2010. *Neoliberalism: A Very Short Introduction.* Oxford, NY: Oxford University Press.

Steger, Manfred B., and Paul James. 2013. "Levels of Subjective Globalization: Ideologies, Imaginaries, Ontologies." *Perspectives on Global Development and* Technology 12 (1–2): 17–40.

Steger, Manfred B., and Amentahru Wahlrab. 2017. *What is Global Studies? Theory and Practice.* New York: Routledge.

Taylor, Charles. 2007. *Modern Social Imaginary.* Durham, NC: Duke University Press.

Thompson, John B. 1982. "Ideology and the Social Imaginary: An Appraisal of Castoriadis and Lefort." *Theory and Society* 11 (5), 659–81. http://www.jstor.org/stable/657343.

———. 1985. *Studies in the Theory of Ideology.* Berkeley, CA: University of California Press. Wilson, David. 2008. "Cities Transformations and the Global Trope: Indianapolis and Cleveland." In *Cultures of Globalization: Coherence, Hybridity, Contestation,* edited by Kevin M. Archer, Martin M. Bosman, and Mark M. Amen, 29–44. New York: Routledge.

Worth, Sol, and Larry Gross. 1974. "Symbolic Strategy." *Journal of Communication* 24 (4): 27–39. http://doi.org/10.1111/j.1460-2466.1974.tb00405.x.

Chapter 6

Infrastructural Urbanism: Ecologies and Technologies of Multi-Layered Landscapes[47]

Nick Dunn

Introduction

The ongoing development of digital technologies has led to new and emerging 'spaces' of expression and production as societal flows of information and communication have assimilated the use of digital networks as an interdependent aspect of everyday life. The 'networked individualism' (Wellman 2001, 238) that affords each person to evolve his or her own community as a bespoke infrastructure with relevant connections enables a mode of structuring and restructuring relationships that goes far beyond what is possible in physical terms alone. Such behaviour has facilitated an unprecedented level of mobility that is at once disconnected from and implicit to the geospatial world. This mobility, Yona Friedman believed, was a basic human need (Banham 1976, 60). His multi-levelled space frames, known as *Spatial Cities*, 1960, hovered over the earth's surface, the detachment from which embodied a deliberate abandonment of the banality below. In an analogous way, this signals a common perception of the disjunctive relationship between digital networks and urban place, although Friedman's language was to be subsequently nuanced by the terminology of the computer industry, referring to the city as a mechanism and to infrastructure as hardware (Friedman 1975, 113–114). As Lars Lerup (2000, 22–23) notes in *After the City*, "The static resistance of traditional architecture in the face of radical mobility demands rethinking rather than escape. The metropolis has replaced the city, and as a consequence architecture as a static enterprise has been displaced by architecture as a form of software."

Indeed, the polemic of Archigram's *Plug-In City*, 1964, was given further momentum by the novelty of its power source: the 'Synthesised Metropolis With Electronic Changeability', aka *Computer City*. Without the infrastructural features of

---

[47] This chapter is an edited version of the essay "Infrastructural Urbanism: Ecologies and Technologies of Multi-Layered Landscapes" first published in *Spaces and Flows: An International Journal of Urban and Extra Urban Studies* 1 (1): 87-96.

the Computer City, Plug-In City would not differ much from any other lifeless componential architecture. The significant characteristic of this project is its depiction of computer technology not merely as a representational tool but as an environmental model. In Dennis Crompton's (1964, n.p.) words: "The activities of an organized society occur within a balanced network of forces which naturally interact to form a continuous chain of change. A METROPOLIS is situated at the point of maximum display of interactive energy and shows the most complex field of forces. In the COMPUTOR CITY this energized field is synthesized at a much higher sensitivity and is programmed to respond to changes in activity". The contours of Computer City were therefore not of information but of how information moved from one place to another. The urban landscape depicted here was thus an aggregate of its numerous sub-networks that connected to form a cohesive system. The sub-networks are a 'multi-layered landscape' in the Computer City axonometric and reinforce the physical presence of the build-up of materiality that affords the development of communications technology (Graham and Marvin 1996; 2001). The lack of centre, or even a primary axis around which the city could orientate itself, was a primary feature of the interminable web, and this characteristic of the Computer City directly challenged the notion of the city centre as being the heart of a place. This position was taken to its logical conclusion in Archigram's later project, *Instant City*, 1968-70, which examined the prevailing attitudes regarding city centre in relation to networks. As Hadas Steiner (2009, 217) has observed, "the urban experience of Instant City was shifting toward a point where information and the city were synonymous. In its ideal form, Instant City would provide a bundle of services; its urban strategy would be connectivity and speed over geographical advantage. To inhabit an advanced network, information and the city would be fully decentralized commodities that travelled the same infrastructure, like computers on phone lines". This development reiterates not only the hardware of infrastructure required to facilitate digital networks but signifies an ontological shift between structure and information and leads us towards the contemporary situation.

Urbanism on the Move

There has been a considerable transformation in our understanding of that which constitutes 'the city', from the pre-modern model with a single centre and clearly defined boundary, through the subsequent sprawl of suburbanization, differentiating between core and periphery, to the emergence of the poly-nucleic model in which the centre and edge of the city are integrated across a variety of urban conditions. This latter model directs us towards what numerous writers now refer to as the 'network city'. This term is, however, rather ambiguous as there has been a propensity to view the physical landscape to have the capacity and behaviour of digital infrastructures, an association rendered complex by the commonality of some features and the applied terminology by which they are described. Whilst it is acknowledged here that such exchange may be useful in certain critical analysis, it does not highlight the distinction between the two that has taken place as a residue of the stacking up and overlays of digital technologies upon extant physical situations to develop a 'multi-layered landscape'. As Page and Phillips (2004, 88) have noted: "The way the city is read is a key issue in uncovering ways one might intervene within the contemporary metropolis. Cities are an ongoing record of many players and forces operating through global, regional and local spheres of influence, utilizing tools and techniques that are permanent, ephemeral, invisible and strategic". From this position, the apparent bifurcation of 'the city' has developed two fascinating, if somewhat confusing, effects. Firstly, the visualization of 'space', as telecommunications and digital technologies have evolved, has led to the mapping of cities as abstracted networks, typically favouring topological relationships over topographical ones. The apparent boundless accessibility of online data about any chosen location has led to a pre-supposed familiarity of terrain that does not exist in a historical perception of 'place' and has contributed to a diminished sense of awe, invoked by new experience (Wilkins 2010). Secondly, the steady erosion of 'place' in the traditional physical sense and in relation to 'the city'; the term has been supplanted by a hybridized definition that is both in contact and disconnected with the physical space.

The discord between the high level of connectivity that pervades digital networks in relation to the increasingly fragmentary nature of the physical urban condition has produced an expansive territory for exploitation for artists, architects and designers who are engaged in operating within this 'in between landscape'. Networks have emerged in the digital age to seemingly restructure societal order and develop new relationships between data, whether as organizing structures, navigational tools, or descriptive mechanisms, for complex matrices of cultural, economic, political, or social activity, or a framework that is often a hybrid of these (Sassen 1998). The scope of networks as mapping instruments to reveal the assembly and nature of previously unknown or dynamic relationships is also reliant on another view of 'space' that is distinct from the definition that has previously enabled urban and cartographic descriptions to be mutually bound (Wigley, 2007). The transformation of the physical landscape towards an increasingly incoherent set of urban conditions and the corresponding flows of endless data into an apparently infinite and united system has implications for what we might consider to be public domain. The tradition of the public domain as a realm of culture, media and politics is a characteristic that has seemingly deteriorated through the increased commodification of place as a consumptive environment (De Cauter 2004). The nature of the public realm, as both a receptive and reflexive domain, may perhaps now be located in digital networks rather than in physical space. The ubiquitous technological presence in our daily communication and other transactions as a correlation of increased growth of broadband in the developed world and the global continuum facilitated by mobile phones, has become manifest in readily accessible, ever-present networks that not only challenge our ideas and experience of 'place' but have precipitated an evolution in relationships of time and distance (Picon 2010). This simultaneous process of dispersal and accumulation, through the use of information technologies, which have been transformative in the ways in which we work, learn, socialise and conduct business, is discussed extensively in Manuel Castells' (2000) *The Rise of the Network Society*. Rather than erasing the city, Castells views the addition of technological layers as enhancing the future development of the urban landscape, albeit with an increased mobility as a direct result of rising flexibility in the workplace and social networks.

Perhaps of greater significance is that this move towards networks of abstracted 'space' rather than urban physical 'place' is not simply driven by technology but is intrinsic to developments across society. Networks have permeated traditional hierarchies within commerce, politics, economics and other organizations, along with their top-down communication systems (Martin and Baxi 2007). A simple indication of this growth is the prevalence of 'network' in the linguistic terminology of everyday life, being used to describe all manner of connections and organizations, albeit with blurred definitions. However, it is important to iterate here that whilst the level of interest in (and use of) topological relationships is increasingly widespread, this may not be quite as radical as it first appears. As Manuel De Landa (1997) explains in *A Thousand Years of Nonlinear History*, the networks of online individuals and communities may be much more 'destratified' than with other forms of media but this does not necessarily mean they have replaced existing structures and modes of connection and communication. Instead, such relationships may actually serve to augment existing hierarchies through reconfiguration, facilitating restratification of the networks in the process. The complexity of the contemporary situation is that shifts and patterns are both emergent and responsive, features intrinsic to the nature of digital networks themselves. As Paolo Fusero (2008, 106) suggests, "If we analyze the effects that the growth of digital networks is having on cities we realize it is neither a process of centralization nor of decentralization of events, but actually a complex process of 'fragmentation' and 'reassembling' of existing urban models". In a sense this has already been played out due to the imposition of physical infrastructural systems across cities the world over that have balanced two aspects of this transformation with varying measures of success. Firstly, the integration of new placeless forms of connectivity enabled by physical and digital infrastructures, and secondly, the fracturing of social structures as communities whose organic growth was historically assured are either included in or excluded from the new mobile, global integration. On this latter point, however, it should be noted that the affordances of ecological niches based on social, cultural, economic and political values are often burgeoning on their own terms even if we are not immediately able to identify them.

Digital Ecologies

Mapping networks has powerful implications beyond the description of a 'datascape' as it also reveals relationship and the extent of connectivity. In particular, the mapping of networks describes the ecological mutuality between digital and physical landscapes, especially with regard to social behaviour and patterns. This 'social' data is an extrapolation of that which exists in the real world: a confluence of cultural, political, economic and religious datasets that explain how we interact within and across systems as well as with each other. The complexity of the situation is increased further as these relationships evolve and form new patterns and networks in their own right. Whilst the dynamic exchange between physical and digital landscapes continues to develop, mapping these networks offers fertile ground for enriching our knowledge and use of such infrastructures. The value of the 'urban imaginary' as part of the instrumentality through which we, as Edward Soja (2000, 234) noted, "think about, experience, evaluate, and decide to act in the places, spaces, and communities in which we live" is inherent in the multiplicitous ways in which we engage with digital technologies. More specifically, in this context it is useful to consider the notion of 'digital ecologies' as constructs or environments that afford effective relationships and behaviour across digital networks to emerge and adapt. By way of clarity, I default here to Mihaela Ulieru's (2010, 1341–1342) definition of a digital ecology as an open infrastructure in which "interconnected interdependent systems of systems weaved by the Internet together with social networks of prosumers (producers and consumers) of applications and services coexist and coevolve, in much the same way as different species share the resources of a common habitat and provide mutual benefits in an ecosystem-like manner. By including the users themselves as key players in the global collaborative ecosystem, its complexity is approaching (if not already reached) the complexity of naturally evolved systems". Accordingly, if we are able to further the knowledge of the spatiality of our interactions within these 'digital ecologies' we may begin to develop the potential of suitable niches within which we may form intelligent and adaptive networking and affect change (Harvey 2009; Soja 2010). It is therefore appropriate at this juncture to discuss the work of two creatives who are establishing new modalities that enrich the instrumentality via which we may better understand digital networks.

Media and communication networks form the primary territory across which the new media artist Lisa Jevbratt operates. Her work is concerned with systems and collectives and is relevant in this context given the intrinsic invisibility of the behaviour and events that occur within digital networks. Across a series of projects exploring the nature of networks, Jevbratt has developed modes of inquiry to enable interpretation of the navigation of Internet users. Interestingly, given the intangible and dissolute character of digital space, she is keen to connect the projects with more defined techniques, "programmers are more land-artists than writers; software are more earthworks than narratives. The 'soil' we move, displace, and map is not the soil created by geological processes. It is made up of language, communication protocols and written agreements. The mapping and displacement of this 'soil' has the potential of inheriting, revealing and questioning the political and economic assumptions that went into its construction" (Jevbratt 2006, 75). With this perspective in mind, Jevbratt's work offers a very different sense of data. Through projects such as *1:1*, 1999 and 2002, and *Infome Imager Lite*, 2002-05, the mapping of dataset to image is an unambiguous process of translation that attempts to utilize graphic visualizations to disclose latent structures. In *1:1*, a crawler or automated web-browser, was employed to catalogue more than 200,000 Internet Protocol (IP) addresses from a huge database of those available. If a site was found it was added to the database regardless of whether it was publicly accessible. In its later incarnation, the web had developed and altered considerably so rather than survey the entire web, five interfaces or mappings were produced to visualize the variants in the database: *Hierarchical, Every, Random, Excursion*, and *Migration*. This database of selected IP addresses was then mapped by assigning a pixel of colour to each IP address. The lowest IP address is located in the top left corner and the highest in the bottom right. The different colour values that emerged through the mappings are a direct correlation of the red, green and blue mixed in relation to the parts of the address. The variables inherent in the dataset are used to produce several different maps by implementing numerous rulesets and observing the visual effects for example; the *Hierarchical* interface of data maps only the top-level domains i.e. .com, .gov, .edu etc. whilst the mapping of *Every* is inclusive of all possible IP addresses. This produces a filtering system of the dataset, affording us to view it as dynamic mappings through which we can turn various layers of information on and off. Visually we are confronted with a series of complex striated patterns of colour whose varied and non-uniform organization have a direct relationship with the topography of numerical space and density. The *1:1* project has implications beyond mapping as it allows us to consider the visualizations as tools, revealing inherent structures and providing the capability to enter the dataset in numerous ways.

The subsequent project, *Infome Imager Lite* develops some of the themes of *1:1* by directly engaging the viewer or user, in the construction of the dataset and visualization process. The visualizations produced are interfaces that directly correlate to the sites crawled, in a similar manner to *1:1*, the main difference exists in the open yet personal dialogue between user and the mapping process. As a result, the software has explicit connections with a user's experience by illustrating personal networks and choices. This raises another key difference between the *Infome Imager Lite* which is localized and contextual whereas by contrast *1:1* is overtly macro and global. In this context such activity acts as a locative device in an apparently infinite and ever-mutating topological framework. A central theme in the content of Jevbratt's work is the hidden information and structures of network data that may be revealed and explored to provide new understandings of the social as well as technical landscapes intrinsic to the Web. The work of Jevbratt therefore echoes that of the architects and urban designers who have sought to intervene and communicate notions of the city, the only shift is one of context that is both autonomous to and interdependent with the physical urban landscape. If this brings us back to themes of 'place' and navigation then it is worth considering the implications of networks for mapping and their ability to provide intelligent maps that are dynamic, reflexive and complex with respect to the information they synthesize. Engaging with the data of digital networks and exploring new methods for communicating this information, whether directly linked to the urban landscape or not, has become a focus for a number of designers and architects.

Stanza is one such figure, whose interest in networks and the visualization of data gathered from cities has led to the production of alternative maps to reveal latent characteristics of urban conditions. A key aspect of his work is the tripartite relationship of handling data in terms of its collection, visualization and display. Relevant in this context is the feedback loop created with the urban landscape as he notes: "Data from security tracking, traffic, and environmental monitoring has been used. These investigations have created new ways of comparing, conceptualizing and visualizing complex concepts related to the relationship of emergent data and real space in the built environment" (Stanza 2010a). In his project *Soundcities*, 2003-08, Stanza recorded found sounds and 'soundscapes' from a number of cities around the world through his interest in how such data is expressive of the identity of particular geographic locations. Whilst highly engaging as a piece of work, *Soundcities* is of specific interest here due to the way its creator evolved and networked its content. The data collecting technology comprises of a system of microphones with GPS and wireless capacity, whose sounds are streamed live to an online server. Keen to retain the fluidity and transformations characteristic of cities, an interactive website, *soundcities.com*, facilitates the ongoing nature of changes in the global urban landscape and enables public participation. Based on the principle of 'open source' software, the website allows its users to create their own mixes of the audio data and upload them into the database for others to create visual collages connecting architecture and people to the specific sounds, further augmenting this digital archive. The resultant collages or cityscapes form mappings of live data from the geospatial world, reassembled online.

Stanza's interest in the interplay between the urban landscape and online networks is more explicitly demonstrated in his project, *Sensity*, 2004-09. The series of works in this project are produced using data from the city: the flows of people and traffic, levels of air pollution, along with the sounds and vibrations of buildings. Describing the intentions of the project, Stanza (2010b) explains, "I want the public to explore new ways of thinking about interaction within public space and how this affects the socialization of space". Using a series of small wireless sensor boards to collect data and upload it to a central server, *Sensity* gathers huge quantities of information directly from the city and affords new interpretations and reconfigurations of urban space by providing access to 'invisible' but important qualities of the city. The project therefore seeks to map and visualize the live real time city through a physical network of sensors that then communicate this data to a digital network, enabling users to work with it in an open source environment. Through the interaction across the digital network, the data may be used to reform and reinterpret experiential aspects of the city and their flux. As Stanza (2010c) describes, the project "leverages the real time data city and represents it online, showing the life of the system, opening up the system, and then publishing emerging changing behaviours of the space". With the potential to run this type of system in cities around the world, the project has the capability to link real time global information and provide monitoring of the urban landscape as public domain data resource as well as possible benefits in terms of addressing social issues and polarization by offering suitable connective tissue. Projects such as this offer a rich platform across which we may be able to better understand our urban landscape by increasing our knowledge of the ebbs and flows that occur around and within the more fixed elements of the city. In addition, they enhance the instrumentality through which we may explore, describe and comprehend 'digital ecologies' as vital environments that may provide affordances in society: formulating change and fostering sustainable relationships.

Surfurbia Redux

The disclosure of the complexity and information of the data in projects such as these affords us the opportunity to think in visual terms and uncover unknown territory (Brook and Dunn 2011). Perhaps the greatest obstacle in this regard is the manner in which digital networks and the physical landscape are described. There is a tendency in recent critical theory and literature on the subject to assume that omnipresent and influential computer technologies have taken over the urban realm and that architecture simply cannot keep up. Of course, a central strand of this perspective is the idea that digital networks and physical conditions are distinct, as opposed to integrative, layers which infers a process of capillarity between the two in which the digital networks syphon the characteristics of the real world, thus emptying it of meaning and value. Is this actually true? Perhaps as Aurigi and De Cindio (2008, 1) in *Augmented Urban Spaces* suggest, the potential revolutionary transformations do not actually become manifest in reality, "Both utopia and dystopia have been heavily involved in predictions on mega-scale transformations of society, cities and space. And yet, when we observe things around us we can notice how cities are not giving any sign of obsolescence, how people are still people who just happen to use technologies, how space has not been replaced by virtual environments … and basically how 'embedded' digital technologies have become, and how 'real' their functions feel". This emphasizes an important feature of networks that, despite a number of proclamations and diverting theories through ongoing technological developments, they form an interdependent part of urban conditions. If anything, this should reassure designers who now face the 21st century city as a mediated landscape of networks, nodes and fluid systems of density, program, and urban space. Whilst the previously held legibility of spatial order may now be very difficult to establish, the integration of mapping and networks provides some clues to future development. Therefore, rather than contributing to a diminished sense of awe, networks have the capability to enrich and extend our everyday experience and understanding of the city. Furthermore, the development of 'digital ecologies' to form adaptive and meaningful relationships has interesting implications for the future planning of the physical city and its stakeholders as Howard Rheingold (2003, 214) has observed, "new technologies always create opportunities for power shifts, and at each stage from writing to the Internet, more and more power decentralizes".

It is therefore much more useful to engage with networks as multiscalar devices that further dialogue around our relationships to, across, and within urban landscapes. Our perception and experience of the networked city is also becoming further nuanced with the development of locative media and handheld devices that enable us to be connected to digital networks and the urban situation at the same time. The likelihood is that this will serve to further increase our social mobility and organizations to affect change through intelligent networking. In summary, we need, as Stephen Read (2009, 19) has raised, to consider "the question of the respective powers of the global and local: are we subject to a macro-physical architecture of technological networks delivering power from above, or are we able to engage technologies of all types to maintain, invent and reinvent microphysical architectures of enabling places offering multiple ways of being and living?". An essential part of the process of our comprehension of the 'externalities' of digital networks is in their use to develop greater instrumentality that affords thick descriptions of scenarios and enables us to develop appropriate design strategies and responses. It is through contributing to our understanding of the way these infrastructures are differentiated and articulated and implementing this knowledge effectively we may deliver a 'multi-layered landscape' of varying niches for relationships and flows of information that celebrate diversity, equality and creativity for all.

REFERENCES

Aurigi, Alessandro and Fiorella De Cindio, eds. 2008. *Augmented Urban Spaces: Articulating the Physical and Electronic City*. Aldershot: Ashgate.

Banham, Reyner. 1976. *Megastructure: Urban Futures of the Recent Past*. London: Thames & Hudson.

Brook, Richard, and Nick Dunn. 2011. *Urban Maps: Instruments of Narrative and Interpretation in the City*. Farnham: Ashgate.

Castells, Manuel. 2000. *The Rise of the Network Society*, 2nd Edition, Oxford: Blackwell Publishing.

Crompton, Dennis. 1964. *Archigram 5*. Self-published and unpaginated.

De Cauter, Lieven. 2004. *The Capsular Civilization: On the City in the Age of Fear*. Rotterdam: NAi Publishers.

De Landa, Manuel. 1997. *A Thousand Years of Nonlinear History*. Swerve editions, New York: Zone Books.

Friedman, Yona. 1975. *Toward a Scientific Architecture*. Cambridge, MA: MIT Press.

Fusero, Paolo. 2008. *E-City: Digital Networks and Cities of the Future*. Barcelona: LISt.

Graham, Stephen, and Simon Marvin. 1996. *Telecommunications and the City: Electronic Spaces, Urban Places*. London: Routledge.

———. 2001. *Splintering Urbanism: Networked Infrastructures, Technological Mobilities and the Urban Condition*. Oxon: Routledge.

Harvey, David. 2009. *Social Justice and the City*. Athens, GA: The University of Georgia.

Jevbratt, Lisa. 2006. 'Inquires in Infomics.' In *Network Art: Practices and Positions*, edited by Tom Corby, 74–95. Oxon: Routledge.

Lerup, Lars. 2000. *After the City*. Cambridge, MA: The MIT Press.

Martin, Reinhold, and Kadambari Baxi. 2007. *Multi-National City: Architectural Itineraries*. Barcelona: Actar.

Page, Scott, and Brian Phillips. 2004. 'By Design: Editing the City.' In *Shifting Infrastructures*, 306090 No 6, edited by Patricia Acevedo-Riker, J. D. Solomon, and A. Briseno, 84–93. New York: Princeton Architectural Press.

Picon, Antoine. 2010. 'The City in the Digital Sprawl.' In *Digital Culture in Architecture: An Introduction for the Design Professions*, 171–208. Basel: Birkhäuser.

Rheingold, Howard. 2003. *Smart Mobs: The Next Social Revolution*, Cambridge: Perseus Publishing

Read, Stephen. 2009. 'Another Form: From the Informational to the Infrastructural City', *Footprint 05: Metropolitan Form*, edited by François Claessens, A. Vernez Moudon, and D. Prosperi, 5–22. Delft: TU Delft.

Sassen, Saskia. 1998. *Globalization and Its Discontents: Essays on the New Mobility of People & Money*. New York: New Press.

Soja, Edward. 2000. *Postmetropolis: Critical Studies of Cities and Regions*. Oxford: Blackwell

———. 2010. *Seeking Spatial Justice*. Minneapolis, MN: University of Minnesota Press.

Stanza. 2010a. Artist's statement. Accessed 3 September 2010.
        http://www.stanza.co.uk/about/statement.html

———. 2010b. Interview with Stanza, March 2010. Accessed 3 September 2010 http://we-make-money-not-art.com/archives/2010/03/do-you-have-a-photo.php

———. 2010c. Project description. Accessed 15 September 2010.
        http://www.stanza.co.uk/sensity/index.html

Steiner, Hadas. 2009. *Beyond Archigram: The Structure of Circulation*, New York: Routledge.

Ulieru, Mihaela. 2010. 'Special Issue on Digital Ecologies', *IEEE Transactions on Systems, Man, and Cybernetics–Part A: Systems and Humans* 40: 1341–1342.

Wellman, Barry. 2001. "Physical Place and Cyber Place: The Rise of Networked Individualism." *International Journal of Urban and Regional Research* 2: 227–252.

Wigley, Mark. 2007. 'The Architectural Brain.' In *Network Practices: New Strategies in Architecture and Design* edited by Anthony Burke, and T. Tierney, 30–53. New York: Princeton Architectural Press.

Wilkins, Gretchen., ed. 2010. *Distributed Urbanism: Cities after Google Earth*. Oxon: Routledge.

Chapter 7

Beijing Parallax: Manifestations of Thirdspace in the Beijing Olympics Opening Ceremony[1]

Steven A. Nardi & Munehito Moro

Mapping Beijing

First Map

In our paper, we are to investigate the consequences of the 2008 Olympic Opening Ceremony. In particular, we will be making reference to the ceremony as film, and current film theory. We became interested in this project through a book, Michael Dutton's *Beijing Time*. We both travelled to Beijing in December 2009 quite literally with *Beijing Time* in hand, retracing the steps of Dutton's argument.

In particular, we became interested in the way Dutton describes the changing cartographies of Beijing as illustrative of different ideological constructions. As Edward Soja writes, "the social-spatial-historical processes that shape our lives do not simply operate *in* and *on* cities, but to a significant degree also emanate *from* cities" (Soja 2000, 18). To paraphrase this, the urban order is a substructure from which "our lives" are derived, while opening up what Soja calls "thirdspace". The core is tracing the intended force that three different configurations of Beijing's space exert on the shape of the political and culture of first China, and now the world. In particular, we will discuss three distinct moments in mapping Beijing.

The first cartography is urban space in classic Beijing constructed in the early fifteenth century. It was designed along a regimented configuration according to Confucianism and the Ying-Yang cosmology. The city, prior to the dissolution of imperial power in 1911, was laid out with a clarity as to the source and distribution of secular and divine power. This city map provides a geographical rendition of an

---

[1] This chapter is an edited version of the essay "Beijing Parallax: Manifestations of Thirdspace in the Beijing Olympics Opening Ceremony" first published in *Spaces and Flows: An International Journal of Urban and Extra Urban Studies* 1 (4): 9-20.

ancient worldview originating from the Han dynasty (202 BC–AD 9). As Jianfei Zhu remarks,

> [imperial] Beijing displays a centrality and a symmetry in its overall composition. [...] A 7,500-metre-long axis, running from north to south through the city is the strongest organizing element of the whole plan. An east-west axis intersects this main axis, defining the centre of Beijing (Zhu 2004, 29).

The "center" is, of course, the point occupied by the Forbidden City, which had functioned as the imperial residence and the political center from 1420 to 1911.

This mapping of the city, in other words, conflates the political center of power with a Confucian cosmology. As Zhu writes, "The king's imperial system resembles the cosmos, and his centrality on earth mirrors that of heaven above" (Zhu 2004, 35). Further, it conflates the historical character of the city with its spiritual character. The map seems to promise that the real character of both city and regime is ahistorical and divinely based, by overlapping a secular order with the heavenly one. To return to Soja's words, it is a city plan (not individual buildings) designed to order society along metaphysical as well as political lines. This conceptual spatiality was inscribed within the city's configuration centering around the axis.

Second Map

It is the organization of power in urban planning that the Communist Party appropriates. Dutton discusses, in particular, the re-centering of the city when Mao Zedong rewrites the Beijing cityscape with the "Ten Great Constructions" of the Great Leap Forward in the 1950s. The Great Hall of the People, for example, is a magnificent building on the west side of Tiananmen Square built to serve as the political hub of Communist China. Dutton discusses the effect of Tiananmen Square, in particular, on Beijing's spatial configuration. Its size and the creation of a new sense of center draws the focus of Beijing away from the Forbidden City. Dutton writes, "The recentering of the city at Tiananmen Square effectively made the old Imperial Palace the northern 'backyard'" (Dutton 2008, 29).

By going against the ancient cityscape, the placement of the Square posed itself as a historical confrontation with the pre-modern relics. Its placement incurs within the timeless imperial map an unmistakable disruption. Whereas the imperial city was designed to appear timeless, eternal, the Square's placement served as the modernist imposition of historical direction upon the axis. In the *Little Red Book*, Mao describes that his communist party is "the most complete, progressive, revolutionary and rational system" (Mao 1966, 23). This imposition of a "revolutionary and rational system" onto history has its analog in the reorientation of Beijing. The "re-centering" process in the city was, in this context, made equal to the development of materialist history. The placing of the Square was, therefore, a physical correlate of modernity's advent, a spatial embodiment of temporality. It was a creation of the city's new center by the spatial cancellation of the old center's authority. The new axis still borrows the determinism of the earlier, divine, directionality of the city, but replaces the divine cosmology with a modern ideology.

Third Map

As imperial Beijing, and then Maoist Beijing, was, so the new Beijing is also inseparable from its new architectures. In fact, the massive amount of re-building in Beijing in preparation for the Olympics is done in such a way as to again reconfigure the axis that Beijing is built upon. The Olympics completes the transition to a third map that represents a third re-configuration of Beijing. If you have visited Beijing, you have most likely felt the energy of the city's development. When we visited, we were particularly looking forward to seeing the China Central Television (CCTV) Headquarters Building which Rem Koolhaas designed.

Image 1: Bejing National Centre for Performing Arts/National Grand Theatre

Source: Hui Lan, Wikipedia, CC BY 2.0

Of course, the Beijing National Stadium (the Bird's Nest) designed by Herzog and de Meuron is famous. On the map, the bird's nest extends the traditional central axis north. But particularly important to the reconfiguration of urban space is Paul Andreu's National Center for the Performing Arts (aka "the Egg"), a huge, cocoon-like oval theater 212 meters in length by 143 meters in width, which opened in 2007. The Egg, in particular, affects the clarity of the layout. Because its vast presence sits at an oblique angle to the central Imperial axis. This addition disrupts the spatial inscription of history carefully built by Mao's urban plan. It disturbs the strict clarity with which the city organized and constrained time. In other words, when the historical development reaches a certain threshold (the end of modernity), it begins to go out of joint. The axis was able to receive a direction either toward the premodern north (Gate of Heavenly Peace) or the modernist south (Square). When the Center was superimposed the "revolutionary and rational system" of history inscribed in the second cartography of Beijing lost its clarity of purpose. Instead of the axis-arrow, we now have a triangle.

Postmodern Mapping

What is at stake in mapping Beijing, therefore, is a relationship to history. In the third map, where the monumental new creations embrace postmodernism, the new relationship to history is a disruption. This remapping reflects a fundamental re-arrangement of history into urban space. It opens up what Soja calls "thirdspace": "a simultaneously real-and-imagined, actual-and-virtual, locus of structured individual and collective experience and agency" (Soja 2000, 11). History, understood within a modernist framework, becomes displaced within Beijing's "thirdspace."

Beijing's historical disconnections are best understood as symptomatic of postmodern social conditions. Frederic Jameson, in *Postmodernism*, argues that the postmodern condition has changed the construction of our relationship to history. The past has become only "a vast collection of images, a multitudinous photographic simulacrum" (Jameson 1991, 18). The effect, Jameson argues, is the past as an object of nostalgic longing: what he calls "'pastness' and pseudohistorical depth, in which the history of aesthetic styles displaces 'real' history" (Jameson 1991, 20). The flow and variation of historical experience, in other words, are replaced by sets of aesthetic effects best embodied in the third map.

This sense of dislocation and the impression on the map of a new, virtual, nostalgic order, is neatly summed up by a controversial image included in the filmed version of the Olympic opening ceremony. During the live broadcast, footage of a set of footprints walking across the city was spliced into the live coverage. These footprints were controversial because computer generated footage was used. Although real fireworks were set off, the ones seen on screen were computer generated, complete with a shaky camera effect to preserve the illusion they were being filmed from a helicopter.

As you can tell, the footsteps begin in southern part of the city, and move north through the same axis as the old imperial city plan. The addition is that they extend the axis up through the city to the "Bird's Nest," the Olympic Stadium where the opening ceremony was held. The dramatic spectacle of the footprints is nothing but the manifestation of Soja's "thirdspace." They are "simultaneously real-and-imagined, actual-and-virtual" (Soja 2000, 11). Despite the controversy, they can neither be called fake or authentic. They serve as the "locus of structured individual and collective experience and agency" in the sense that the spectacle itself creates a new locus from which Beijing is experienced (Soja 2000, 11).

History as Simulacra

One way of understanding what happens in the text of the opening ceremony, therefore, is that in invoking an image of Beijing on the screen, the opening ceremony blurs the distinction between the real urban environment, and its phantasmagoric shadow. In Jameson's terms, the real history is displaced by the aesthetics; we see this displacement enacted in the footsteps superimposed upon the live event of the opening ceremony. In the power demonstrated in the sheer size of the spectacle, that displacement is written into both the individual and collective experience of the viewer.

The text of the opening ceremony, then, extends into space the qualities of film. Produced by a famous film director, created with the camera in mind, marketed afterwards as a DVD set, the ceremony is an odd hybrid of history, film, and live event. In this aspect, the construction of this text is best understood as a giant, enormously expensive, nostalgia film. In particular, we found the work of Rey Chow useful. In *Sentimental Fabulations*, Chow writes,

> [...] the ever-expanding capacities for seeing and, with them, the infinite transmigrations and transmutations of cultures—national, ethnic, rural, illiterate—into commodified electronic images are part and parcel of a dominant global regime of value making that is as utterly ruthless as it is utterly creative (Chow 2007, 165).

Chow's emphasis is upon the ruthless fact that no one can avoid being seen; nonetheless the impact is also a creative one with regard to identity formation. It is not simply that we are powerlessly subsumed into a homogenized, "Americanization," but that our cultural identity is inevitably doubled: local and global, by the instant mediation of commodification. We have to contextualize the Beijing Olympics into this "ruthless" but "creative" formation of identity.

The ceremony is also, however, a staged political demonstration along the lines of Maoist Red Guards assembling in Tiananmen Square in the sixties and seventies: the reduction of politics into spectacle. Therefore, what we are witnessing now is the permeation of spectacle into everyday perception of the world. As an extension of a film, the opening ceremony provides a new constitution of spatiality.

In a postmodern city it is the perceived that has gained ontological depth. That reversal, that perceptions shape what is seen rather than what is seen shapes perceptions, is particularly evident in a story Dutton tells about the Gate of Heavenly Peace, which was damaged beyond repair in a 1966 earthquake (Dutton 2008, 72). Faced with the prospect of demolishing the gate, a symbol of the legitimacy of the political order, and only a short time after the Cultural Revolution had been proclaimed from its walls, the regime balked. Instead, the decision was made to keep the demolition of the gate a secret. Between December 1969 and March 1970, the gate was covered by a scaffold, surreptitiously dismantled, and then replaced by a perfect replica.

The story provides a literal analog of the process of demolition and creation of meaning. In the rebuilding of the gate, the appearance of history is produced as a spatial domain. The Maoist project of historical determinism conceals the elevation of image; the gate, too, has become part of "a vast collection of images, a multitudinous photographic simulacrum" (Jameson 1991, 18). Even Marxist history is known only as an arrangement of images.

Beijing Parallax

This example also shows that history in Beijing involved false surfaces even before the third cartography; the Imperial and Maoist city, in a manner of speaking, were equally arbitrary constitutions of spatialities. The only change in the historicism of the postmodern map is that its embrace of fiction is no longer hidden under a scaffold.

At the core, therefore, these three distinct maps are intimately related despite their disparate ideologies. In *the Parallax View*, Slavoj Žižek discusses a similar phenomenon. His example is taken from Claude Levi-Strauss's account in *Structural Anthropology* of a tribe in the Great Lakes. Members of the tribe drew two very distinct maps of their village, depending on their social position. These two maps, Žižek argues, do not merely show a difference in their point of view; but they also describe a hidden truth shared within the community, as the three maps of Beijing also do. Žižek writes,

> [...] The very splitting into the two 'relative' perceptions implies a hidden reference to a constant—not the objective 'actual' disposition of buildings, but the traumatic kernel, a fundamental antagonism the inhabitants of the village were unable to symbolize, to account for, to 'internalize,' to come to terms with, an imbalance in social relations that prevented the community from stabilizing itself into a harmonious whole (Žižek 2006, 25-26).

Žižek calls the shared truth of the Great Lakes villagers, the "traumatic kernel," a parallax. The parallactic "Real," he writes, "is the traumatic core of some social antagonism which distorts the tribe members' view of the actual arrangement of the houses in their village" (Žižek 2006, 26). Similarly, the three maps of Beijing represent three disrupted points of view that in their totality provide a vision of Beijing's own capitalized "Real."

The mutability of historical surfaces in Beijing also helps to understand why film has been so important in Beijing and China's emergence as such an important cultural product in the last two decades. Films since 1987's *The Last Emperor* and *Red Sorghum* have moved from generally factual depictions of the past, to increasingly fantastic constitutions of the pastness.

1998's *Crouching Tiger, Hidden Dragon*, for example, presents Beijing as a space of fantasy and sorcery. The act of remembering has been replaced by the construction of fantasy; the more satisfying truth is the constructed truth. The cinematic projection of Beijing has become more and more imaginary. It is no longer possible to see the city in the same way because we have been so influenced by the cinematic perception.

In this context, even the Forbidden City, a place we usually conceive as one of the city's best-known ancient relics, begins to appear differently. Although it was not torn down and rebuilt in as literal a way as the Gate of Heavenly Peace, the historical authenticity of the Forbidden City is also something of a production.

The site began widely welcoming large numbers of foreign tourists after the release of Bernardo Bertolucci's *The Last Emperor* in 1987: the year when the site was registered as one of China's first World Heritage sites. As the historian Geremie R. Barmé says, "The success of that film came at a time when the Palace Museum was learning to market itself, and it had a profound impact on how this was done" (Barmé 2008, 179). With the dust blown away, the site began to shine again, but this time as a commodity in the global market. International exhibitions held by the Palace Museum have gained enormous popularity overseas, with increasing frequency within the last thirty years.

What has happened is a constitution of intelligibility, namely, the norms of regulation within which objects are arranged and then discovered. We now witness the City as simulacra of the place: images in tourist guidebooks, exotic films, or news coverage circulating in what Rey Chow would call the "global regime of value making."

Global Ritual/Local Ritual

The context of the ceremony is, therefore, an imaginary spatiality onto which hues of pastness have been painted. We can examine, particularly, the reconfiguration of the meaning of "China" within the global system of intelligibility--or the "global regime of value making". From here, we can delve into the genealogy in which history and geography have been intertwined by referring to the ceremony's cinematic precursor, *The Road Home*, created by the same director Zhang Yimou in 1999. *The Road Home*, like the ceremony, defines our lived environment (the present) from the perspective of pastness.

The film is about a woman's life in a rural village during the fifties. It is structured as a complicated set of enfolded narrations. The mother's story has become part of local legend, and in the film this old narrative is retold by the son. The movie opens as the son travels back to the village after the news that his father, who has been a teacher in the village for many years, has died. His mother is insisting on a traditional funeral procession, in which the father's body would be carried back from the distant hospital to the village by hand. The village mayor says that because all the young people have moved to the city, there is no one left able to carry the casket.

At the end of the film, the son comes around to his mother's way of thinking and agrees to insist on the ritual. In a warm, sentimental ending, former students, colleagues, and friends from all over the region hear of the procession and come to pay their last respects. The film ends with images of this restored sense of community brought back by a rural ritual.

The ritual represented also leads to understanding the film's further relevance in our argument. As a communicative practice, the funeral procession in *The Road Home* operates on a principle similar to what James Carey, in his book *Communication as Culture*, names the "ritual" aspect of communication. The "ritual function" of language, Carey argues, aims "toward the maintenance of society in time" (Carey 1989, 18). It generally consists of the repetitive participation in social gatherings in order to confirm the "underlying order of things" across time.

In this sense, *The Road Home* makes an argument about the importance of ritual in structuring the way the past is experienced in contemporary China. In the movie, the mother's point of view is that of a mythical, heroic, eternal peasant. When her apparently irrational determination is deciphered and turns out to present a pseudo-genealogy that explains why the past is relevant, we come to understand that pastness still remains vital to ordering our present experience.

The insertion of the son's gaze functions also as a cinematic apparatus to introduce the global gaze into the film's world. The son, as well as audiences, gradually comes to understand his mother's life and the meanings of the rituals she clings to. Through repeating an apparently pointless rite, the son finds a connection to his mother's story. This sentimental ending also works for the viewer, who comes to feel that through watching the movie has granted insight into a seemingly lost Chinese culture. The viewer feels gratifyingly connected to a pastness that beforehand had seemed erased and lost. In this point, the whole theme of the film is devoted to the cinematic/visual transmission of a local, ritualistic life into the global regime of intelligibility.

The film thus centers around the translation of the local into the global: a translation which gives a new meaning to old, ritual practices. In short, the film's hidden theme is about how to subsume locality into visibility: how the local rituals can be rendered intelligible through being revealed by the global circulation of visions. The connection the viewer feels to the community created in *The Road Home* might feel, to a Western viewer in particular, as if he or she is involved in the community being created. However, it is only the intervention of the globalized point of view that enables that vicarious connection.

In *Cosmopolitanism and the Geographies of Freedom*, David Harvey writes, "The production of space, in short, proceeds alongside of, as well as through, the production of places" (Harvey 2009, 191). In Harvey's context, the film is about the production of locality in the global space of consumption. Watching *The Road Home*, even a Western audience feels as if they are witnessing the revelation of authenticity; but the voyeuristic pleasure, inevitably entailed in the visual experience, nonetheless confirms that this experience of authenticity is feasible only in the context of commodification. That experience is created by, as Harvey writes, "the dialectical character of this space-place connection" (Harvey 2009, 191). The experience of authenticity that seems to characterize the local is actually an encounter with the global regime of value making.

Parallax Olympics

While the Road Home, as a "mere" film, succeeds in marketing an image of Chinese identity, both externally and internally, the filmic version of the Beijing Olympics, and the event itself, should be seen not as the expression of genuine cultural heritage, but as a much more profound act of cultural formation. The Olympics here function as a ritual. The product of that ritual is the formation of a new identity that circulates in a global marketplace. While the NBC commentators watch the movable type dancers, one exclaims, "Again, the reconciling of opposites". The other replies, "Absolutely, and again the desire to replace one image of China with another one". Included on the official DVD, this exchange goes to the heart of how this event is marketed.

Through the lens of the ceremony, Beijing has become a site that is both global and local, fashionably contemporary as well as charmingly quaint. We want to look at the opening ceremony as the spatial extension of nostalgia films. The ceremony and a nostalgia film are similar, in both cases evoking a past experienced as authentic, while functioning entirely within the global logic.

The Opening ceremony is structured as a series of the parallax. Human and machine, the past and the present, virtual and real, are brought into a relationship that defies their conventional oppositions. Instead, the ceremony opens up a space of connection in which these oppositions are, at least apparently, reconciled. In *The Parallax View*, Žižek found a "traumatic kernel, a fundamental antagonism," binding the disparate visions of the villagers into a whole. This same "traumatic kernel," also forms the antagonistic oppositions of the opening ceremony into a single spectacle which appears united.

Mass and Individual

This theme is introduced early in the piece when it begins with the spectacle of thousands of drummers in unison hammering away at their drums. The drummers appear as an army of mechanized humans, all set on a single task. (The NBC commentators mention that the drummers were so grim at first that they were told at the last minute to smile).

In the opening sequence, where each drum is lit, and as the lights go out, when the swinging sticks of the drummers glow red, the drummers appear as if they were pixels on a giant screen. Yet at the end of the segment, each of the drummers stands up and enthusiastically waves to the crowd. The ceremony repeatedly blurs the line between mass and individual.

The drummers' transformation is a foreshadowing of one of the most memorable moments—the scene with the movable type. Again, the distinction between individual human and mass is blurred; the dancers appear as part of a mechanical whole, forming a single image as counterparts with the two computer screens which bracket them. Further, the dancers take the role of individual pieces of a machine. The scale, precision, and aesthetic quality, give a sense of the inhuman to the spectacle. The commentator's tone as the dancers shed their costumes is revealing. For a Western viewer, who until this point might have mistaken the dancers for actual machines, the revelation of the humanity at the end may well serve as a surprise. The suddenness of this reconciliation is the key to understanding the logic of parallax. The sudden dissolving of the mass into individual faces unsettles the opposition between the dehumanized image of an enormous automaton and a fully expressive human.

In the same way that the opposition between individual and mass breaks down, so does the opposition between the past and the present. The disruption in the spectator's sight provides a vicarious experience analogous to feeling a part of the flow of history. Specifically, the sheer size of the spectacle works as a metaphoric substitution for history. The scale of China's history is sensed through the immensity of the performance.

The size, setting, and stage of the ceremony give the experience an impact that cannot be contained for the viewer merely as spectatorship. One is unable to maintain the distance from the scene implied in that word. Instead, one is inevitably a participant in something much greater, a ritual enacted on a global stage, a ritual that transforms the viewer into a member of a newly formed community.

Global Ritual

In *Global and Local Cultures*, Mike Featherstone claims that it is still possible to accentuate a distinct sense of national identities. Although globalization is frequently taken as Americanization, experiences such as the FA Cup final, or national spectacles such as the Olympics, are events that create a sense of national unity. He associates this creative force with the idea of mediated ritual. He writes,

> [The rites and ceremonies] that were spectacles which have become commodified and promoted to wider audiences need not be taken to imply that they have induced passivity amongst citizens who are essentially manipulated spectatorship should not be understood as passive, or remote from the bodily enacting of rituals (Featherstone 1993, 178-179).

In the context of the globalized marketplace, in other words, these national differences manifest themselves as commodified and salable pleasures. Featherstone's idea is that rituals work even through commodified, technological ways of seeing.

Featherstone's argument misses the dialectical interaction between global space and national locality: the location in which they encounter with each other, namely, thirdspace. We add to his argument, therefore, this transnational dimension, which is inevitably superimposed on the national. National place and global space influence one another through a specific logic.

In the context of the Beijing Olympics, the limitations of his argument would be seen. In this case, "Chinese identity" is given another twist in addition to the mere construction of the national identity. What's being formed through this televisual ritual is not an indigenous concept of "China". The ceremony proves that the national identity is not achieved unless it becomes globally intelligible. This globally intelligible local identity is emerging from what Rey Chow calls "the every-expanding capacities for seeing and, with them, the infinite transmigrations and transmutations of cultures" (Chow 2007, 165).

Conclusion: The Visual Construction of a New Beijing

Therefore, our final task is to associate those capacities with the argument of Beijing as thirdspace. The concept of thirdspace should not be reduced into the mere uniqueness of geography, such as Asia or China or Beijing. Rather, it should be found in the intersecting location between the local and global; in our case, it is the Olympics and its consequences in forming the new sense of spatiality. The visual coverage of the ceremony worked as a performative act of cartography, by which Beijing's locality was introduced into global space. It was the vision-based construction of the new global city.

Referring to Rey Chow again, the ceremony shattered the experience of the city "into commodified electronic images [that] are part and parcel of a dominant global regime of value making that is as utterly ruthless as it is utterly creative" (Chow 2007, 165). The balance Chow insists on, the one between "ruthless" and "creative", neatly sums up the doubled functioning of the ceremony: sweeping reduction of the entire place into a sentimental product, but simultaneously opening up the transcultural framework to the world, that is, thirdspace.

REFERENCES

Barmé, Geremie. 2008. *The Forbidden City*. London: Profile Books.

Bertolucci, Bernardo, dir. 1987. *The Last Emperor*. Hemdale Film Coporation.

Carey, James W. 1989. *Communication as Culture: Essays on Media and Society*. New York: Routledge.

Chow, Rey. 2007. *Sentimental Fabulations, Contemporary Chinese Films: Attachment in the Age of Global Visibility*. New York: Columbia University Press.

Dutton, Michael Robert, Hsiu-ju Stacy Lo, and Dong Dong Wu. 2008. *Beijing Time*. Cambridge: Harvard University Press.

Featherstone, Mike. 1993. "Global and Local Cultures." In *Mapping the Futures: Local Cultures, Global Change*, edited by Jon Bird, Barry Curtis, Tim Putnam, George Robertson, and Lisa Tickner, 169–88. New York: Routledge.

Harvey, David. 2009. *Cosmopolitanism and the Geographies of Freedom*. New York: Columbia University Press.

Jameson, Fredric. 1991. *Postmodernism, or the Cultural Logic of Late Capitalism*. Durham: Duke University Press.

Levi-Strauss, C. 1963. *Structural Anthropology*. Translated by Jacobson, Claire and Schoepf, Brooke Grundfest. New York: Basic Books.

Mao, Tse-Tung. 1966. *Quotations from Chairman Mao Tse-Tung*. Peking: Foreign Languages Press.

Soja, E W. 2000. *Postmetropolis: Critical Studies of Cities and Regions*. Malden, MA: Wiley-Blackwell.

Žižek, Slavoj. 2006. *The Parallax View*. Cambridge: MIT Press.

Zhang, Yimou, dir. 1999. *The Road Home*. GuangXi Film Studio.

———. *2008 Olympics: Beijing 2008 Complete Opening Ceremony*. Ten Mayflower.

Zhu, Jianfei. 2004. *Chinese Spatial Strategies: Imperial Beijing, 1420–1911*. New York: Routledge Curzon.

Chapter 8

Hybrid Spaces in China's Mega-Urban Regions: Rural-Urban Synthesis as a Foundation for Sustainability[1]

Andrew M. Marton & Terry McGee

Introduction

This chapter explores one of the main challenges facing China as it moves rapidly to become a modern developed society in the 21st century namely how to grow economically while at the same time creating a more equitable, just and sustainable society. Central to this task, despite the fact that China is one of the most rapid economically growing societies in the world, is that is has not yet resolved the ongoing problems of rural-urban inequality that are demonstrated in the ongoing spatial inequality between the predominantly rural areas of Western and Central China and the eastern coastal zone of China. Of course, the Chinese government recognizes this challenge and has made vigorous efforts to reduce these rural-urban disparities in the 11th and 12th Five Year Plans. But at the same time the main focus remains upon the rapidly urbanizing coastal zone and in particular on the growth of large mega-urban regions.

In this respect China is repeating a model of development that has and is occurring in the East Asian region that stretches from Korea and Japan through China to Southeast Asia. In such areas there is an increasing concentration of population in the large zones of urban activity or mega urban regions (MURs) located in deltaic coastal zones that developed throughout history as the "food baskets" of their countries. Mega-urban regions include one or more core mega-cities (usually over 10 million), up to several medium and large secondary cities (over 1 million), a number of smaller cities and towns, and large areas in between of mixed agricultural and non-agricultural land-use. This is part of the urbanization process that has accompanied the surge in economic growth that has been occurring at an uneven pace across most of the East Asia since 1960.

---

[1] This chapter is an edited version of the essay "Mega-Urbanization in China: Rural-Urban Synthesis as a Foundation for Sustainability" first published in *The Global Studies Journal* 10 (2): 1-19.

In recent years as the global economy has undergone radical restructuring in the face of global economic volatility the East Asian region has emerged as one of the pivotal regions that is leading the global economic recovery. However, this process is happening in the context of a number of global environmental, economic and social challenges that will be particularly acute in the 21st century and threaten the sustainability of the MURs.

This chapter positions the Chinese urbanization experience within the context of the urbanization processes of the rest of East Asia. These developments are discussed under six broad headings:

1. The growth of Mega-Urbanization in East Asia

2. Urbanization Processes in East Asia

3. Mega-Urban Regions in East Asia

4. Special Features of the Urban Transition in China

5. Rural Urban Relations and hybrid spaces in Chinese Mega-Urban Regions: The Example of Food Production

6. Policies for Rural Urban Synthesis in China's Mega-Urban Regions as a Foundation for Sustainability

The main argument of these six sections is that the growth of mega-urbanization is producing major changes to rural activities that have characterized the deltaic regions into which urban activities are spreading. These challenges are occurring because of increased urban demand for diversified food and industrial crops, loss of good agricultural land, changes in the food distribution system in response to increased urban demand, and increased competition for resources of these regions such as land and labor in addition to the many environment problems caused by climate change and pollution. While some economists see this as an inevitable process that is leading to increased economic rewards these developments pose both challenges and opportunities for the sustainability of mega-urban regions. The final section of the chapter argues for developing policies of rural-urban synthesis that will be sensitive to issues of sustainability using the concepts of *synergetic capital* and *eco-capital*. These concepts capture some of the elements of the Chinese concept of "harmony" that are embodied in the most recent development plans.

The Growth of Mega-Urbanization in East Asia

The first part of our argument is that the urbanization process at a global level is an inevitable part of the process of development that is now gaining momentum in the developing countries of the world. Four facts support this assertion:

1. For the first time in human history the twenty-first century has more than 50 percent of the global population living in urban places.

2. This urban shift will involve a decrease in the proportion of people engaged in rural activities in developing countries as the process of development encourages the movement of rural people to urban areas. This will mean an increase not only in urban populations but will also an increase of the employed people in non-agricultural activities in areas that remain defined as rural.

3. This urban shift will involve an ongoing increase of the number of people living in mega-urban regions.

4. The growth of large mega-urban regions poses many challenges of governance, environmental sustainability and economic and social development particularly in developing countries.

China is a microcosm all these global trends. By 2020 China will have more mega-urban regions than any country in the world and this will involve a large increase in the proportion of urban population in a time-frame that is much shorter than that experienced by Western countries at comparable periods of rapid urbanization. The implications of these facts concerning contemporary urbanization are obvious to most East Asian governments and China. Their responses have been driven by a position that sees the economic advantages of increased urbanization to be a central concept that drives policy formation. This position is supported by the economic arguments that emphasize the importance of economies of scale, the creation of mass urban markets, the encouragement of foreign investment and the higher productivity that occur in urban places. Of course these developments have been heightened by the growing integration of the global economy and the restructuring of the economies of the developed world that are part of the much debated process of globalization (Olds et al. 1999; McGee and Watters 1997). The results of these urban-orientated development strategies in the more developed East Asian economies have been the decline in the proportion of the employed population in agriculture, the depopulation of rural areas, a sharp reduction in the number of family farms and a restructuring of agriculture with growing emphasis on capital intensity, off-farm employment, the employment of migrant farm labor and food imports and increased agricultural productivity Another result is an increase in rural-urban income disparities that accentuates out-migration from rural areas.

In this context China's institutional framework of "market socialism" (which it shares with Vietnam) makes it distinctive in the East Asian region. On the one hand, the historical experience of socialism encourages a form of gradualism that emphasizes efforts to decrease rural-urban differences through policies of improvements in infrastructure, new delivery systems for education, health and social welfare in rural areas and investment in increasing agricultural productivity. This is supported by policies of regional development focused on improving the economic conditions of disadvantaged rural areas as, for example, in Western China. But at the same time these pro-rural policies are being implemented, accelerated economic growth in urbanizing areas of the Eastern coastal region have been the drivers of national economic growth fueled by both international, national and domestic investment and have led to a rapid "marketistation" of this region. Thus, at the national level this model of development seems to offer no alternative but to encourage structural shifts to the industrial and service sector locating in urbanizing areas. Despite ongoing commitment to rural development there is still a strong belief that urbanization is an inevitable part of creating a modern state.

Urbanization Processes in East Asia

We argue that in the 21st century these national policies need to be combined with regional responses, particularly at the level of the mega-urban region, which place emphasis on developing "synergies" between rural and urban activities. Development should aim to increase linkages within and between rural and urban areas to produce regional transformation as part of a strategy that is designed to create a sustainable region (Douglass 1998). These synergies and linkages are influenced by three main processes driving urbanization in East Asia:

1. Structural change in East Asian economies.

2. The "transactional revolution" in communications and transportation (Marton 2000).

3. The emergence of urban-like formations outside core cities which we have labeled "diffuse urbanization" (McGee 2016).

Structural Change in East Asian Economies

This brief summary of the prevailing developmental wisdom of East Asia is supported by a quick overview of the relationships between urbanization and structural change in East Asia. Table 1 presents an overall picture of the relationships between urbanization trajectories and structural change in the contribution of the three main economic sectors of agriculture, industry and services to GDP in selected East Asian countries for the forty-year period between 1960 and 2000. These urbanization trajectories are organized into (Type I) developed post-industrial societies with urbanization levels of above 70 percent; (Type II) developing societies with urbanization levels of between 30 and 70 percent; (Type III) underdeveloped societies with under 30 percent levels of urbanization, and; (Type IV) China, with the most rapid growth in urbanization levels since 2000 reaching more than 50 per cent by 2011.

Table 1: Changes in Distribution of GDP and Urbanization Levels 1960-1980-2000 (%)

	Agriculture			Industry			Services		
Year	1960	1980	2000	1960	1980	2000	1960	1980	2000
TYPE I *(Urbanization above 70%)*									
Taiwan	28	9	3	29	46	35	43	49	62
Japan	13	4	1	45	43	32	42	53	66
South Korea	37	16	5	20	39	44	43	45	51
TYPE II *(Urbanization 30 to 70%)*									
Malaysia	36	23	9	18	39	51	46	47	40
Thailand	40	22	9	19	28	42	41	50	49
Indonesia	54	26	16	14	39	46	32	35	38
Philippines	26	22	16	28	36	32	46	42	52
TYPE III *(Urbanization below 30%)*									
Myanmar	33	48	57	12	13	10	55	39	33
TYPE IV *(Urbanization 46% in 2009)*									
China	39	33	15	38	47	46	23	20	39

Sources: World Bank (various years) World Development Report. Washington. Taiwan (China) data from Taiwan Statistical Data Book (various years). Source: Own Figure.

Note: Figures for Singapore and Hong Kong (SAR, China) not included because both are considered as 100 percent urban. Figures for Laos, Cambodia and Vietnam not included.

From the point of view of the arguments developed in this chapter it is the group of post-industrial East Asian societies in trajectory Type I that appear to be the model that China and other East Asian countries will follow. In particular it is the development of the urbanized corridors that run between the major urban centres (Tokyo-Osaka; Seoul-Pusan; Taipei-Kaoshiung) that is important. Thus, for example, while the population of Greater Seoul and Pusan was 14 percent of the national population in 1960, by 2000 it was more than 50 percent. Similar patterns were also true of Tokyo-Osaka and Taipei- Kaoshiung.

The Transactional Revolution

East Asian countries in trajectory Type I of the urbanization process have been very successful in breaking down the "friction of distance" reducing transportation costs, extending urban subway systems, implementing improvements in digital informational systems and national and local highway infrastructure (McGee and Lin 1993). It is important to note that China has been dramatically successful in a much shorter time in introducing these improvements. In all these countries transactional corridors have been formed linked by super-fast railway systems. While current accounts lay much emphasis upon the role of globalization and national policy in this urbanization process, the major fact that effects the urbanization transition is that it is occurring at a very much faster rate than that urban transitions of developed countries. Marcotullio and Lee have argued with respect to the urban transition that the "...unique feature of the present era is the compression of the time frame in which the transitions are occurring" (Marcotullio and Lee 2003, 331). What is important in the China case is the large volume of population that will be involved in this urban transition with creates great challenges to managing the urban transition.

Such transitions are being driven by accelerated transactional flows of people, commodities, capital and information between, and within, countries. The international components of this transactional revolution are generally referred to as part of a new era of globalization in which foreign investment encouraged by national states is an important component. The different character of the transactional revolution places much more emphasis on the flows of people, commodities, information and capital within national space economies. Thus, development is seen as occurring in a dynamic sense as a process of transformation of national economic space in which interactions and linkages are a more accurate reflection of reality than the idea that rural and urban areas are undergoing somehow spatially separated transitions (Marton 2000).

In contemporary East Asia the rural-urban transformation is fundamentally driven by a network of linkages that provides a dynamic spatial frame of flows of people, commodities, information and capital. This involves the recognition these "transcending networks" are restructuring urban space in a way that emphasizes the emergence of intensely transaction networks particularly focused on mega-urban regions. This is leading to very rapid economic growth rates focused on these mega-urban regions but at the same time is creating many environmental and social problems and increasing disparities at the level of individual nations.

Diffuse Urbanization

A third component of the overall urbanization process is linked to the emergence of urban-like formations outside traditional city cores that have been labeled "diffuse urbanization" (McGee 2016). This is occurring in both developed and developing countries of East Asia and China. This has resulted in radical changes to regional urban space which, in addition to territorial extension from core urban areas and the expanded territory of the city, has also led to the reconfiguration of urban space with the creation of areas outside the core cities of mixed agricultural and non-urban activities that include industrial estates, residential settlement and increased commercial activity such as shopping malls This region of diffusing urbanization has been called "desakota" by McGee (1991). In the early phases of the urban transition these regions (previously largely rural) have been characterized by an increase of "in-situ urbanization" with informal sector activities including building and renting accommodation for in-migrants, creating petty enterprises in retailing and industry. But in the latter phases of the changes in desakota spaces urban activities in industry and services have increased and this has led governments to create organized urban spaces such as new towns and industrial estates that have increased the demand for middle and high income housing. This has also resulted in an increase in income for the population of these desakota spaces that have created opportunities for local entrepreneurialism. But at the same time, this has created conflicts that are reflected in rural opposition to urban development, economic and social inequality, and environmental problems that create difficulties of administration and governance (Brenner 2014).

At the urban level, the way exogenous actors such as developers and facilitative administrators drive expansion, and the degree of their interaction with endogenous local actors, needs to be set in the particular context of specific "desakota spaces". Past theory has attempted to universalize these realities of urban spaces by creating zonal models, often drawn from the North American experience, of core cities, peripheral zones, and mixed rural-urban zones on the margins of urban places. But the latest phase of urbanization is dominated by the rapid growth of urbanization in the Global South, occurring in a new phase of global capitalism globalization of the market system which has created a multiplicity of capitalisms which Jessop labels "variegated capitalisms" (Jessop 2014). This makes comparison between different sites of desakota change a complex task. It is these extended rural-urban spaces created by "diffusing urbanization" that are the crucial "sites" of the changing features of rural-urban relations in China today. Before taking a closer look at the Chinese context, it would be useful to briefly highlight key features of mega-urbanization across East Asia.

Mega-Urban Regions in East Asia

In order to understand the challenges of rural-urban relations in mega-urban regions of East Asia it is necessary to discuss briefly how such regions may be defined. At its simplest, formation of mega-urban regions are linked to a process whereby an increasing proportion of a country's GDP and urban population are concentrated in one or more extended spaces. As was highlighted earlier, this must include not only one or more core mega-cities, but other secondary and smaller cities, and regions in between which account for significant proportions of GDP. The only statistical database that enables the temporal measurement of these large urban regions is the UN Population Division's bi-yearly publication that provides data on urban areas of more than one million in size, including information for agglomerations of more than 5 to 10 million people which may be classified as mega-urban regions (MURs). Analysis of the estimated increase in the number of large cities between 2000 and 2015 show the importance of China at a global scale. However, this data-base is limited for measuring MURs because it relies upon administrative definitions that do not always include cities and other areas which are part of an integrated spatial network in its definition of urban agglomerations.

A more satisfactory definition is based upon the measurement of functional integration in MURs as measured by transport flows, economic linkages (industry, service and agriculture) labor markets and population movements that make-up the "transactional space" of the MUR. Because MURs usually have the most well developed "transactional space," the main concentrations of human, social and economic capital, as well as a developed infrastructure, they offer an environment that is attractive to both domestic and foreign capital.

A major feature of MURs is the ongoing spread of urbanization from built up city nodes that arises from improvements in transportation systems and economic growth. Initially in East Asia (with the exception of Japan), transportation systems were dominated by automobile systems but now many countries, including China, are beginning to adopt the Tokyo model of subway systems linked to buses in the outer areas. This urban spread is also associated with an increasing dispersion and insertion of industry into the urban margins and a restructuring of the urban cores towards service functions. Residential decentralization is also important as urban cores are restructured from industry to service functions displacing inner city population.

At a global level there are also processes facilitating the emergence of mega-urban regions which force them to become increasingly competitive so as to attract more investment and establish their branding image globally. While industrial investment has dominated much of this process of international integration, as the global service economy becomes more integrated there is a need to attract part of these national and global transactions through the development of financial services, tourism and conferences. While this competition for "transactional capital" was initially led by individual cities it is increasingly being realized that it is necessary to develop marketing campaigns that emphasize opportunities across the wider region.

Because of these processes MURs are increasingly becoming the "engines" of economic development of their countries often contributing above 50 percent of the national GDP. In part because of their very success, MURs present policy challenges that are focused on four main areas: (1) Developing effective governance and management systems for mega-urban regions; (2) Making mega-urban regions sustainable in the face of environmental deterioration and global economic competition; (3) Making MURs livable in terms of employment, services infrastructure and effective social policy, and; (4) Developing new policies for rural-urban relations in MURs. However, there are distinctive features of the urbanization process in China that are at present shared by only one other East Asian country, Vietnam, that stem from the nature of the transition from socialism to a market economy. These are discussed in the following section.

Special Features of the Urban Transition in China

At present China appears to be exhibiting many of the same features of the rural-urban transformation that occurred in the case of Japan, Korea and Taiwan. Since 1978 China has been experiencing increasing urbanization fueled by rural-urban migration both legal and illegal, rapid industrialization and increased agricultural productivity in city margins, and structural change with an increase in services in the large core municipalities such as Shanghai. By 2000 China had a population of 450 million people defined as urban a level of urbanization of 36.9 percent. By 2030 it is estimated that this urban population will nearly double to 883 million reaching an urbanization level of 60 percent. However, with the acceleration of urban growth since 2000, China had already reached an urbanization level of 60 percent by 2015 much earlier than predicted. In addition, it may be argued that these figures are an under count of actual urban populations because they do not take into sufficient account the spread of urban activities into the surrounding countryside of many cities in China creating a form of rural-urban hybridity (Marton 2016).

These margins serve as locations for new land development projects including residential and industrial estates that are often located alongside proliferating small industries (township and village enterprises) that developed during the 1980s. Such areas can be defined as assemblages of urban and rural activities that are characterized by an intense mixture of rural and urban activities (Marton 2002). This pattern of urbanization is not evenly distributed throughout China with much of the surge of urbanization since 1978 occurring in the eastern zone which has the highest rate of increase of cities of all sizes in China, particularly large cities defined on the basis of non-agricultural population in excess of 1 million in population. They have received over 60 percent of the national fixed asset investment in the period since 1978 and a high proportion of total national foreign investment (McGee et al. 2007, 53-65).

There is considerable interest in China in the emergence of these large mega-urban regions. They were first recognized by Zhou (1991) who suggested they had some similarity with the urban region between Boston and Washington D.C defined as *megalopolis* by Gottmann (1961). However, Zhou also recognized there were important differences between China and the USA including China's high density in-situ population and the development of market socialism. He used the following criteria to define what he called "interlocking metropolitan regions (IMRs)", including: (1) two or more cities with more than 1 million population; (2) an important port; (3) convenient lines of communication that act as a development corridor; (4) numerous small and medium sized cities; (5) intensive interaction between rural and urban. Based on these criteria Zhou delineated four interlocking metropolitan regions: (1) Nanjing-Shanghai-Hangzhou in the lower Yangzi River delta; (2) Hong Kong-Guangzhou in the Pearl River Delta; (3) Beijing-Tianjin in the North China Plain; and (4) Shenyang-Dalian in central and south Liaoning Province. He also delineated two incipient IMRs in the Shandong peninsula and Fujian coastal zone. Data from the 2000 census suggests that the latter two IMRs now fulfill the criteria. In addition, the interior IMR of Chengdu-Chongqing should now be added. These seven IMR's contain 15 percent of China's population, account for more than 50 percent of China's GDP and are the major drivers of the economic success of the last fifteen years (McGee et al. 2007).

The prospect that China may be duplicating the developmental trajectories of the East Asian NICs raises serious concerns at a national and global level for environmental sustainability. China became the world's second largest economy in 2010 and thus is a key player in the global economy. This advance has been accompanied by a rapid growth in trade and investment. It is projected that China will become the world's largest consumer of global fossil fuels by 2030. Even with the "new normal" of relatively slower economic growth around 6 to 7 percent, as China continues to move rapidly towards higher levels of GDP per capita and becomes more urbanized, demands on the environment and resources will continue to increase substantially.

One of the arguments supporting this assumption has been that China's commitment to the development of auto-centered transport systems, including private cars, motor-bikes, trucks and various forms of public transportation such as buses and mini-buses, will place increasing pressure on land and energy as China continues to urbanize (Freud and Martin 1999). Despite a rapid growth of alternative forms of transportation leading to an expansion of national super-fast rail communications between the major cities and a large increase in urban and suburban rail systems, the rate of auto-centred transportation has continued to increase and will place increasing pressure on land and energy in China particularly in the mega-urban regions. These auto-centered systems encourage the outward spread of urban-based activities (residence, work and leisure) that are complemented by state policies of industrial decentralization to urban margins and the need for linkages to transport nodes such as ports and airports. Spatially, these forces are focused on the urban margins of Chinese cities and particularly in the coastal zones of China where some of the most fertile and productive agricultural land is located.

Although China's land area is huge, cultivated land accounted for only 122 million hectares in 2008, or 12.7 percent of China's land surface, with most of the best quality arable land located in the eastern region the region of the most rapid urbanization and the greatest loss of good agricultural land (Cui and Kattumuri 2010). This creates great demands on available resources such as water, land and energy that are needed as inputs for a rapidly urbanizing society. In addition, growing disparities between rural and urban areas will encourage rural-urban migration that is estimated to be of the order of 500 million over the next 25 years. Most of this movement will be to the cities of the coastal zone that face ongoing pressures focused on mega-urban regions. For example, it is estimated that some 20 to 23 percent of agricultural land has been lost to urban expansion over the twenty years to 2008 (Cui and Kattumuri 2008), and despite China's size there are limited possibilities to expand cultivated land (Lin and Ho 2005). The growing use of intensive chemical reliant farming systems is beginning to affect water systems. At the same time the by-products of urban and industrial growth are leading to increased environmental problems that affect agricultural production.

These challenges precipitate a careful consideration of the management of rural-urban relationships in China's mega-urban regions, and it can be argued that China has several advantages in accomplishing this rural-urban transformation. First, China is a late arriver in the development process and therefore has the opportunity to take advantage of previous transformations and look for positive examples from other countries that are most suitable for its local context. Secondly, China is experiencing rural-urban transformation at a unique period of globalization that gives the government access to information and technologies that can be applied to the management of the rural-urban transformation. Thirdly, China is able to engage the management of urbanization as a state project that is part of what has been called "a high modernist ideology." that offers more opportunities for planning and guiding urbanization. Fourthly, rural-urban transformation is being filtered through a series of administrative scales from national to local that is increasingly characterized by decentralization and local control.

In this respect China is experiencing an urban transition within an institutional framework which may be described as a mixture of socialism and capitalism (socialist-market economy) which retains elements of the previous socialist system. This institutional system offers both positive and negative possibilities for policy formation designed to advance national goals of creating an economically developed, modern, sustainable and just society. For example, since the beginning of the reform period China has adopted "endogenous solutions" to these challenges that offer local areas more local control of the development process. This means there is much more opportunity for local involvement in urbanization and in developing policies. This point is particularly important in China's mega-urban regions where there is a mixture of urban and rural activities around a poly-nucleated urban system dominated by one or more very large urban cores. These MURs serve as locations for new land development projects including residential and industrial estates outside the urban core areas that are now being implemented at a national level. These include greater assistance through policies of regional development focused on Western China and policies designed to decrease the social and economic differences between rural and urban areas, and differences within rural areas and urban areas. Such ideas are being driven by the desire to achieve balance in these relationships and are framed by the concept of "harmony" articulated by the Chinese leadership.

Fifthly, while economic decisions on investment are an important part of this process the rural-urban transformation is primarily an institutionally driven process and China has been very successful in making institutional adaptations in the post-reform period. This is accomplished through the creation of provincial level municipalities (e.g. Chongqing), expansion of existing municipalities (e.g. Guangzhou), reclassification of counties to municipalities (e.g. Dongguan, Kunshan) and the creation of new urban spaces (e.g. Shenzhen, Zhuhai) and the amalgamation of townships (Ma 2005). This process of reshaping of administrative space is thus extending the spatial control of urban areas over former rural areas creates both opportunities and problems in the rural-urban transition. It is this process of reshaping of administrative space is that is extending the spatial control of urban areas over former rural areas creates both opportunities and problems in the rural-urban transition. This expansion of urban space has been facilitated by state-led opening-up of a new market track by increasing use of rural land for non-rural activities and the spread of urban political power into these rural areas adjacent to municipalities. This is further accentuated by state efforts to rationalize land-use to avoid environmental problems and create more livable societies that has led to a proliferation of industrial zones in the margins of the city cores. These programs are further promoted by the need to increase the quality of production to conform to the regulatory environment that has to be set-up as a consequence of the admission to the WTO in 2001 (Lin and Ho 2005).

Sixthly, despite the size of its population China has been able to successfully reduce the rate of population growth because of its One Child Policy and in addition, largely avoided an unmanageable surge of rural migrants to urban areas in the first decade of the reform era through a residential registration system (*hukou*), thus minimizing the growth of extremely large informal squatter settlements that are a ubiquitous feature of urbanization in other developing countries.

A final element in the management of the urbanization process has been the rapid incorporation of China into the global economy which Allen Scott describes as creating a new "social grammar of space in which the whole edifice reposes upon a geographical foundation that can be best described as a mosaic of city regions constituting the economic motors of the global economy" (Scott 2001). What we are describing here is an intensely competitive system in which the mega-urban regions of China, like those in other parts of the world, are competing to capture some portion of these transactions generated at both a national and international level. As such, there is increasing pressure upon governments at both national and city level to create an urban environment that will increase the flow of transactions to the mega-urban region. Olympic venues, major attraction sites such as Disneyland, new airports, convention centres, multi-media corridors, urban renewal and industrial estates in peri-urban areas are all part of packages that are designed to make urban regions more attractive. In some of the transformed NICs such as Japan, Korea and Taiwan (China) this creates an ongoing tension between growth-orientated policies and those directed towards creating more livable urban regions that includes persistence of rural activities (Ma and Wu 2005).

This tension begins to assume a spatial dimension in the imbalance in investment between the MURs nodal cities and its surrounding rural areas. This is, of course, an accommodation to the forces of globalization involving major investments of public and private capital in the enticing-built environment of globalization. For example, at a national meeting held in 2005, Wang Guangtao, Minister of Construction criticized these strategies claiming 183 cities had vowed to build themselves into international metropolises with so-called "show-off projects" such as squares, luxury office buildings and airports. As one report noted, most of urban China has been built in the past 25 years at a rate of 150 million square metres per year, often on large projects. This rate of urban expansion is unprecedented. This surge of urbanization is generating a huge demand for capital. The same report estimates the annual costs of Chinese urbanization at 300-500 billion yuan (US$ 37 billion) which is roughly 2-4 % of the Chinese GDP in 2004 (Sustainable Development Research Group 2005). This growth in capital demand has generated a huge amount of borrowing at various administrative levels.

Rural Urban Relations and Hybrid Spaces in China's Mega-Urban Regions: The Example of Food Production

As we have shown in the preceding section, the growth of urban activity in the MURs of China has led to substantial restructuring of agricultural activity within these regions changes characterized by features of food production in most of the large MURs of East Asia. This is not a new phenomenon. We have argued elsewhere that these densely populated deltaic environments with high densities were in fact large cheap labor reservoirs waiting to be tapped by international, state, and local capital. Most successful in this respect were Japan, Korea and Taiwan where efforts to increase rural income in mega-urban regions were made through the introduction of higher yielding crops, guaranteed prices, diversification into non-staple crops and increased possibility for employment in rural industries. These efforts were aided by physical infrastructure investment, improvements in roads, electrification, improvements in irrigation and institutional changes particularly in land reform. In addition, the state invested in major transportation linkages such as freeways and electrified railways (largely for non –agricultural activities such as industry and residential development). Of course, these developments did not prevent the movement of labor out of agriculture that accelerated in Japan in the 1960s, in Korea and in Taiwan in the 1970 and 1980s. In other mega-urban regions of East Asia such as the Bangkok, Jakarta, Manila, Hanoi and Ho Chi Minh MURs, these processes occurred much more unevenly but have accelerated in the 90s and first decade of the 21st century. Allowing for the distinctive elements of its rural-urban transition, it is clear that China has been exhibiting similar patterns since the 1980s.

What are the common features of the previously rural margins, labeled "deaskota" by McGee (1991) around the major Chinese cities? (1) They have all been characterized by large small-holder population primarily engaged in the cultivation of rice but also characterized by non –agricultural activity such as craft industries etc. (2) They have all experienced an increase in the non-agricultural activities that are very diverse including employment in trading, transportation and industry. This increase in non-agricultural activity is characterized by a mixture of activities often by members of the same household. Thus, for example, one person may move to the main urban node of the MUR to work as a clerk, another engage in full-time farming, a third work in industries that are close to the farm and another look after the sale of vegetables in nearby markets. (3) These zones of mixed activities are generally characterized by increased fluidity and mobility of the population. The availability of relatively cheap transport such as two-stroke motorbikes, buses and trucks that becomes more affordable as family incomes increase enable farmers to access markets and employment over much larger distances. Thus, these areas are characterized by two levels of transportation movement. At one level the building of freeways and fast rail linkages is integrating the MUR, while at the local level an intermediate form of transportation is integrating sub-parts of the region around local urban nodes that are increasingly interactive. (4) In these rural areas of these MURs there is an increase in household income that depending on the expenditure decisions of the household (e.g. saving/expenditure ratios) means that there may be a greater demand for local goods (food, furniture etc.) or goods from larger urban centres (refrigerators etc.). (5) There is an increase in the participation of females in non-agricultural activities as more diverse sources of employment become more available such employment in factories etc. There is ample evidence that the contribution of these female workers to family income through remittances greatly adds to the household income and increases internal migration to work in these areas. (6) The growth of urban centers in the MUR is an important cause of these changes in rural activities particularly the production of food. Chinese MURs (and indeed beyond) are experiencing consumption changes that effect food suppliers, the food supply chain and the retailing of food in urban areas. (McGee 1991). (7) Finally, in the last two decades the rural margins of Chinese mega-urban regions have been changing rapidly as the result of processes of the growth of secondary cities in the urban hierarchy and the consolidation of housing, industry and agriculture (Webster et al. 2003)

This produces three main results that affect the food producers in the desakota regions of China's MURs. First, historically in the Asian context most food has been produced close to where it is consumed. But as transportation improves food can be conveyed over long distances, which means there is an increasing competition for urban markets. Secondly, previously most food that was consumed in the urban centres of MURs was purchased from wet markets or smaller dry-goods outlets which led to a daily pattern of supply. This is now changing as urban households can store food in refrigerators and buy processed foods from supermarket outlets. Thirdly, increasing urbanization has been shown, generally, to be accompanied by the consumption of processed foods that are a response to the limited time available to spend in food preparation especially as the proportion of women workers in urban areas increases. This means that the retailing structure in urban areas is increasing with a growth of "supermarkets" and larger grocery stores. The retailers increasingly rely upon contracts with "intermediaries" to contract the provision of food to their firms. This process is radically changing food production systems particularly leading to more capital-intensive operations in the MURs of East Asia. This is facilitated by the need to adopt acceptable standards of quality control for food.

These processes also have negative effects at a broader scale. First, China has lost more than 20 percent of its first-class agricultural land to non-agricultural uses since the early 1980s (Cai and Kattumuri 2010). While many economists argue that the greater wealth earned from an increase in non-agricultural use more than compensates for the loss of agricultural land, it still may be argued that in intensely crowded MURs there is a need to increase food production as urban demand increases. While national food security policies often subsidize the production of rice that encourages farmers to continue to produce this staple there is increasing pressure to shift from mono-crop production resulting in growing diversity with production of livestock, vegetables and fruit. This is characterized by capital intensity. Thus, in the MURs the number of concentrated animal feeding operations (CAFOs) has increased in response to urban demand and the changing food system (Ellis and Turner 2007). There are many reports of the waste, particularly from livestock operations such as pig farms, from CAFOs polluting water systems.

Secondly, the increase of industrialization and urbanization create increasing demands for resources such as land, water etc. for which rural households located MURS cannot compete. This may be further accelerated because of the effects of climate change including droughts, flooding and other environmental challenges particularly water supply, pollution from industry and chemical fertilizers used in agricultural production (McGee 2008; De Sherbinin et al. 2007; Gu et al. 2010). Thirdly, because the zones of mixed land use in MURs are often administrative "grey zones" in part because "urban" regulations, are more difficult to apply in "rural" areas it is more difficult to develop management responses. (Zhong and Zhu 2004; World Bank 2007). Fourthly, political fragmentation and internal competition between different levels of government in these MURs is often a major deterrent to creating national and globally successful economic regions. To reduce these problems new forms of collaborative governance, need to be introduced which are inclusive of different sectors of society (Asian Development Bank 2008). Research on these problems by Luo and Shen (2009) and Shieh (2011) give detailed information on the nature of these problems.

Thus, there are many challenges to rural–urban relations that are emerging in the contemporary urban regions of China. At a national level, the details of these challenges are more obvious and acute in China's MURs: (1) The proportion of population working in primary occupations (principally agriculture) decreased substantially in the period between 1980 and 2011; (2) The proportion of the contribution of regular non-urban wages to rural household incomes rose from 18.1 percent in 1985 to 32.6 percent in 2007; (3) The area planted to rice declined by 21 percent between 2000 and 2007. There is increasing evidence that the food systems of the MURs are undergoing rapid change particularly as the urban areas consume food from supermarkets and large grocery outlets. It is well known that large retailing chains, both national and international, increasingly source their food nationally and internationally and this poses a threat to local supply chains (PECC 2007).

The remainder of this discussion focuses on the largest and most economically successful mega-urban region in China the lower Yangzi River delta. This region is made-up of Shanghai Municipality and the provinces of Jiangsu and Zhejiang that in 2008 had an estimated population of 150 million (7 percent of China's total) equivalent to the 9th largest country in the world by population. It is estimated that this region produced 25 percent of China's GDP in 2008. Historically one of the "heartlands" of Chinese rice production, the region has lost some 30 percent of its rice land since 2000. Much of this loss is attributed the expansion of rural industry and residential development. Meanwhile, agriculture is rapidly diversifying as consumption demands of the rapidly urbanizing region shift to a greater emphasis on vegetables, live-stock and fish. In this respect, the region shows a pattern of structural change in agriculture characteristic of other MURs of the East Asian region. Today it is one of the most urbanized regions in China and has a highly developed urban system which is increasingly interconnected by fast railways and freeways. The lower Yangzi delta urban system is made up of the largest cities of Shanghai, Nanjing and Hangzhou, and many other important secondary cities. They form part of an "economic circle" of linked urban centres which have regular meetings to coordinate economic activities (Luo and Shen 2009).

In addition to the growth and spatial proliferation of rural industry, the restructuring of agriculture and food production systems has coincided with the development of leisure activities pivoting on so-called eco-tourism sites. Arising in part from national policies promulgated in 2006 to "Build a New Socialist Countryside" the dualism of commercial food production and leisure consumption spaces has become pervasive in China's lower Yangzi delta. Consolidation and commercialization of the food production landscape, often with foreign direct investment, coincides with the proliferation of new spaces of outdoor leisure activity where in-situ rurality is consumed. The resulting hybrid spaces of production and consumption activity systems are a key characteristic of diffuse urbanization in the lower Yangzi delta. Efforts to promote leisure consumption in China, and elsewhere, are not new China moved to a five-day work week in 1994 partly to stimulate the domestic economy. Rural tourism development in China has been led with great zeal by the local-state and is often associated with extensive forced relocation and spatial concentration of rural residents both living and ancestral. This separation of people from the land is juxtaposed by counter imperatives which bring urban residents back to the countryside to consume (re-)constructed natural or traditional agricultural landscapes (Marton 2020).

As with elsewhere in China, farming and food production since 1949 in the lower Yangzi delta have undergone profound and, at times, deeply traumatic transformations. Vacillating national-level policies prior to 1978 were largely insensitive to local conditions and were often re-cast or simply ignored (Sun 2002; Zhou 1996). While introduction of the household production responsibility system in agriculture after 1978 led to significant increased output of staple grains at the national level, grain output in the lower Yangzi delta had already peaked by the late 1970s (*Jiangsu rural economy: 50 years*, 1999). Data which clarify the details of commercialization of food production were more difficult to obtain, but with a review of the available information combined with thirty-five years of field observations, it is possible to sketch a general picture of the key changes in agriculture. There has been a striking shift away from staple grain production (almost entirely winter wheat and summer wet rice) in the lower Yangzi delta to a level of output slightly below what it was in 1949. Enormous efficiency gains, however, meant that total grain production in 2017 was grown on the equivalent of just 42% of the sown area in 1949. Production of other traditional crops in the lower Yangzi delta such as rapeseed and silk show precipitous declines since peak post-reform levels of output. Meanwhile, between 1978 and 2017 the output of tea, fruit and aquatic products grew nearly four, thirty-six and nine times respectively (*China statistical yearbook*, various years). The dramatic increase in fruit production, in particular, is tied to investments in greenhouse and other agricultural technologies by subdistrict, town and village collectives, new forms of land leasing and organization of labour input, new commercial processing and food distribution networks linked to modern supermarket retailing, and a nascent form of rural grass roots tourism known as *nongjiale* involving peasant families hosting urban guests for fruit picking, rustic meals and lodging (Ding 2017; Park 2014; Field notes).

Another key characteristic of the food production landscape across the lower Yangzi delta since the early 2000s has been the spatial consolidation of agricultural land. Smaller family-run plots, formerly managed by households under the household production responsibility system, have been merged into much larger farming areas. These larger farms are usually managed through new commercially focused local agricultural cooperatives with links to specialized markets. The key driver for this restructuring has been the creation and promotion of forward linkages with food product processing firms, often at the invitation of local governments through their economic cooperation offices. Local governments in China employ vigorous place promotion and deal-making to attract partnerships in commercial agriculture, especially in the lower Yangzi delta and are themselves often directly involved through ownership and management of locally established commercial entities. This agricultural restructuring coincided with ongoing efforts to promote rural tourism formalized in national policies to stimulate "leisure agriculture," food product processing, services, transportation, construction and cultural sectors (Ding 2017, pp.36-37). There have been at least two key outcomes of these policies in the lower Yangzi delta. The first is the development of agricultural research and production networks with firms constructing sites where large-scale commercial agriculture, product research, food processing, and agri-tourism co-exist. The second outcome is rapid growth in the number of local state-led and state-owned rural eco-tourism, folk customs and culture parks since 2009 (Marton, 2020).

There are many factors which have contributed to the decline in output of the previously dominant farm crops, intensive spatial consolidation of farmland with growth in commercial agriculture, and the proliferation of constructed sites for rural tourism in the lower Yangzi delta. These hybrid spaces have coincided with the growth and diffusion of urban space. However, the evidence strongly suggests that processes and patterns of urban diffusion are not entirely hegemonic decimating agriculture and denuding the countryside of jobs and people. Rather, the story emerging is more nuanced one of resilience, innovation and adaptability, perhaps signaling implications for the persistence of rural forms albeit highly modified hybrid forms and possibilities for social and ecological sustainability.

The emergence of mixed activity systems across hybrid spaces in the lower Yangzi delta highlights the issue of food provision in large mega-urban regions which remains crucial to China's goals of creating a sustainable, just and economically developed society. A central element of the provision of food is affected by the changing character of food consumption in urban areas in in the mega-urban regions of the coastal zones of China although increasingly secondary cities are also experiencing the similar patterns (Veeck and Veeck 2000). Earlier work on Hong Kong by Macleod and McGee (1990) demonstrate that food consumption can change very rapidly from a diet heavily reliant on traditional foods such as rice, vegetables, and limited fish and meat products (such as pork and chicken) to one that shows an increasing consumption of imported meats (especially beef), wheat and milk products and imported processed foods such as instant noodles and cereals. The growth of middle- and upper- income earners are the main consumers. Among lower income urban households, increasing food prices have meant that traditional food outlets small stores, public markets and "illegal hawker markets" offer foods at cheaper prices. A more general trend is the growth in the commitment of more household members to urban wage labor which means there is less time to prepare meals. Access to traditional food outlets and the purchase of instant food such as processed noodles and take-out meals also increases. This has created what has been described as an "industrial palate" which relies increasingly on the international food chains, distributors and producers which begins to displace traditional food consumption practices. Hong Kong could afford this embrace of globalization because they were integrated in a regional and national open trading economy, had higher household incomes and sufficient income to buy in international markets.

In contemporary China food retailers are divided into five main groups: hypermarkets; supermarkets and convenience stores; on-line markets; wet markets, and illegal markets. Foreign companies are largely concentrated in the hypermarket, supermarket and convenience store sectors, but there is also evidence that national and local companies are commanding an increasing proportion of sales (See Zhang and Wei 2015). While the more traditional food markets are dominated by small family enterprises, research by Zhang and Pan (2013) in Shanghai Municipality has shown that the rapid growth of commercial retailing and residential development have led to the closure of and reduction in their number by some 30 percent. Illegal hawker markets have also been subject to increasing pressure from the city government to stop their activities because they are regarded as a danger to public health and create congestion in city streets. While wet markets persist in Shanghai, the number has reduced by two-thirds since the late 1990s and is mostly administered by the municipal authorities.

The Chinese government wishes to avoid an undue reliance on food imports and has adopted three main policies to support this objective. Firstly, at the national level in China policies which stress the need to ensure food security in staple grains, particularly rice, remains central to national planning and are reiterated most recently in the 13th Five Year Plan (2016-2020). The 13th Five Year Plan also places much emphasis on the demarcation of Farmland Preservation Zones and support for agriculture as the foundation for the preservation and increase in food production needed for the increasing urban population. Earlier policies designed to preserve agricultural land, first introduced in 1986, had limited success in preventing the conversion of agricultural land to other uses. These were radically revised in 1997 by a plan that shifted the responsibility for approval of farmland conversion in excess of 35 hectares to be the responsibility of the national and provincial governments. The downgrading of the role of local governments in this process was also closely linked to national and provincial efforts to encourage the process of settlement consolidation.

Secondly, these policies have led to major changes in the margins of the mega-urban regions in an attempt to gradually produce a more rational organization of consolidated spaces of different land-uses (agriculture, industry, urban administrative, and commercial centres) that contrasts sharply with the mixture of fragmented land uses typical of desakota areas in the 1980s and 1990s (Marton 2016). As discussed above, areas of the lower Yangzi delta have undergone a process of readjustment (*tiaozheng*), whereby spaces of mixed land use, including villages, family farm plots and ancestral resting places, have been relocated to allow for the consolidation of agricultural land. Significant changes in the spatial structure of agricultural production in the landscapes of diffuse urbanization in the lower Yangzi delta are linked to newly re-emphasized policies to protect and enhance food production for urban consumption discussed in the next section. Indeed, there is evidence of a significant increase in both the scale and intensity of commercialization of agricultural production, particularly for high quality and high value output such as mushrooms and medicinal products, and inputs for cosmetics production, including for international markets

(Marton 2016). However, in the peri-urban zones of China's MURs it is also clear that local interests exercised through informal institutional frameworks continue to result in excessive conversion of agricultural land for other uses (See Zhu and Guo 2014).

Thirdly, changes in food production and supply, and patterns of food consumption in urban areas indicate that China's socialist-market system is adapting and accommodating to provide a framework for ensuring that food for urban areas in China will remain largely in national hands. At the same time China appears to be continuing to enforce standards of food quality that increasingly meet international standards. However, it is also clear in the 13th Five Year Plan that China recognizes there are many challenges to food security. In response there has been a shift towards advocating for a new people-centred urbanization project designed to increase participation and co-operation in the urbanization process at the local level. This will necessarily involve engagement with the extensive spaces of urbanizing activity outside the municipal cores of the mega-urban regions like the lower Yangzi delta.

Policies for Rural Urban Synthesis in China's Mega-Urban Regions as a Foundation for Sustainability

Like other mega-urban regions in East Asia, rapid changes in the lower Yangzi delta have created challenges to the persistence of rural life and sustainability in the wider region. These challenges primarily focus on threats to the eco-system, threats to food security, threats to rural life and systems of food production, distribution and consumption. The issue is how to put in place policies that can improve this situation. Part of the answer lies in recognizing three key elements:

1. That the changing economic structure of the region is creating a situation in which the decline in agriculture will occur as the region moves to a post–industrial economy in which services and high technology industries will dominate.

2. That the loss of agriculture and agricultural land is a major threat to the food security of the region.

3. That the changing structure of the region is going to lead to a post-industrial society in which the majority of the population will be urban.

As highlighted in the previous section, our arguments are that China is already taking steps to strengthen policies that will create a sustainable national food system. In this respect it is suggested that greater emphasis be placed upon the ability to utilize the "synergetic capital" of mega-urban regions to develop interaction between rural and urban areas that will give greater strength to policies of food security and strengthen the retention of rural areas as a major part of the overall sustainability of the region's social organization. Policies which utilize existing "eco-capital" of the resource systems that constitute the lower Yangzi delta mega-urban region. This approach is informed by the Chilean economist, Sergio Boshier (2001), who suggested that the most important form of capital to be found in a region is "synergetic capital" which denotes a region's capacity to develop a sustainable relationship between its natural capital (the endowment of renewable and non-renewable natural resources (land, etc.) and environmental "services" such hydrological systems, atmospheric carbon cycles, etc., and various forms of what may be labeled "societal capital". Boshier has suggested that there are seven forms of societal capital that can help this process of adaptation. First, "economic capital" that is the stock of financial resources available for investment in a region that includes national, regional and international capital. The second is "cognitive capital" which is the endowment of scientific and technical knowledge available within a region. The third form is "cultural capital" which has three aspects: (1) historical development of cultural features that give distinctiveness to the region; (2) the culture of development that exists in the region, including a particular set of attitudes towards work, risk, investment, etc.; (3) symbolic capital which is the capacity to construct a region, and mobilize latent recognition of a region both locally, nationally and internationally.

The fourth form of capital is "institutional capital" which relates to what Boshier calls the "institutional fabric of a region" that relates both to the "institutional chart" of a region including government, law, etc., but also includes the capacity of institutions to interact with each other and their degree of flexibility and resilience. The fifth form, "social capital", is the ability of human beings to associate with each other to achieve common goals that involves such components as trust, social participation and ability to negotiate for a common result. The sixth form, "physical capital", includes both rural and urban infrastructure such as urban waste disposal systems and rural irrigation systems. And finally, "human capital" which is rather narrowly defined by Boshier as knowledge and skills of individuals in a region that defines the "quality" of a region, intellectual, practical etc., that can embody a regions creative powers. More generally it can be defined as the ability to nurture healthy productive humans, livable environments and education.

To this we would add the concept of "eco-capital" representing the capacity of a society to adapt and preserve eco-systems in the face of the challenges of development and environmental change. The growth of "eco-capital", of course, results both from the ability to utilize the strengths of the combined forms of capital in the synergies of eco-capital. However, it is also suggested that a central assumption would be the acceptance of agriculture as a major plank of the development of eco-capital and the development of harmonious rural-urban relations.

Framed by this conceptualization, three main policy areas can be identified. First, there must be a commitment to preservation of the eco-systems of mega-urban regions which, in most East Asian milieus, are characteristically deltaic areas which are more vulnerable to global climate change, including sea level rise, increased fluctuations in water supply and land deterioration due to over extraction of ground water, etc. (De Sherbinin et al. 2007; Gu et al. 2010). This means that preserving threatened parts of the eco-system (e.g. rivers, lakes, coastal areas and sub-ecosystems such as forests and marshes etc.) is essential. Add to this preservation of sustainable agriculture which will be the only way to prepare for the increasing challenges to food security that are likely to be the result of climate change. These underlying challenges are exacerbated by competition between different levels of government in China (Luo and Shen 2009) and reinforce the need to create some form of regional co-operation institutions that can facilitate policy development and implementation (Otsumi and Sano 2009). One example might include the formation of Metropolitan Regional Authorities which are given the responsibility of coordinating between different agencies and levels of governments in areas such as the environment, transportation, public services such as water, power and waste removal, social policies and developing sustainable and livable regions. Similar organizations need to be set-up to deal with economic planning at a regional level to reduce duplication, and to encourage a level playing field with respect to land taxes and investment. Regional trade associations can facilitate this process through developing regional branding at a global level. These processes of institutional change can also be applied to rural areas.

Secondly, it must be recognized that the process of diffuse urbanization is inevitable even in the special situation of the Chinese transition to full market socialism, and can occur at the same time as policies of sustainability in agriculture and eco-systems can be put in place. As the number of MURs increases in China, urbanization is increasingly characterized by an urban hierarchy typically having one very large urban core, a spreading pattern of secondary cities, and a large number of third level cities and smaller towns. Urbanization is spreading outwards from large and secondary city cores into the surrounding territories and along transportation corridors between them. Diffuse urbanization is thus increasing throughout the hinterlands of MURs. Historically, as these delta areas have developed, close relationships have emerged between rural and urban areas. However, as this pattern grows, urban market demands are causing major challenges to agricultural food production and distribution systems. The central issue is whether food producers in the MURs will be able to keep up with changes in food systems and urban demand which could be characterized by increasing concentration of the suppliers who increasingly source their supplies in other parts of China, or internationally. This is already occurring in many of the developed countries of East Asia.

The issue of whether food producers in the MURs will be able to remain an important part of food system of their region as urban demand changes is central. Already, we see in China an increase of the proportion of food sales that is processed and sold through large food producers and retailers both domestic and international. Some argue that traditional Chinese dietary preferences for fresh food will slow down this process, but research in Hong Kong in the 1970s and 1980s indicates that these changes can occur very quickly even in a cultural context that historically placed great emphasis upon fresh food in their diets (McGee 1967; Macleod and McGee 1990). In a region such as the lower Yangzi delta there are several components of synergetic capital at the regional level that offer opportunities for local producers. There are already many examples of local farmers that form various types of associations to enter into contracts with food companies to supply output. These groups have responded in a very entrepreneurial manner to the needs of larger urban markets for more diversified food. But this could be strengthened by more vigorous government support, including extension services, credit provision, infrastructure provision and the recognition that this "new agriculture" demands some redirection of fiscal resources from the present urban focus. At the local level policies can also be put in place to strengthen the local marketing of food in secondary and smaller urban centres (Douglass 1998). Support can be given to the already well-developed system of wet markets and small dry-goods stores by imposing restrictions that require supermarkets to locate in areas at some distance from these small market sellers. Such progressive policies have already been put in place in other MURs in East Asia.

The third area of policy focus proposed would utilize the new concept of *eco-capital*. Just as the inevitability of urbanization should be accepted, the concept of "eco-capital" must be linked to the acceptance of the co-existence of urban *and* rural areas within MURs during phases of rapid economic and urban growth. This is not a new idea in the history of the attempts of planners and policy makers to resolve the contradictions between rural and urban areas. For example, the idea of green belts was fundamentally driven by the desire to create barriers to urban expansion and preserve rural areas rather than develop policies that can enhance the co-existence of urban and rural activity. In this respect, the experience of Japan's policies that have attempted to emphasize the positive aspects of agriculture within urbanizing areas may be of some relevance to the current experience in China (Nakai 1988). The arguments for these policies are strong: environmental sustainability; food security and a synergy between rural and urban areas that will strengthen the capacity of the MURs of East Asia to respond to the new challenges of the 21st century and build sustainable, livable regions.

In the last two years the Chinese government has become increasingly aware of these challenges and is making determined efforts to enforce regulations on the loss of farmland in the periphery of mega-urban regions. In an announcement on November 3rd 2014 the Ministry of Land and Resources and the Ministry of Agriculture jointly declared that areas of prime arable land near cities and traffic routes should be characterized as "permanent basic farmland" and would be protected from urban development (Peng 2014). Such protected land typically has intensive features such as greenhouses and aquatic farming that are prone to expropriation for urban construction, but highly important for the supply of food to cities. This policy was reiterated by Chinese Premier Li Keqiang in a speech on January 5th, 2015 in which he emphasized the importance of the implementation of these policies in fourteen of China's largest cities by the end of 2016 (TBP 2015). This commitment to preserving land for food production, combined with ongoing improvements in the implementation of environmental policies in these areas, suggest that China is moving to adopt strategies which seem to recognize the key elements of eco-capital creating viable solutions to the challenges of providing food for its rapidly growing urban population.

REFERENCES

Asian Development Bank. 2008. *Managing Asian Cities.* Manila: Asian Development Bank.

Boshier, S. 2001. "Territorial Development and the Contribution of Synergetic Capital: A Contribution to the Discussion on the Intangibility of Development." In *New Forms of Regional Development Paradigms,* edited by A. Kumssa and T.G. McGee, 17-32. London: Greenwood Press.

Brenner, N., ed. 2014. *Implosions/Explosions: Towards a Study of Planetary Urbanization.* Berlin: Jovis. *China Statistical Yearbook.* Various years. Beijing: State Statistics Bureau [in Chinese].

Cui, S. and Kattumuri, R. 2010. "Cultivated Land Conversion in China and the Potential for Food Security and Sustainability." *LSE Asia Research Centre Working Paper 35.* London: LSE Asia Research Centre.

De Sherbinin, A., Schiller, A., and Pulsipher, A. 2007. "The vulnerability of global cities to climate hazards." *Environment and Urbanization* 19(1): 39-64.

Ding, K. 2017. "Agriculture-food-tourism industry clusters in China." In *A multi-industrial linkages approach to cluster building in East Asia: Targeting the agriculture, food, and tourism industry,* edited by A. Kuchiki, T. Mizobe, and T. Gokan, 33-55. London: Macmillan.

Douglass, M. 1998. "A Regional Strategy for Reciprocal Rural-Urban Linkages: An Agenda for Policy Research with Reference to Indonesia." *Third World Planning Review* 20(1): 1-33.

Ellis, L.J., and Turner, J.L. 2007. Environmental and Food Safety Concerns of China's Aquaculture and Animal Husbandry. Working Paper, Woodrow Wilson Center for International Scholars, Washington, D.C.

Freud, P., and Martin, G. 1999. "Driving South: The globalization of auto-consumption and its social organization of space." *Capitalism Nature Socialism* 11(4): 51-71.

Gottmann, J. 1961. *Megalopolis: The Urbanized Northeastern Seaboard of the United States.* New York: Krauss International Publications.

Gu, C., Zhang, X., Wang, X., Guo, J., and Hu, I.L. 2010. "Climate Change and Urbanization in the Yangtse River Delta." Working Paper, Lincoln Institute of Land Policy, Cambridge, MA.

Jessop, B. 2014 "Capitalist Dominance and Variety: Variegation, the World Market, Composssibility and Ecological Dominance" *Capital & Class* 31(1): 45-58 *Jiangsu Rural Economy: 50 Years.* 1999. Beijing: State Statistics Bureau (in Chinese).

Lin, G.C.S., and Ho, S.P.S. 2005. "The State, Land System, and Land Development Practices in Contemporary China." *Annals of the Association of American Geographers* 95(2): 411-436.

Luo, X., and Shen, X. 2009. "A Study on Inter-city Cooperation in the Yangtse River Delta." *Habitat International* 32: 52-62.

Ma, L.J.C. 2005. "Urban administrative restructuring, changing scale relations and local economic development in China." *Political Geography* 24(44): 477-497.

MacLeod, S., and McGee, T.G. 1990. "The last frontier: The emergence of the industrial palette in Hong Kong." In *Economic Growth and Urbanization in Developing Areas,* edited by D. Drakakis-Smith, 304-335. London and New York: Routledge.

Marcotullio, P.J., and Lee, Y.S. 2003. "Urban environmental transitions and urban transportation systems: A comparison of the North American and Asian experiences." *International Development Planning Review* 25(4): 325-354.

Marton, A.M. 2000. *China's Spatial Economic Development: Restless Landscapes in the lower Yangzi Delta.* London and New York: Routledge.

Marton, A.M. 2002. "Local Geographies of Globalisation: Rural Agglomeration in the Chinese Countryside." *Asia Pacific Viewpoint* 43(1): 23-42.

———. Marton, A.M. 2016. "Diffuse Cities in China: Hybridity, Porosity and Eco-Urbanisation in the Lower Yangzi Delta." Unpublished paper presented at the *International Roundtable Conference on Territories of Metropolis: Compactness, Dispersion, Ecology,* April 5-7. Available from the author <amarton@uvic.ca>.

———. Marton, A.M. 2020. Re-landscaping the Chinese countryside: Hybrid spaces and the possibilities of projective ecologies in the lower Yangzi delta. In Esposito, A., Idt, J., Monin, E., Palmioli, A. & Pellegrino, M. (Eds.) *Figures of diffuse urbanization: Territorial dynamics and governance issues.* Paris: L'Oeil d'Or – Urban Futures, 2020 (In French).

McGee, T.G. 1967. *Hawkers in Hong Kong: A Study of Planning and Policy in Hong Kong.* Centre of Asian Studies occasional papers and monographs, no. 17. Hong Kong: University of Hong Kong.

———. 1991. "The Emergence of Desakota Regions in Asia: Expanding a Hypothesis." In *the Extended Metropolis: Settlement Transition in Asia*, edited by N.J. Ginsburg, B. Koppel, and T.G. McGee, 3-26. Honolulu: University of Hawaii Press.

———. 1995. "Metrofitting the Emerging Mega-Urban Regions of ASEAN: An Overview." In *the Mega-Urban Regions of Southeast Asia*, edited by T.G. McGee, and I.M. Robinson, 3-26. Vancouver: UBC Press.

———. 2008. "Managing the Rural-Urban Transformation in East Asia in the 21st Century." *Sustainability Science* 3(1): 155-167.

———. 2016 "Citta Diffusá and Desakotasasi: Comparing Diffuse urbanization in Europe and Asia." Unpublished paper presented at the *International Roundtable Conference on Territories of Metropolis: Compactness, Dispersion, Ecology*, April 5-7. Available from the author <tmcgee@geog.ubc.ca>.

McGee, T.G., and Lin, G.C.S. 1993. "Footprints in Space: Spatial Restructuring in the East Asia NICs 1950-90." In *Economic and Social Development in Pacific Asia*, edited by C. Dixon, and David Drakakis-Smith, 128-151. London: Routledge.

McGee, T.G., Lin, G.C.S., Marton, A.M., Wang, M.Y.L., and Wu, J. 2007. *China's Urban Space: Development under Market Socialism.* London and New York: Routledge.

McGee, T.G., and Watters, R.F., eds. 1997. *Geographies of the Asia-Pacific Region.* London: Hurst.

Nakai, N. 1988. "Urbanization, Promotion and Control in Metropolitan Japan." *Planning Perspectives* 3: 197-216.

Otsumi, K., and Sano, J. 2009. "The Shanghai Economic Sphere and its Evolution as a Mega- Region: Geographical Expansion and the Rising Added Value in Shanghai." *RIM Pacific Business and Industries* IX (33): 1-28.

Olds, K., Dicken, P., Kelly, P.F., Kong, L., and Yeung, H.W.C., eds. 1999. *Globalization and the Asian Pacific: Contested Territories.* London: Routledge.

Pacific Economic Cooperation Council (PECC). 2007. *Pacific Food System Outlook 2007-2008: Linkages to Growing Urban Markets Spur Rural Development.* Singapore: ISEAS.

Park, C. H. 2014. "Nongjiale tourism and contested space in rural China." *Modern China* 40(5): 519-548.

Peng, F. 2014. "China bans cities from encroaching on nearby farmland." Accessed May 30, 2016. http://news.xinhuanet.com/english/china/2014-11/03/c_133763130.htm.

Scott, A.J., ed. 2001. *Global City Regions: Trends, Theory, Policy.* Oxford and New York: Oxford University Press.

Shieh, L. 2011 "Becoming Urban: Rural-Urban Integration in Nanjing, Jiangsu Province." *Pacific Affairs* 84(3): 475-494.

Sun, W. 2002. "Discourses of poverty: Weakness, potential and provincial identity in Anhui." In *Rethinking China's Provinces*, edited by J. Fitzgerald, 153-177. London: Routledge.

Sustainable Development Research Group. 2005. *China Urban Development Report 2005.* Beijing: Chinese Academy of Sciences.

The Brics Post (TBP) 2015. "Focus on Protecting Farmland, Ensuring Food Security: Chinese Premier." Accessed May 30, 2016. http://thebricspost.com/focus-on-protecting-farm land-ensuring-food-security-chinese-premier/#. V0vSI_krKM8.

Veeck A and Veeck G. 2000 "Consumer Segmentation and Changing Food Purchase Patterns in Nanjing." *World Development* 28 (3): 457-471.

Webster, D., Cai, J., Muller, L., and Luo, B. 2003. "Emerging Third Stage Peri-urbanization: Functional Specialization in the Hangzhou Peri-Urban Region." Working Paper, Asia Pacific Research Center, Stanford University.

World Bank. 2007. "Special Focus: Sustainable Development in East Asia's Urban Fringe." Accessed May 30, 2016. http://siteresources.worldbank.org/INTEAPHALFYEARLY UPDATE/Resources/550192-1175629375615/EAP-Update-April2007-sp-focus.pdf.

Zhang, L., and Wei, Y.D. 2015 "Foreign Hypermarket Retailers in China, Spatial Penetration, Local Embeddedness and Structural Paradox." *Geographical Review* 105(4): 528-550.

Zhang Q.F. and Pan, Z. 2013. "The Transformation of Urban Vegetable Retailing in China: Wet markets, Supermarkets and Informal Markets in Shanghai." *Journal of Contemporary Asia* 43(3): 497-518.

Zhong, F. and Zhu, J. 2004. "Diversification and Sustainable Development in Chinese Agriculture." *Chinese Journal of Population, Resources and the Environment* 2(3): 45-49.

Zhou, K. X. 1996. *How the Farmers Changed China: Power of the People*. Boulder: Westview Press.

Zhou, Y. 1991. "The Metropolitan Interlocking Region in China. A Preliminary Statement." In *the Extended Metropolis*, edited by N. Ginsburg, B. Koppel, and T.G. McGee, 89-112. Honolulu: University of Hawaii Press.

Zhu, J. and Guo, Y. 2014. "Fragmented Peri-Urbanisation Led by Autonomous Village Development Under Informal Institution in High-density Regions: The Case of Nanhai, China." *Urban Studies* 51(6): 1120-1145.

Chapter 9

[Un]buildable Redux: Speculative Animations in Cinema and Architectural Research[1]

Maciej Stasiowski

Introduction

"For a long time, architecture was thought of as a solid reality and entity: buildings, objects, matter, place, and a set of geometric relationships. But recently, architects have begun to understand their product as liquid, animating their bodies, hypersurfacing their walls, crossbreeding different locations, experiencing with new geometries." (Bouman 2005, 22). In this statement taken from an article published in *4d. space* issue of "Architectural Design" magazine, Ole Bouman summed up what could be regarded as a proposal for a new definition of architecture. As stated, it should include much more than just built environments merely settings for architectural practices organized around and inside them. Our daily interactions mainly take place in an entangled space, which conjoins material, tactile surroundings with virtual strata. The ontological shift that Bouman hints at namely, an undoing of built practice through its segmentation into adjacent art forms (music [architectural acoustics], performance art, painting, film) was already inscribed into the postwar 20th century landscape, having only intensified in architectural discourse. Such interdisciplinary networks of meaning, resulting from connecting areas of interrelated concepts, span decades. They link up such works as Kurt Schwitters' *Merzbau* with Zaha Hadid's early paintings [*The World (89 Degrees)*, *Vitra Fire Station*], on the premise of their constructivist backdrops. What each of the art objects (set apart by merely six decades) put forward although each in the manner adjacent to its medium is the incorporation of a time-based factor into the design; despite representing it statically (Schwitters's crashing planes versus Hadid's dromoscopic and though

---

[1] This chapter is an edited version of the essay "The [Un]buildable Redux: Speculative Animations in Cinema and Architectural Research" first published in *Spaces and Flows: An International Journal of Urban and Extra Urban Studies* 6 (2): 63-73. This has been reworked into a slightly expanded version entitled "[Un]buildable Redux Speculative Animations in Cinema and Architectural Research" included in this reader as a chapter.

unwieldy perspective). At the same time, they challenge traditional definitions of built form. Had they ever been implemented as accurately as they were conceived, skylines of our cities would have been altered beyond recognition. Instead, they stand as time markers in discipline's alternate history that paved its way through sketches, plans and models into the utopian realm of the "unbuilt".

This history of architectural experiments materialized mainly in the form of drawings (Giovanni Battista Piranesi, Claude Nicolas Ledoux, Antonio Sant'Elia), paintings (Constant Nieuwenhuys), narrative fictions (Bernard Tschumi, NaJa & deOstos), and, even more profusely, as gallery exhibits (Walter Pichler, Diller Scofidio + Renfro, Lebbeus Woods) or films (FORM, XEFIROTARCH, Nic Clear). Clearly, with such examples architecture seems to exceed categories mainly associated with the practice, namely the creation of blueprints for future habitats, flowing into provinces of different art forms. Especially cinema can serve as a prime research site for maverick architectural thought that strays beyond the material and the static.

The idea behind brief case studies of a handful of animated films analyzed here is not to focus on reasons for such concepts' marginalization or incompatibility with built practice, or proposals how could they be made more practical (and thus concrete), but on the practice itself, which is usually regarded by the architectural tradition as a "sketchpad" for serious projects. This immaterial, cinematographic area literary becomes a construction site for utopian/dystopian concepts that can reveal their true nature only through working, literally animated description of their inner workings. With a number of architects today pursuing projects not only in the virtual environment of the software at hand, but for virtual environment *per se*, we shouldn't redundantly question notional boundaries between the actual and the immersed. New ways to grasp unbuilt potentialities should be devised, encompassing cultural texts (projects) implied by the aforementioned discursive turn in the arts.

I would argue that these examples of "threshold architectures" (along with their speculative predecessors) are in fact serious proposals, as they encapsulate all inconsistencies and dynamic shifts observable in contemporary life, which can only partially be reflected in built/material form. Main ideas behind the speculative drive have been distilled by architectural historians as a venture aimed at perfecting draftsmanship, giving form to purely theoretical concepts by deploying media and modes of representation predominant at the time (*capriccios* of the 18th century, gallery exhibitions in the 1950s, collage paintings and photomontages in the 1960s). Peter Cook reflected on this 20th century's shift in the approach to drawing practice. "Once we see a completed piece of graphical representation, we are usually satisfied to take it for itself; only the connoisseur of 'method' may be more fascinated by the means by which it was achieved. That is, until recently. The effect of photography and film in alerting our minds to the idea of architecture as part of an unravelling experience is now vastly accelerated by the ability to 'freeze' and 'unfreeze' architectural information in an unending stream via computer processes. The 'drawing' can simply be one of a million possible choices of line arrangement drawn from the logged criteria or 'model'." (Cook 2014, 210) Through the depiction of non-existent, fantastic sites, the classical drawing or its surrogate media turn into a *test site* for radical visions. Due to the emergence of cinema and simultaneously through gradual incorporation of cinematography and filmic strategies of depicting space into design practice, this *test-site* becomes a double, cross-breeding area, in which some architectural animations lose their commercial grounding, while, in turn, certain movies become significantly more concerned with visualizing daring, or even impossible architectural surroundings, than with standard preoccupations, like the plot.

Paper Architecture

When we look back at the utopian and speculative traditions, we can instantly recognize the flare with which the drawings/designs carried out their attack on contemporary built forms. In Piranesi's series of Roman-inspired ruins, we find altered source material that reminds us of the excavation sites' findings. This personal archaeology was elaborated upon by the artist through the years and subsequently reconfigured into a series of "Pompeian Fantasies". The images are filled with Gargantuan archways and a proliferation of columns, pilasters, caryatids and rubble, juxtaposed in order to carry out an attack and comment the 18th century's tendency to praise the architecture of Ancient Greece over that of the Roman Empire. In equal measure, the drawings taunt architects who blindly copied from ancient styles, with no regard to an initial purpose or context. Piranesi's critique of contemporaneity, similarly to the notions present in utopian literature of the previous centuries (Thomas Moore, Francis Bacon, Tomasso Campanella), employs the means of exaggeration and extremity. Piranesi and his Neoclassical followers (Ledoux, Boullée) created labyrinthine structures (as was the case in *Carceri* series), which in a *trompe l'oeil* fashion deluded their audience's attention, drawing the inspecting eye into the picture frame, while complying to compositional rules and apparent clarity of traditional architectural plans, at the same time mocking their delusional absolutism. "Not only did they represent geographical locations and architectural details, they are first and foremost stories. A ruined arch is not just a clever rendering of an abandoned and crumbling Roman structure, it is an episode in an epic dedicated to decadence and vainglory, stories of ruin as well as ruins, prelude to a later century's idly Romantic musings." (Howe 2010, 13) Anyone trying to "read" the drawings, and in consequence, building a spatial representation of these architectural structures in his mind, eventually would find himself disappointed by the spatial conundrums. Illusionary tradition in art had always pointed outwards of itself. It hinted at a world much more complex, from which all urban issues arise. In comparison, most architectural interventions in all of their idealistic glory are all in all deemed to failure.

What is then the main reason for drawing, if not creating architectural blueprints? The first one had already been mentioned–graphic experiments of this kind contest the prevailing ideology of the age. We can relate this idea to subsequent centuries, taking

Ebenezer Howard's "garden cities" as an example. His concentric towns were laid out along railway tracks, banning all motorized traffic from their cores. The idea itself was a reaction to what Howard observed as a contemporary trend towards a densification of urban fabric the overcrowding, jamming and polluting of city centres, together with an increase in accidents towards the end of the 19th century. The 20th century's mindset, in contrast, proved to be set not just on mobility's threat to historical towns, along with their subsequent expansion, but also directed at the functionalist city model, zoning, and Modern Movement's vision of postwar renewal, traced along the lines of the Athens Charter (1934). This, for example, became the prime mover for Lebbeus Woods' pictorial rebellion against the *tabula rasa* policy of reconstruction projects, opting for eradication of both ruins and undamaged buildings, if they were seen as obstacles to urban planning. His *radical reconstruction* series were conceived in the form of site-specific interventions (into disaster, war-affected, and traumatized areas like Sarajevo or Kobe (the latter affected by the earthquake in 1995), and confronted the viewer with a look of "patched up" buildings, asymmetrically deformed structures displaying scab-like constructions on their facades. New spaces formed inside structures' cavities (Woods called them *freespaces*) were supposed to host any kind of program a war-scattered reality wanted to assign to it.

Piranesi's second aim was to depict contemporary trends in architecture and urbanism as to simulate their future outcomes–dystopian simulations made centuries beforehand, showing contemporary threats to the city blown-up to catastrophic proportions. We can find Piranesi's spiritual and conceptual accomplice in Hugh Ferriss and his renderings of Manhattan's skyscrapers. After the introduction of the "zoning resolution" in 1916, new buildings had to be erected in a way that wouldn't seal off the sunlight, thus plunging sidewalks into darkness. Therefore, the size of the lot, being reproduced as the spatial basis of the building's floors, had to get smaller and smaller until buildings began to resemble urban stalagmites. This fuelled Ferriss's imagination, allowing him to envision New York as a metropolis of spires, with buildings postured like rock formations, climbing ceaselessly towards the sky. Flats would serve as vertical supports for bridges, while the metropolis would have been put on display with all its Egyptian monumentality.

The third purpose of speculative projects would simply be the creation of an alternative visual discourse. Each era has its dominant and subsidiary trends, which can disappear and then resurface decades after their inception. Some showing more of an expansive than expensive nature would be put forever on hold due to economic crises[2]. New Brutalism begun to dominate over the postwar British landscape, yet in the shadow cast by the acolytes of Peter and Alice Smithson, new ideas of Archigram's "walking cities", assembly-kit towns and portable homes would sprout

----

[2] This was often said of the 1980s' generation of deconstructivist architects, with critics remarking that inability to realize commissions created perfect conditions for architectural theory to flourish.

even though hardly any of the projects were ever to compete with their adversaries for the city's skyline. Still, due to their pop-art vividness as well as due to their extraterrestrial look the drawings remain a breath of fresh air in the context of grey, load-bearing seriousness of *béton brut*.

Utopias

As the admirers of Piranesi already remarked, each set of his visionary etchings implies a narrative (even if not necessarily a progression). The narrative can explain the project's initial conditions and purpose, or it can grow on the compacted premise of a backstory for the proposed construction. In *Carceri* we can see human figures, torturers and the tortured citizens of an infernal prison world, giving us a sense of wicked hierarchical society observed by the artist from his 18th century studio. Piranesi's perspectives are a series of theatrical stage sets often "mistaken" for film frames, especially by directors the magnitude of Sergei Eisenstein that present a conceptual framework for a visual, as well as inherently spatial criticism of his times. "The eye travels up, enjoys the illusion of looming cornices and overhanging entablatures, and returns to the horizon, to earth. With Piranesi, once the gaze has been directed upward, it does not easily descend again, but remains lost in the fragmented vista that is perhaps Piranesi's greatest revolution. Were we to strip away the walls of his prisons layer by layer, from the foreground back, until the farthest planes are uncovered, we would discover a vista geometrically whole, but sequentially fragmented." (Howe 2010, 14) Among the themes addressed by 20th century creators of *paper architecture* there are however quite different concerns with notions such as programme and its introduction to architecture as a set of objectives for a building to fulfill. Be it a hospital or an opera house the roles prescribed for patients and music lovers don't seem interchangeable. Towards the end of the millennium though, there increased the number of architects challenging functionalist dictum, deeming it too rigid and insufficient, especially in times of massive revitalization enterprises. Buildings should stay flexible to some extent, let alone user-oriented; with inhabitants responsible for broadening the range of activities ascribed to its space.

The challenge of narrativity in architectural/urban proposals, expanding upon the notion of programme, becomes most evident in utopian fictions (also ones of architectural origin). Traditional utopian literature, dating back to Thomas Moore's *Utopia* (1516) or Tommaso Campanella's *The City of the Sun* (1602), take on spatialized forms to map out new idea sets, and project them onto the topography of not simply foreign, but a hypothetical (is)land, country, or government. Either the main character, or the eavesdroppers flocking around the storyteller, is usually invited on a guided tour around Bensalem or any other Utopia, being offered a glimpse at mechanisms and apparatuses behind this prospected society. Evidently this route changed very little as even contemporary *science-fiction* films follow similar guidelines.

In contrast to the panoply of subjects in speculative drawings, the narratives in literary utopias are more overt. Moore's book introduced the name for the genre, while following a narrative thread uncoiling into a long list of features far superior to ones his English countrymen grew accustomed to gradually revealing the 'engine' underneath utopian 'software' by means of a report on the political/social/cultural differences between the reality of Moore's book and reader's own. Since its inception, cinema has been interested both in representing/illustrating utopian fictions, and in reconstructing a sense of spatiality conveyed by architectural forms. One of the most deliberate attempts to do so was the "city film" genre. "City films" of the 1920s proved that it is possible to "narrate a city", from dawn to dusk, showing all nooks and crannies, frequently in accelerated motion. Thus, we behold rush hour traffic and empty squares as crowds disperse from fish markets' bustle to shots of couples promenading by moonlight. Alberto Cavalcanti's *Nothing but the Hours* (1926), Walter Ruttmann's *Berlin: Symphony of a Great City* (1927), and most explicitly Dziga Vertov's *Man with a Movie Camera* (1929) depict the city as a montage of sites. From a fast succession of views we construct the general image of the city. Frames are usually linked by content (storytelling progression), but most often they are connected through a string of associations. Bordwell and Thompson regarded the associational style as an alternative to continuity editing, that is, to joining the scenes in logical order of storytelling.

Both associational and abstract forms of editing (often ambiguous and contradictory) are most characteristic of experimental cinema. Their legacy becomes evident in architectural animated shorts, which are less concerned with social reception of architecture (and ritualistic practices assigned to it), and more with spatial relationships of texture, lighting, and the shapes light carves out in building interiors (*The Third & The Seventh* by Alex Roman, *Luce/Light* directed by Francesco Mansutti). Like in city films of the 1920s, architecture shown in them is again rendered abstract, whereas story wraps itself around the structure.

Each of the aforementioned films was shot in real life interiors, however their look was subsequently enhanced in post-production (light correction, saturation, creation of fluid CGI forms, which serve as reflective surfaces of "liquid shapes" manifesting their presence in space). The films are far from proposing any alternatives to constructed environments. Being apprehensive to volume, void and mass, they prefer to make architectural space malleable, bending and moulding it, therefore I only mention them as a "live action" alternative to animated speculations of the case studies to come. They, on the other hand, state their central themes with a progression of shots. By means of casual plot lines any design of a prospected building can possibly be explored and depicted in motion, even ones that are in use. The characters in these shorts are most often building's inhabitants; either victims (as in *Carceri*) or perpetrators of relationships formed in and around spatial domains. Treated not as surplus but as essence of this discourse is a digital space of communication, layered over daily and casual encounters on the urban plane.

Approaching Architecture (Differently)

The other important factor that opened architectural practices up for the medium of film was itself immaterial. It has changed the way of thinking about built environment and of architecture in general. Probably it wouldn't have come into being, if it weren't for the economic crisis. It was triggered by an emergence of the "generation" of deconstructivist architects–a formation whose name was to recall Soviet constructivism and Jacques Derrida's notion of textual deconstruction in the same line. It was a reconfiguration of avant-garde typologies, though this time channeling directly into unconscious agendas (as in Coop Himmelb(l)au's and Daniel Libeskind's projects, where a sense of psychological unsettlement of users was induced by apparent instability of constructed settings). Despite taking on commercial projects not sooner than in the late 1980s, architects such as Peter Eisenman, Bernard Tschumi, Zaha Hadid, Rem Koolhaas, Daniel Libeskind and the aforementioned collaboration between Helmut Swiczinsky and Wolf D. Prix begun to deconstruct architectural language, reassembling its "building blocks", exploring through their projects the notions of program/event, typology/archetype, façade/skin-interface, time resistance/decay. One can see an evident shift towards temporality, as the time-oriented perspective became an important part of the projects themselves. It came much easier to speculate upon issues of immateriality when, with the advance of communication technologies, the real/virtual dichotomy grew more apparent.

In effect, the architecture, as discipline, *set sail on a sea of gestures* (as Hadid used to describe her painted architecture), leaving the post-structuralist harbour to navigate towards a mediated phenomenology. If the perspective of Steven Holl's and Juhani Pallasmaa's writings owe a debt to Maurice Merleau-Ponty or Edmund Husserl (and therefore can be regarded as works of rather classically-minded researchers, studying sensual experience of one's presence in a space), the concepts of Paul Virilio, along with the projects of NaJa & deOstos or Bouman turn the polemic more feisty, arguing that our presence is already thoroughly mediated, and we should treat telepresence, televised representations, along with the impact of cinematic strategies on our perception on equal basis with sensations researched by Holl and Pallasmaa (light, space, tactility).

As time-based technologies of cinema, video and streamable media started to become inseparable from the architectural designs, an issue was raised on how to make the screen-mediated, interface-based representations more homogeneous, intrinsic to designs. Were we again to deal with *decorated sheds* before we would be allowed to move on to *ducks* to use the distinction made by Robert Venturi? Ole Bouman proposed four possible solutions to this problem, outlining types or adaptation stages of embedding time-based technologies into architectural design. First one of these strategies confronts us with a flat animated space in the form of large displays and moving façades. In the second instance, the space itself turns interactive. "I tried to deal with the way in which spaces have become speeded up, quickened, and now tend towards a more liquid condition." writes Bouman (Bouman

2005, 16). Space of speed, which Virilio calls *dromosphere*, has already surfaced in architectural drawings under various guises: free-flowing forms of Zaha Hadid, the *cinégrams* of Bernard Tschumi (serving as design graphs, potential form generators capable of creating "event spaces"), Michael Webb's *Temple Island Project*, or the media-infested interactive *Ada Intelligent Room*, created by the Institute of Neuroinformatics in Zurich for the Expo exhibition in 2002.

On a more general level, the concept of dromosphere, where physical dimensions collapse into a temporal plane, could easily suggest that film–a time-based medium from the outset–has been the most competent language of expression, since its very inception. Thus, it can not only convey a sensation of velocity through a rapid succession of images or sped-up, uninterrupted shots (the example of *Oh, I Can't Stop!* (1975) by Zbigniew Rybczyński). Certain architectural spaces themselves accentuate this notion by making the outer shell/skin appear motion-blurred (as in Daniel Libeskind's *Denver Art Museum*). *Dromosphere* is not merely a concept for transmitting "high energy particles" to architecture, but a cognitive aid to describe our inconstant and endlessly "updated" relationship with the artificial surroundings, which are themselves already immersed in new multimedia technologies and multi-layered representations. "[N]ew technologies such as television, live satellite broadcasts, video-surveillance or [...] the observation of minute or sub-atomic spaces, 'light up' the world in a different way and transform our (purely phenomenological) apprehension of space and time." (James 2007, 36). When navigating *cyberspace* (the term may seem obsolete, yet remains fitting in this context), we find physical dimensions collapsed and substituted by temporal progression. Bouman calls it the "asynchronicity" of present age, pointing out our propulsion to communicate mostly via social media. The creators of experimental architecture evidently decided that it is high time to make dromosphere visible in material space as well.

The final two stages in Bouman's concept are about overlapping. Environments can overlap (projecting one space in order to animate the space in another place), or they can prompt the user to literally "go online" (stage four). The last instance is what John Andrews called "performative architecture", heralding an amalgamation of physical and digital environments like *Ectoplasmatic Housing* by NaJa & deOstos, or *Ada*. Through constant interactions provided by the attendees, this intelligent environment measures currents passing through the room, as well as room's own temperature; it maps human movements around the space, and interacts with them by means of sound effects and flashing lights, after having processed input data from multiple cameras and microphones installed in its walls. *Ada*'s reactions are then projected onto monitor screens that surround users/visitors. In ONL's (Kas Oosterhuis) *trans-ports* this responsive room typology has been taken to logical extremes, as walls are curved surfaces with embedded screens and structure becomes womb-like. Because surroundings aren't flat but folded, convex or concave, room's responses are modelled in such a way as to appear, as they tried to encapsulate the user.

Immerse in the Post-Cinematic Case Studies

With such a surge of augmented reality technologies, among various other media that consequently remodel architectural practice, it is only rational to turn now to films selected for this study, because each combines characteristic features derived from: utopian literature, speculative drawing, architectural/urban representations, and multimedia; in essence, from all adjacent areas to the practice discussed above. Each sets out to explore an idea that is utopian by nature, illustrating it with either urban or architectural form.

Each is an animated short, made with extensive use of CGI. Some combine live-action sequences or treat them as "source material" to be altered in post-production. This genre, if one could call them that, evolved from the fly-through animations used as architectural visualization tool since the late 1970s. However, they usually drift far away from that original purpose (project's presentation to the contracting party), as well as from conventional language of architectural representations; indeed, fly-through animated sequences–portraying the structure from various angles, ground points and aerial views–were diversified by introduction of solutions from a vast history of filming techniques. This way they began to make frequent use of cutting edge cinematography and framing that take after mainstream productions, which in turn came to incorporate techniques from experimental films of the European avantgardes of the 1920s (city films among them), American Experimental West Coast movement (Harry Smith, Kenneth Anger, Bruce Baillie) and the New York scene (Jack Smith, Andy Warhol, Jonas Mekas), as well as the post-structuralist cinema of Hollis Frampton, Michael Snow and others.

By restricting the choice to short CGI animations, I was able to outline a tendency that becomes apparent due to constraints imposed by form: short time span, single narrative thread, a shared theme based around a personal experience of a partially-augmented, semi-material architectural space. *Algorithmic Architecture* (Charlie Behrens, 2012), *Augmented City 3D* (Keiichi Matsuda, 2010), *Golden Age: Somewhere* (Paul Nicholls, 2011), *Synaptic Landscapes* (Dan Farmer, 2009) speculate upon the premise of space that blurs boundaries between material and virtual realities, therefore conceptualizing an emerging seamless experiential territory; an augmented reality or a streamlined haptic cyberspace. If this is an updated version of *paper architecture* (as the "unbuilt" tradition has been often referred to), then paper-making technologies should be regarded as their skeuomorphic analogy. In this kind of CGI-permeated cinema there is an additional level of deceit underlying visual representation. The image, in regards to its source, is both *motion captured* (animating objects created in a digital environment), and *rotoscoped* (film frames of moving objects are drawn over). Every part of the frame is digitally altered. What we're seeing resembles a simulation, yet at the same time is firmly rooted in an already-mediated corporeality.

Some of the works I analyze in this chapter were made by the graduates of Nic Clear's course at the Bartlett School of Architecture, during which they worked on projects combining architectural design processes with film analysis, interpretation, and creation. Their standpoint is especially important, because it evidences a shared double perspective. It enables them to make films about architecture, while simultaneously conceiving of architecture works that reflects the post-cinematic experience we are all immersed in.

Intelligent Environments/Ephemeral Representations

The cross-pollination between the real (material) and the virtual might be regarded as province of science-fiction writers, nevertheless none of them is able to refrain from depicting them in purely spatial categories, thus engaging readers with futuristic buildings set dressed with blinking though at times quite discrete hi-tech. Downloadable furniture, for example, are the main narrative 'prop' and thematic concern in a short film by Paul Nicholls, *Golden Age: Somewhere* (2011). Floating around the city, we see crystalline structures growing above buildings. We descend to earth, from an exterior shot to home interior. William Turner's painting (*Rain, Steam and Speed*, 1844) is transformed from a meagre entry in a browsed folder into a domicile environment, a kind of 3D wallpaper, yet this decoration can be switched off just as easily. The character of this futuristic home staging episode downloads templates, adjusting them to her leisurely mood, whereas messages and calls pop up on her communication terminal. Without warning, a dystopian edge sinks in, disrupting this fable, while downloading a new dress, a virus infects the entire domestic OS (operating system). It crashes, resets and restarts itself in a Cartesian grid's "DOS mode". In Nicholls's short the space that humans inhabit becomes a hardware structure with a built-in operating system. In the futuristic visions of Archigram a group conducting their research out of London in late 1960s, homes were transformed into detachable capsules or modules, resembling to space station units, as in Peter Cook's *Plug-In City* (1964). Connecting mechanisms included pipes supplying all indispensable media (electricity, water, sewage, etc.). As of today, we could compare their drawings to images of prototypical USB drives, by the very look of the schematics evidencing peripheral devices "powered" by a central (processing) unit. On the other hand, *Suitaloon*, envisioned by Michael Webb, was intended as a wearable design comparable to an inflatable tent. Whenever a future denizen was feeling tired and needed a quick nap, one could indeed easily find him- or herself at home thanks to the content of this backpack. In creating a personal, comforting space, Nicholls's film draws from such projects, reassembling them into a sort of Apple-friendly to-morrow land.

An extreme take on this subject is displayed in a different short film, created by Dan Farmer, called *Synaptic Landscapes*. Its extremity lies in the fact that it transgresses the real/virtual opposition via deconstructing our perception of places down to chemical processes taking place in the cerebral cortex. In Farmer's view both spatial layers–the material and the virtual–undergo the same process, that is, they are constructed in a similar fashion in terms of brain's processing of input from the environment. While material reality prioritizes senses of smell, touch, and balance, their virtual manifestation relies solely on sight and hearing. It is akin to a relation of packets of stimuli versus similar, though already mediated packages. Farmer argues that our perception of space relies on processing stimuli from the environment and translating them into visual/acoustic/tactile sensations. For example, we perceive colours as manifestations of the way surfaces reflect particular wavelengths of visible light spectrum or mixtures thereof.

Therefore, it is hypothetically possible to simulate the stimulation, as does the protagonist of *Synaptic Landscapes*, although primarily applying all the "tech" to perspective cues. Images generated through such manipulation are literary transformed into a holistic physical environment. In the cinema of German Expressionism (*Golem* [1920] by Paul Wegener and Carl Boese, *The Cabinet of Dr. Caligari* [1920] and *The Hands of Orlac* [1924] by Robert Wiene) it was common practice to project protagonist's anxieties and desires onto one's surroundings. In *Synaptic Landscapes* this process not only refurbishes perceived space but alters its outer shape in accord with a deranged psychic state.

In Farmer's film a non-diegetic narrative introduces us to what could be described as conceptual doubt expressed by the working model of the perceptual apparatus. The architect/filmmaker uses cinematic devices, like dissolves, disruption of forced perspectives, and cutting out small fragments of continuous shots. In consequence, jerky movements of the camera indicate to the viewer that only key stages of motion are shown. The camera's pace is slow, despite forward and backward tracking shots zooming in on the action or, simply, revealing what lies on the outside of the frame. At about 2'56" we see a model Renaissance linear perspective, composed of straight lines that partition the space into a grid, yet along with camera's panning around the scruffy interiors (panorama) this ideal perspective breaks down. Gradually, it is deconstructed into a series of parallel lines and geometric outlines. Eventually, this is revealed as a 3D installation consisting of "materialized" beams, rims and outlines in physical space, apparently suspended in mid-air. We listen to the main character's soliloquy: "*brain is not a camera; it doesn't record pictures. It recognizes and identifies forms. It looks for particular spatial and temporal correlations within lines and patterns,* [which are treated as] *index cards in its search for clarity.*" (film dialogue) Narrative-wise, viewers are meant to behold the patterns gradually emerging along with incremental movements. Each new shot dismantles the optical illusion of its predecessor. As we forsake realities of fixed perspectives, strange non-symmetrical spatialities are revealed to us. Before our eyes, the Cartesian grid's framing device suddenly decomposes into a mesh of lines and ellipses. This way the director questions our mind's automatism in constructing spatial representations.

Similar traces, in terms of designing the drawing, could be seen in Piranesi in his engravings' montage of perspectives that constitutes his imaginary prisons. Both in Nicholls and Farmer one is able to discern the utopian drive (even a rudimentary plot), echoing speculative novels' device in inventing unfamiliar settings, simulated realities, and technologically-induced transgressions, departing from architectural frameworks towards internal landscapes. Indeed, we leave a "good place" (*eutopia*) for a non-existent place; for no place at all.

"The Language of Waves and Radiation" a nod to Don DeLillo

"Space becomes electromagnetic, chemical, sensorial and atmospheric with thermal, olfactory and coetaneous dimensions within which we are immersed." (Bevan 2009, 52). Having investigated conditions by which we communicate through social media, it is time to look into the attempts to map those relationships, and to strategies of mapping in real time what once was cartography's domain. Charles Behrens's *Algorithmical Architecture* uses Google Maps and Google Street View algorithms to create a somewhat impossible urban landscape, literally bringing out tectonics above infrastructure. His aim is to uncover their code(s) by visualization of glitches (this way revealing the constructed nature of image space). What Behrens notices is the facility with which we take representations for facsimiles of authentic places, casting our interpretational nets upon the world at large; eventually, more restrained than freewheeling by such post-technological perception. This way our point of view (POV) descends in *Algorithmical Architecture* from an aerial shot, by means of infinite zoom, down to serpentine roads, sidewalks, squares, over- and underpasses, valleys and hilltops, leaving residential areas for the edgelands. Behrens's sight-lines cross paths with Kevin A. Lynch's *the Image of the City* (1960), as both campaign for practical and aesthetic layout of the city. A layout that seems to be at odds with imaging technologies, rooting for picturesqueness, which Lynch calls *imageability*. Describing urban infrastructure from a pedestrian's point of view, Lynch views the city through its landmarks, rational arrangements of streets and quarters, and a narrative implied by a sequential configuration of sidewalks, roads and bicycle routes. Whenever we consider taking a shortcut or detour, we decide on a particular sequence of sites (and, simultaneously, of events taking place). Following his argument, we can say that either by walking, driving, or riding, we perceive the city as a series of images. From the surveys conducted by Lynch, a conclusion could be drawn that citizens' inability to imagine their own city is caused by nothing other than chaos in urban planning. On daily basis we have to deal with an overabundance of images, and our own mental mapping algorithms in this context are crucial in discerning the "valid path".

But *Algorithmical Architecture* refrains from setting off into some unspecified future to make its point. It does so by simply overlaying present-day images in a fly-through journey across highways, suburbs, and city centres. Often, the shape of terrain doesn't match the aerial image, which ardently emphasizes the film's main argument. This results in a wildlife of abstract and illogical imagery of flattened road junctions placed high upon mountain ranges, or crossroads located at the bottom of a crater. But this imposition of 3D "street views" over aerial 2D images reveals much more than just mismatched mappings. Only here we can see the topographic spacing between buildings, voids in urban fabric, as well as zones of extremely dense concentration.

This is the view Lynch might have wished for, if only he knew satellite imaging would be two clicks away some day. Such discrepancies make us aware that there is still a great gap to be bridged between the planner's and streetwalker's viewpoint, and a beneficial connection would not merely be a wishful advantage, but a rudimentary bottom-up solution for a 21st century's *Image of the City*.

As a supplement to this digital rendition of New Urbanism comes *Augmented City 3D* created by Keiichi Matsuda. In this animation rotoscoped over live-action footage, we are taken on a journey around town; one that starts in a snack bar and ends up with the meeting at a train station. Visible are the digital/virtual space "markers", superimposed on material surroundings, as if the main character had been equipped with a built-in GPS application that projected navigation tags onto buildings and sidewalks. As he strolls down the street, advertisements littering the pavement subside. He can change tenement houses' fronts, even alter graffiti patterns, whenever and wherever he likes. The characters in Matsuda's short live in an age of asynchronous communication, which necessitates multitasking in both material and virtual environments. Already today we catch ourselves red-handed when checking email accounts, while rushing downtown; add to that a quick review of Facebook statistics, a Skype/WhatsApp session with a friend, and/or glimpsing at a game of virtual chess in the background. Here we get a glimpse of where our dispersed/distributed attention is likely to end up in near future. But then again, is Matsuda's film really intended as a dystopian bed time story, or have we always been hardwired for this kind of tiered reality, only waiting for proper technology to arrive?

Both *Augmented City 3D* and *Synaptic Landscape* fill concrete space(s) with abstract designs that transform themselves in real time. These films reflect on our condition of semi-grounding, or conditional submersion in everyday life. Paul Virilio introduced the term "simultaneity", which demonstrates this shift in a somewhat apocalyptic context of the "information bomb". Hopefully, we haven't yet reached a state of sensual overload, stepping over the threshold. Similarly, in *White Noise* (1985), Don DeLillo described the state in which we inhabit an electromagnetic and acoustic wilderness; one that is permeated with flows of electromagnetic radiation. "I was suddenly aware of the dense environmental texture. The automatic doors opened and closed, breathing abruptly. Colors and odors seemed sharper. The sound of gliding feet emerged from a dozen other noises, from the sublittoral drone of maintenance systems, from the rustle of newsprint as shoppers scanned their horoscopes in the tabloids up front, from the whispers of elderly women with talcumed faces, from the steady rattle of cars going over a loose manhole cover just outside the entrance." (DeLillo 1998, 295). Animated shorts described above allow us to recognize and perceive this flux; an environment already penetrated to the furthest degree with virtual architectures of inconstancy.

Conclusion: Tactile Signals Leave Permanent Traces

What DeLillo described as an ascending trend of technological permeation is now considered the *status quo*. In turn, it is architecture that turned immaterial; new projects convey a sense of being less concerned about the static and the solid than their antecedents. As stated in the opening paragraph, architectural practice keeps on expanding into areas of augmented ephemerality and dynamics, often inspecting and reaffirming itself through the lens of other media. What emerges at this point is genuinely an architecture of flows. Para-architectural projects that explore our partial grounding in both realities are gaining momentum with such executed designs as the aforementioned *Ada Room*, NaJa & deOstos' *Ectoplasmatic Housing/Library*, Kas Oosterhuis' *trans-ports* or *Son-O-House* by NOX, where one's movements and actions alter musical cues played in the interiors.

2008's Venice Biennale captivated audiences with a similarly sounding theme of *Architecture beyond building*, which best sums up this tendency to pursue projects analyzing relationships between invisible environments of datascapes with habitats we move through on daily basis. They give rise to architecture popping out of our cellphone displays and iPad screens. What comes as most intriguing is their use of film footage and recorded image as main input for more tactile interactions. As immaterial "architectures" of data are in the course of being materialized or realized as installations and art projects in real space, the animated films do exactly the opposite. They adopt and visualize those datascapes, conjoining them with artificial spaces reconstructed in 2D with the aid of cinematic means. They remain subversive, as most of the films presented here vastly rely on glitches and optical illusions in visually reinforcing their polemics. Cinematic space, although immaterial, has the advantage of representing non-existent, *trompe l'oeil* constructions. Whenever building from virtual blocks, i.e. conceiving of a drawing, not just the object it is meant to represent, means realizing both the structure and the optical illusion underlying it. Therefore, the architectural assembly in such cases doesn't exist independently from the observer (as in Farmer and Matsuda). This brings about an unexpected twist to issues concerning space, taken up in articles and books by both Holl (2001) and Pallasmaa (2012). Both authors emphasized the importance of phenomenological experience to true engagement with architectural space. Digital phenomenology might be much more than just an algorithm then.

Speculative architectural drawings, since their very first rendition as Piranesi's engravings, were supposed to suggest an alternative to the discourse, a different order. They were meant to formulate critical points, re-presenting them to the practice, while investigating new methodologies and codes of architectural language. The style of these designs (drawings, collages, films, models) evolved in conjunction with technologies and media employed in design practice. Nevertheless, many architects were making even greater leaps into realms of pictorial avant-gardes, performance and video art; namely, to territories far removed from the "immediacy" of design/construction pipelines. Especially film, considered as medium, briefly became a fashionable tool in the 1960s and 70s, useful in visual analysis of highways and roadside landscapes seen from driver's perspective, most explicitly applied in the famous study *Learning from Las Vegas* (1972) by Robert Venturi, Denise Scott-Brown and George Izenour. Contemporary studies of houses in motion reach back to that art-architectural tradition, whereas engaging with experimental, wildly speculative projects. Just like the atmospheric renderings created at the École des Beaux-Arts in the 19th century, architectural animations set out to convey both sensual and conceptual characteristics of space; the pedestrian point of view and the moving panorama perceived from the backseat. Cinema greatly facilitates this task due to its predilection to represent motion, as well as by manipulating the flow of images with devices such as framing and editing. These strategies reconstruct, mimic, even enhance the way we build mental images of architectural spaces.

Animated films concerned with architectural space bring forth their arguments via dystopian narratives. They comment on the shortcomings of urban planning and architectural investments, waste sites (drosscapes) and large-scale construction projects. They vary in scope from landscape engineering to domestic appliances and smart technologies, critically engaging with the semantics of visual culture. As these short films suggest, we should ask primarily about reasons why instances of cutting-edge architecture still remain (un)built, especially as the artificial environments we've grown used to inhabiting ceased to meet our expectations? One of the highest advantages of speculative architectural animations, along with other para-architectural practices oriented at representing events taking concrete place(s), as part of their futuristic mise-en-scène, is therefore their central argument; the argument that space has always been (and with new technological advancements turns even more so) a half-architectural, half-mental construct.

REFERENCES

Behrens, Charlie, dir. 2012. *Algorithmic Architecture.*

Bevan, Richard. 2009. "The Carbon Casino." *Architectural Design* 79 (*Architectures of the Near Future*): 50–55.

Bordwell, David, and Kristin Thompson. 2008. *Film Art: An Introduction.* New York: McGraw-Hill.

Bouman, Ole. 2005. "Architecture, Liquid, Gas." *Architectural Design* 75 (*4dspace: Interactive Architecture*): 14–22.

Coleman, Nathaniel. 2005. *Utopias and Architecture.* London and New York: Routledge.

Cook, Peter. 2014. *Drawing: The Motive Force of Architecture.* Chichester: Wiley.

DeLillo, Don. 1998. *White Noise.* New York: Penguin Books.

Farmer, Dan, dir. 2009. *Synaptic Landscapes.*

Holl, Steven. 2001. *Parallax.* New York: Princeton Architectural Press.

Howe, John. 2010. "Preface." In *the Prisons/Le Carceri*, by Giovanni Battista Piranesi, 11–17. Mineola, New York: Dover Publications, Inc.

James, Ian. 2007. *Paul Virilio.* New York: Routledge.

Lynch, Kevin. 1990. *The Image of the City.* Cambridge, MA, and London: The MIT Press.

Matsuda, Keiichi, dir. 2010. *Augmented City 3D.*

Nicholls, Paul, dir. 2011. *Golden Age: Somewhere.*

Pallasmaa, Juhani. 2012. *The Eyes of the Skin: Architecture and the Senses.* New Jersey: Wiley.

Smith, Kendra Schank. 2005. *Architect's Drawings: A Selection of Sketches by World Famous Architects Through History.* Oxford: Architectural Press.

Smith, Kendra Schank. 2008. *Architects' Sketches: Dialogue and Design.* Oxford: Architectural Press.

Tschumi, Bernard. 1994. *The Manhattan Transcripts.* London: Academy Editions.

Virilio, Paul. 2005. *The Information Bomb.* London and New York: Verso.

Venturi, Robert, Denise Scott Brown, and Steven Izenour. 1988. *Learning from Las Vegas: The Forgotten Symbolism of Architectural Form.* Cambridge, MA, and London: The MIT Press.

Chapter 10

Reexamining Zipf's Law from a World Historical Perspective: Urbanization, Complexity, and the Rank-Size Rule[1]

Daniel Pasciuti,

The Urban Distribution

During much of the twentieth Century, increasing urbanization throughout the world was highly correlated with industrialization. The growth of cities, such as New York, matched the industrial development of the United States. Urban development, as a manifestation of American dominance, was easily identifiable and explainable in this context. New York was the largest city in the world because the United States was clearly the leading industrial force upon which the world moved.

Under this condition, Zipf outlined a universal law of complex systems, specifically identifying its relationship to the distribution of city sizes conforming to a power law, where the size of a city is inversely proportional to its rank (Zipf 1949). Thus, the probability $P(s) = Pr\{S>s\}$; meaning that the value S, the size of a city in the urban distribution, is greater than s with the probability density function p(s) exhibiting a power law dependence $p(s)\sim 1/s^q$ (de Vries 1984, Gabaix 1999, Saichev 2010).

Economic theory defines Zipf's Law as a steady state distribution of cities in a geographic area which forms a power law. Under this argument, urban forms will take on a log-normal, straight-line distribution, based upon the logged population size, where the largest city in a geographic region constitutes the top of the distribution, the next city will be half the size of the largest city, and so on down the entire urban distribution of the region. "Zipf's law for cities is one of the most conspicuous empirical facts in economics, or in the social sciences generally" (Gabaix 1999, 739).

---

[1] This chapter is an edited version of the essay "Reexamining Zipf's Law from a World Historical Perspective: Urbanization, Complexity, and the Rank-Size Rule" first published in *The International Journal of Interdisciplinary Global Studies* 7 (4): 29-40.

Paul Krugman has argued that Zipf's Law is an empirical fact in the United States but one without a theoretical explanation. "The size distribution of cities in the United States is startlingly well described by a simpler power law: the number of cities whose population exceeds S is proportional to 1/S. At this point we are in the frustrating position of having a striking empirical regularity with no good theory to account for it" (Krugman 1996, 399).

This is related to the rank-size distribution, expressed as $S=K(R)^{-q}$, where R is the city rank, q and K are constants, and S is city size. "The values of K and q can be estimated as a simple linear regression by ordinary least squares. If the array of cities arranged in order of their size yield a good fit, the city size distribution can be represented by a straight line with a slope of –q, and is called a lognormal distribution" (deVries 1984, 87).

> To visualize Zipf's law, we take a country (for instance, the United States), and order the cities by population: No, 1 is New York, No, 2 is Los Angeles, etc. We then draw a graph; on the y-axis we place the log of the rank (N.Y. has log rank ln 1, L.A. log rank ln 2), and on the x-axis the log of the population of the corresponding city (which will be called the "size" of the city) the slope of the curve is very close to -1 In terms of the distribution, this means that the probability of the size of a city is greater than some S is proportional to 1/S (de Vries 1984,739-740).

Figure 1: Theoretical Distribution for Zipf's Law

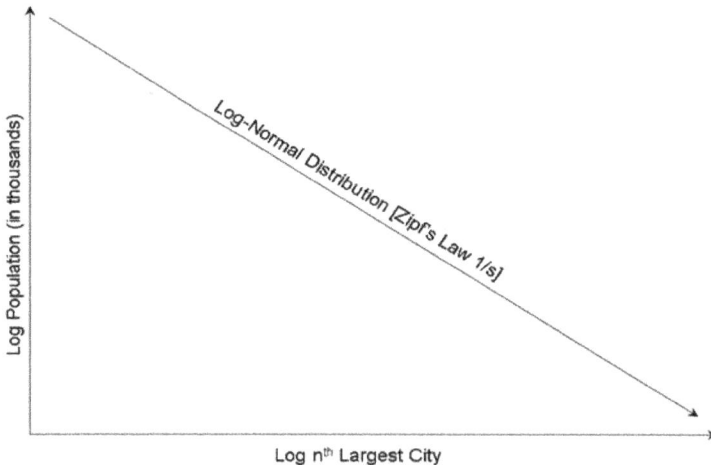

Source: Author

Brian Berry linked the formation of this type of urban distribution, specifically Zipf's rank-size rule, as being consistent with central place theory where an urban system should attain a steady state equilibrium whose individual cities vary in size in a stochastic process. Thus, while the future size of individual cities cannot be determined, the overall process of urban development should remain stable. Berry uses the concept of entropy maximization; that any system is subject to constraints and thus the rank-size rule is the most likely probability pattern, to justify the likely spatial distribution within that system which represents a finished or efficient form of urban development in a system of cities (Berry 1961, de Vries 1984, Hohenberg and Lees 1985).

However, with rapid urbanization in the South over the past several decades, with little or no corresponding industrial development to match, this basic property has seemingly failed. Cities such as Mexico City, Rio de Janeiro, and others witnessed the explosion of massive slums and shadow cities and appear incapable of using their newly acquired labor force into the production and consumption practices or maintaining a stable urban distribution. Although the global context of this event is acknowledged and identified by authors such as Davis, "urbanization-without-growth is more obviously the legacy of a global political conjuncture the debt crisis of the 1970s and subsequent IMF-led restructuring of Third World economies in the 1980s than an iron law of advancing technology" (Davis 2006a, 9). It is also dismissed as an explanation; "'Modernization', 'Development' and now, the unfettered 'Market' have had their day. The labour-power of a billion people has been expelled from the world system, and who can imagine any plausible scenario, under neo-liberal auspices, that would reintegrate them as productive workers or mass consumers?" (Davis 2006a, 27). However, it is precisely these conjunctures which illuminate the changing nature of the global urban form:

> The hectic pace of capitalist development over the past decades has taken tangible form in the transformation of the world's cities: the epic expansion of coastal China, deindustrialization and suburbanization of the imperial heartlands, massive growth of slums. From Shanghai to São Paolo, Jerusalem to Kinshasa, cityscapes have been destroyed and remade— vertically: the soaring towers of finance capital's dominance—and horizontally: the sprawling shanty-towns that shelter a vast new informal proletariat, and McMansions of a sunbelt middle class. The run-down public housing and infrastructural projects of state-developmentalism stand as relics from another age. Against this backdrop, the field of urban studies has become one of the most dynamic areas of the social sciences, inspiring innovative contributions from the surrounding disciplines of architecture, anthropology, economics. Yet in comparison to the classic accounts of manufacturing Manchester, Second Empire Paris or Reaganite Los Angeles, much of this work is strikingly depoliticized. Characteristically, city spaces are studied in abstraction from their national contexts. The wielders of

economic power and social coercion remain anonymous. The broader political narrative of a city's metamorphosis goes untold (Davis 2006b, 46).

This draws upon a central theme; that cities are inexorably linked to the political and economic systems within which they operate. As Richard Blanton once described, cities are "a manifestation of the growth of institutions capable of organizing vast regions into integrated systems" (Blanton 1997). Therefore, we must begin from the premise that the demographic changes of the world today are intertwined with the changing nature of the world economy and historical capitalism. Urbanization is divorced from neither an economic logic nor the political influence of the state, it is part and parcel of understanding the entire dynamic of global capital and urban transformation in time and space.

Instead, cities are manifestations of social, political, and economic power represented in the world economy. They offer an accessible window into the organization of any geographical social system in time based upon their development, expansion, and decline. Further, there is no reason to assume this manifestation is uniform throughout history; rather its changing dynamics through time must be understood in world historical perspective.

Reexamining Zipf's Law

Volker Nitsch argues there are two lines of research dealing with urban hierarchy distributions, specifically Zipf's Law. One is to provide an economic rationale for the development of city distributions where "[t]he basic aim is to build a model which generates a city size distribution that obeys Zipf's Law. However, while it may be possible to show that an urban hierarchy model produces a Zipfian distribution for certain specific parameter assumptions, the main difficulty of these attempts is that they do not explain the actual key feature of the rank-size rule: the robustness for a wide range of countries and time periods and, in effect, economic conditions" (Nitsch 2001, 20).

The second line of research for dealing with Zipf's Law is to mathematically derive the rank-size rule as the result of a random growth process. Citing Paul Krugman, Nitsch argues that "[t]he basic underlying idea is that there is scale invariance in the growth rate of cities. Because cities display on average the same pattern of growth at all scales, size would be more or less irrelevant. If this assumption is correct, however, then it is possible to show that the resulting distribution of cities is also scale-invariant and can be described by a power law" (Nitsch 2001, 20).

Deviations from these log-normal distributions are not taken as alternative urban development processes but instead are argued as symptoms of disorder; the most common is the presence of cities which are 'too large' and thus distort the distribution; outliers to the empirical regularity of the distribution. Numerous explanations for these deviations have come from multiple disciplines in the social sciences including sociology. Charles Tilly (1964) attributed this symptom of disorder to 'political instability'. While Alejandro Portes (1976) attributed it to colonial domination in Latin America and E.A Johnson (1970) to an impoverishing economic imbalance; all of which created an imbalanced urban system where one or more central cities became 'too large' in comparison to their corresponding counterparts; the 'primate city'.

Others simply choose to ignore these cities as aberrations which cannot be accounted for but do not undermine the overall value of the rank-size distribution. "Zipfs law is not quite as neat in other countries as it is in the United States, but it still seems to hold in most places, if you make one modification: many countries, for example, France and the United Kingdom, have a single "primate city" that is much larger than a line drawn through the distribution of other cities would lead you to expect. These primate cities are typically political capitals; it is easy to imagine that they are essentially different creatures from the rest of the urban sample" (Krugman 1996, 41).

Recently, research has emerged which examines city-size distributions at the sub-national and supranational levels (Gisen and Südekum, 2011; Subbarayan and Kumar, 2015; Ye and Xie, 2012; Vallabados and Subbarayan, 2016). Soo (2012) explored the size distribution of cities in US states finding strong evidence of a lognormal distribution of city sizes within states. While Devadoss and Luckstead (2016) examined the size distribution of smaller US cities from 2000 to 2010 and found a strong association at the lower tail for Gibrat's law; meaning that the proportionate growth rate of cities from 2000 to 2010, irrespective of their absolute size, produced a log-normal distribution in the US.

While these studies have updated and expanded the research on Zipfian distributions in the 21st century, they focus solely on the contemporary structures of urban spatial arrangements. Thus, Arshad et.al, conclude in their meta-analysis of studies of city-size distributions that there are mixed results from studies of Zipfian distributions and much of the research lacks a theoretical grounding for both adherence to and deviations from a log-normal distribution. The ultimately argue that existing empirical evidence "is not robust" and future studies must use "bias corrected empirical methods and better definition of cities to examine Zipf's law" (Arshad et. al. 2018, 90).

However, we should reconsider the nature of proportionate growth and urban development in the context of the historical dynamics of the world-economy. In this context we can consider both adherence to and deviations from a log-normal, Zipfian distribution. We must explain the continued existence of and even the increasing presence of these outliers in our theoretical understanding of urbanization. Thus, Hohenberg and Lees argue that if the rank-size rule is to be something "more than a mathematical curiosity, it should have some sort of normative property. For one thing, *the rule can serve as a standard against which to describe actual urban size distribution"* (Hohenberg and Lees 1985, 347 *emphasis added*).

Several attempts have been made to this effect. Robson (1973) examined the upper end of the size distribution to order cities between oligarchy and primacy. While de Vries (1984) periodized early modern European urbanization into stages based upon movement in the rank-size distribution. However, these attempts still identify alternative urban distributions as 'incomplete' and ultimately progressing towards the steady state equilibrium envisioned by Zipf's Law. Instead of theorizing deviations from this log-normal distribution as a symptom of disorder, I argue we should instead embrace these deviations as important elements of an overall pattern which must be completely explained.

In a pure economic situation, a city would only represent the needs of a geographic region to produce and facilitate production and exchange between different economic and social groups. Thus, any urban system would have a limited amount of merchants, bankers, and production capabilities as well as social and cultural institutions based on the spatial distribution of the population as a whole. An urban system which develops beyond these limited functions represents a social-political process to organize, extract, and concentrate more functions in the urban environment than would thus be otherwise needed."[W]e have reason to believe that relations of power, domination and exploitation do affect the distribution of human populations in space. Many large cities are as large as they are because they are able to draw upon far-flung regions for food and raw materials. If a city is able to use political/military power or economic power to acquire resources from surrounding cities it will be able to support a larger population than the dominated cities can, and this will produce a city size distribution" (Chase-Dunn et al. 2005).

Supporting this thesis is the work of Doug White and his collaborators. White and his colleagues examined urban hierarchy distributions between 430 BCE and 2005 CE using the data from Chandler and Fox (1974) and UN estimates of populations from 1950, to create a q exponential model of urban hierarchy development. Basing their measure on work in fractality, which deals with a "broad class of hierarchically organized and self-scaling processes and satisfies our requirements for a suitably general function with which to model city size distributions historically" (White et al. 2006, 2-3). They argue that by creating generalized monolog plots based upon a function of q, a logarithmic function, the slope of the distribution can be measured as the function approaches a power law.

In this instance, the log-normal, Zipfian distribution, is only one instance of the power functions of the model, where Beta reaches a value of approximately 2, and thus other power functions of the distribution can also be traced out. (White et al. 2006, 3). "Thus, the Zipfian distribution for large cities becomes a special case subsumed under a more general distribution for cities of any size with a parameter q, relevant to urban hierarchy theory and not sensitive to size but to region or historical period, along with a parameter k that is relevant to historical change in the scale or total populations of differently sized cities in an urban hierarchy" (White et al. 2005, 3).

I hypothesize that successive conditions of capitalism produce successive urban stratification patterns where the urban distribution itself is an intertwined part of the economic and ideological processes of the world historical process. The existence of cities which exhibit a non-Zipfian distribution must be understood as embedded within politically, economically, and socially dominant power(s) and/or nation state(s) based on alternative historical conditions of capital from that seen under the United States in the twentieth century. Therefore, the expanding urban development of the latter part of the twentieth century and the beginning of the twenty-first, does not represent the dislocation of urban development from the conditions of capitalism but rather the reorganization of urban development's as a new political and economic order emerges from the shadow of U.S. hegemony. The 'slum cities' of the third world and the 'world cities' of the first world are not disparate elements of competing interests but unified elements of the integrated global process of historical capitalism.

That political and economic organizations can operate in distinct spatial formations based upon different distributions of power requires some clarification of the concept of complexity. Drawing from the critique by Crumley, who criticized definitions of complexity as being focused solely upon hierarchical structures and patterns of inequality and should instead focus on the dialectics of state formation on existing structures like coalitions, federations, or democracies (Crumley 2001), we should consider different organization complexities in spatial formations. Thus, complexity can consider more than a Hierarchical structure, such as Zipf's Law, to include a Heterarchical structure, where increasing complexity in time and space does not necessarily correspond to an increasing rank-ordered system of organization. Crumley defines heterarchy as.

> [T]he relation of elements to one another when they are unranked or when they possess the potential for being ranked in a number of different ways. For example, power can be counterpoised rather than ranked. Thus, three cities might be of the same size but draw their importance from different realms: one hosts a military base, one is a manufacturing center, and the third is home to a great university. The relative importance of these community and individual power bases changes in response to the context of the inquiry and to changing (and frequently conflicting) values that result in the continual reranking of priorities (Crumley 1995, 3).

This provides a comparative conceptual tool to consider the configurations of complex power relations in urban development in world history as more than the 'mathematical curiosity' of Hohenberg and Lees. If Zipf's Law is invariant to the historical conditions of urban development, we need a conceptual model capable of considering alternative arrangements of power in the built environment and the spatial organization of complex urban distributions. In Figure 2, below, I have sketched out how these new urban stratifications can be understood; as Hierarchical Urban Distributions and as Heterarchical Urban Distributions.

A Hierarchical distribution that focuses power into a concentrated and highly ranked spatial formation where the economic, political, and social power of the urban system is concentrated into a single urban form, the 'primate city', and thus achieves a level of complexity and size within the urban system far beyond that of any alternative cities. The city of London under the British Empire in the nineteenth century would be one of the most conspicuous examples of this form in world history. As a world entrepôt, a major industrial center, and the center of government for both the Kingdom of Great Britain and the British Empire, the city of London concentrated social, economic, and political power in a way few other urban centers have ever achieved.

A Heterarchical distribution differentiates complexity, power, and therefore size, throughout the urban distribution resulting in a more egalitarian spatial relationship between cities sizes. This does not imply such a stratification pattern is more socially equitable. Rather, that there are several large cities whose population sizes are relatively equivalent and exist under a counterpoised distribution of power, usually through specialization of various social, economic and political functions. The Dutch Republic of the seventeenth century has been called a 'decentralized metropolis' (Dierderiks 1990) as many cities within the provinces performed specialized roles. Thus, even the most famous city of the period, Amsterdam, was neither the political capital of the Republic nor the only major commercial port; The Hague being the political capital and Rotterdam, among others, operating as a the central point for international commerce.

Figure 2: Theoretical Hierarchical and Heterarchical Urban Distributions

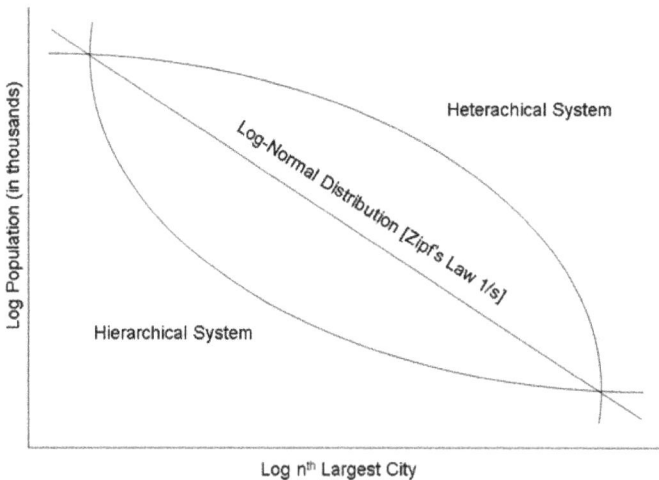

Source: Author

The comparison of the two urban systems and their associated periods clearly demonstrates this fundamental difference in their stratification patterns. As seen in Table 1 below, English urbanism was always highly concentrated on London, forming a Hierarchical Urban Distribution where the city of London never represented less than two-thirds or more of the total urban population in the nation. While Amsterdam, in contrast, possessed less than one third of the total urban population of the Dutch Republic throughout the seventeenth century and early eighteenth centuries. If the development of London represents a supremum example of hierarchical, concentrated, urban development (meaning London was the peak of the subset of British urbanism), then Amsterdam and the cities of the Dutch Republic represent its antithesis through a heterarchical, counterpoised, urban formation. Thus, while Amsterdam was never the largest of cities in the global urban distribution, the cities of the Dutch Republic represented a total level of urbanism that cumulatively surpassed their single city counterparts.

The changing nature of the urban built environment, the development and redevelopment of the city in time and space, reflects the strategies of power that a state organization embarks upon to redevelop the capitalist system in its own image. If we accept London as an important urban space in the seventeenth and eighteenth centuries and not dismissed as an anomaly of overurbanization, why are the present global urban anomalies of the South dismissed as imbalanced or unstable urban systems rather than as an alternative urban development process under specific historical and contemporary conditions of capital?

Table 1: English and Dutch Urbanization, 1600-1750

	1600		1650		1700		1750	
Number of towns of 10,000+								
England and Wales	6		8		11		21	
United Provinces	19		19		20		18	
Population Living in Towns of 10,000 +								
England and Wales	Thousands	% of Total	Thousands	% of Total	Thousands	% of Total	Thousands	% of Total
excluding London	55	21.57%	95	19.19%	143	19.92%	346	33.89%
London	200	78.43%	400	80.81%	575	80.08%	675	66.11%
Total	255	100.00%	495	100.00%	718	100.00%	1021	100.00%
United Provinces								
excluding Amsterdam	299	82.14%	428	70.98%	439	68.70%	370	63.79%
Amsterdam	65	17.86%	175	29.02%	200	31.30%	210	36.21%
Total	364	100.00%	603	100.00%	639	100.00%	580	100.00%

Source: Adapted from Ormrod (2003) Table 1.1

Under this theoretical conceptualization it is possible to hypothesize that the current urban developments are the result of a new emerging urban distribution which directly reflects the changing political and economic conditions of the world towards Asia and the growing importance of cities in the Global South. David Satterthwaite has observed, "[t]he growing number of large Asian cities reflect the region's growing importance within the world economy (and Asia has many of the world's largest national economies). In addition, historically, Asia has had most of the world's largest cities for most of the last three millennia" (Satterthwaite 2005, 2). If East Asia and specifically China represent the new dynamic function of global capitalism, then the rise of East Asian cities is both a reflection of their power and a lens into the future of orientation of the 21st century. After all, you do not redevelop the political and ideological center of a nation (i.e. Beijing) simply for international games but rather for the focus of the world to see what can be offered in the 21st century. The new spires of success must push the limits of our imaginations, even as the new shanties of the poor challenge our sensibilities.

Reinterpreting Historical Urban Complexity

The reinterpretation of previous historical analyses of urban distributions rests upon the reconceptualization of urban distributions as being variant based upon the political and economic conditions of world history. Hierarchical ordering of urban development represents one possible political and economic strategy for capitalism. Alternatively, I conceptualize an alternative spatial arrangement to the urban distribution through a heterarchical organization of cities, where the counterpoised dimension of power facilitates capitalism and urbanization through an alternative formation of city sizes.

This historically contingent urban spatial arrangement between hierarchy and heterarchy can now explain the numerous anomalies and outliers which have been identified. Specifically, attempts to explain the historical development of urban distributions through measures of urban hierarchy by Zipf's Law alone can be reconsidered to see if a longer temporal consideration of urban change and a broader conceptual prism for urban organization provide alternative explanations for the perpetual existence of anomalous outliers.

Building upon the patterns discussed in Table 1, a recent comparative historical attempt to examine Zipf's Law was undertaken in the Netherlands at three-time points; 1600, 1900, and 1990. The authors find marked differences in the historical urban distribution at different times and attempt to align the historical changes in the rank-size rule to structural changes in historical economics for the Dutch state and as such represent a compelling precursor to the attempt here (Brakman et al. 1999).

The authors develop three regression models, one for each time point, and achieve model fits of .96 or better. However, the predicted slope of -1 closely fit only one regression model, in 1900: a q-slope of 1.03 and an R^2 of .97. The two other regressions obtained lower values for the slopes; in 1600 a slope of .55 and in 1990 a slope of .72 both with an R^2 of .96 (Brakman et al. 1999, 187). Thus, representing a less hierarchical and possibly more heterarchical distribution, to reorient the reader to the terminology described above, of cities in the Netherlands during the time periods of 1600 and 1999.

One of the more recent attempts to consider historical urban development and organization through urban distributions was by Volker Nitsch (2001). Nitsch develops a series of Transition Matrices for his selected countries in Europe. A transition probability matrix starts from an initial distribution of cities in a nation divided into different size groups. The matrix then describes how the given cities are redistributed over time into different categories. (Robson 1973, de Vries 1984, Eaton and Eckstein 1997, Nitsch 2001). "Specifically, each cell of the matrix gives the proportion of cities which start with a given size in an initial year (rows) and move to a particular size group in the final distribution (columns). Thus, each row, for example, shows the probability that a city remains in its size groups or transits to any other group" (Nitsch 2001, 44-45).

Nitsch examines 10 European countries transition matrices using data from 1870-1990. He considers the changing matrices' in 40-year periods and finds an intriguing pattern to the overall results. In describing the first 40-year interval of 1870-1910 he states,

> [T]here is convincing evidence that large cities tend to grow faster than the rest of the distribution. Thus, existing differences in city size increase further between 1870 and 1910. The later years, however, the pattern of divergence appears to fade out. While the sign of the relationship between initial size and subsequent population growth is ambiguous for the period from 1910 to 1950, the results become unequivocal in the final 40-year period [1950-1990]. In all countries, the coefficient on the initial level of population is negative, suggesting that the size distribution of cities is getting more equal over time. The finding of convergence is statistically robust for six of the ten countries in the sample: Denmark, Italy, the Netherlands, Portugal, Sweden and Switzerland (Nitsch 2001, 57-59).

Nitsch explains this changing pattern of divergence in the first 40 years and convergence in the last 40 years based upon historical stages of industrial development. Arguing that in the initial stages of industrial development large cities benefited from the growing urbanization but that later improvements in transportation allowed a more balanced system of urbanization to develop and the smaller cities to begin to catch up to the larger ones; thus creating a convergence in the last part of the twentieth century.

However, the argument of transportation improvements alone seems limited to explaining a convergence in the urbanization rates of European countries when a major transportation revolution, the building of the railroads, had already occurred in the nineteenth century leading to a well-documented expansion of cities and urbanization in England and the United States (North and Thomas 1968 & 1973, Pred 1980, Schivelbush 1986, Krugman 1996). That a transportation 'revolution' of the nineteenth century, where the speed of the transportation, over previous modes of transport, created a dynamic impetus for new urban expansion and offered the possibility of ever more interconnected urban network both within nation states and transnationally throughout Europe cannot be ignored (Schivelbush 1986) but is of itself, an incomplete causal explanation for urban convergence.

Hohenberg and Lees also attempted to understand the historically changing conditions of urban dsitribution from 1750 to 1950. They developed a series of urban ratios using the logged values of the city populations and various cut-off points over five time periods. They begin by noting the development of a clear urban hierarchy distribution in the early period of their dataset and proceed on the assumption that this represented a move towards an economically integrated urban distribution. "[N]ote that the ratios decrease toward those of a perfect rank-size pattern between 1800 and 1850, only to move away from it again in the twentieth century" (Hohenberg and Less 1985, 347-348). In other words, they begin with a flattened (more heterarchical) distribution in 1750 which then moves towards a rank-size (hierarchical) distribution between 1800 and 1850, only to reverse itself and become more heterarchical between 1900 and 1950.

They go on to argue that this rhythmic pattern may correspond to the rise and fall of free trade which peaked in the 1860's and consider if the rise of nationalism may have slowed and reversed the process of developing a more unified European urban system between 1850 and 1950. We are left with the assumption that urban development must proceed towards linear convergence, where urban development and economic development have only one possible end point. Similar to classical theories of economic development, the scale of urban development is to be explained by a simple economic state; the more resources an urban development has access to, the larger it will become.

However, these arguments remain trapped in an assumption that a Zipfian, power law, distribution is the penultimate end point in the historical development of urbanization; anomalies must be explained away rather than embraced and interrogated. Instead of taking these historical patterns as anomalies, we can hypothesize this as a changing urban dynamic related to a larger political and economic change in the world economy itself.

As Europe transitioned from a political-economic system dominated by the British Empire, in the waning decades of the nineteenth century, to the rise of a system reoriented around U.S. dominance in the twentieth century. From a world historical perspective then, the movement from extreme hierarchy towards heterarchy is part of the larger history embedded in the movement from a British centric urban world to an American centric urban world. The divergence of city size, which Nitsch and Hohenberg and Lees identified in the 1870-1910 period, is no longer an outlier but rather an integral piece of understanding alternate urban developments in world history.

Conclusion

Krugman stated that Zipf's Law was an empirical reality without a theoretical explanation, but I have shown here that the 'empirical reality' comes with numerous outliers. To reincorporate these key outliers, I conceptualize Zipf's Law as only one dimension of urbanization and urban development capable of emerging based on unique conditions of power in the world economy. Hierarchical urban distributions represent a possible outcome of urban development based on complex political, economic, and social conditions in world history, where the largest city in the urban distribution concentrates economic, social, and political power to reach a level of population size that far outstrips other cities in the system. In contrast, a Heterarchical urban distribution represents an alternative stratification pattern where the complex dimensions of the world economy are now distributed across several cities to form a counterpoised distribution of political, economic, and social power, where each of these centrally important cities may be relatively equivalent in population size.

By theorizing historically contingent urban spatial distributions, I have argued that we can begin to pursue a more complete understanding of both historical urban development and the potential new dimension of urbanization in the twenty-first century; the rise of the Global South. In this way, anomalies and outliers of Zipfian distributions are no longer limitations to a mathematical formula but central aspects of urban development to be understood and explained. In this way we move beyond Zipf's Law as an empirical oddity to achieve a theoretical approach grounded in world historical perspective.

REFERENCES

Arshad, Sidra, Shougeng Hu, and Badar Nadeem Ashraf. 2018. "Zipf's Law and City Size Distribution: A Survey of the Literature and Future Research Agenda." *Physica A: Statistical Mechanics and its Applications* 492: 75–92.

Bairoch, Paul. 1988. *Cities and Economic Development*. Chicago: University of Chicago Press.

Bairoch, Paul, Jean Batou, and Pierre Chevre. 1988. *La Population des Villes Europeennes de 800 a 1850*. Geneva: Librairie Droz.

Berry, Brian, Joe, Lobley, and Allen Pred. 1961. *Central Place Studies*. Philadelphia: Regional Science Research Institute.

Brackman, Steven, Harry Garretsen, Charles Van Marrewijk, and Marianne van den Berg. 1999. "The Return of Zipf: Towards a Further Understanding of the Rank-Size Distribution." *Journal of Regional Science* 39: 183–213.

Chandler, Tertius, and Gerald Fox. 1974. *3000 Years of Urban Growth*. New York: Academic Press.

Chandler, Tertius. 1987. *Four Thousand Years of Urban Growth*. The Edwin Mellen Press.

Chase-Dunn, Christopher. 1985. "The System of World Cities: AD 800–1975." In *Urbanization in the World Economy,* edited by Michael Timberlake, 269-292. New York: Academic Press.

Chase-Dunn, Christopher, and Alice Willard. 1993. "Systems of Cities and World-Systems: Settlement Size Hierarchies and Cycles of Political Centralization, 2000 BC–1988 AD." Paper presented at the Annual Meeting of the International Studies Association, Acapulco, March 24.

Chase-Dunn, Christopher, Alexis Alvarez, and Daniel Pasciuti. 2005 "Size and Power: Urbanization and Empire Formation in World Systems." In *the Evolution of World-Systems*, edited by Christopher Chase-Dunn, and E.N. Anderson, 92–112. London: Palgrave.

Crumley, Carole L. 1995. "Heterarchy and the Analysis of Complex Societies." In *Heterarchy and the Analysis of Complex Societies*, edited by Robert Ehrenreich, Carol Crumley, and Janet Levy, 125-121. Arlington: American Anthropology Association.

———.1987. "A Dialectical Critique of Hierarchy." in *Power Relations and State Formation,* edited by Patterson, Thomas Carl, and Christine Ward Gailey, 155-169. Washington D.C.: American Anthropological Association.

Davis, Mike. 1990. *City of Quartz: Excavating the Future of Los Angeles*. London: Verso.

———. 2006a. *Planet of Slums*. New York: Verso.

———. 2006b. "Fear and Money in Dubai." *New Left Review* 41: 46–68.

de Vries, Jan. 1974. *The Dutch Rural Economy in the Golden Age, 1500–1700*. Yale University Press.

———. 1984. *European Urbanization, 1500-1800*. Cambridge: Harvard Press.

———. 1989. "Renaissance Cities." *Renaissance Quarterly* 42: 781–793.

Devadoss, Stephen, and Jeff Luckstead. "Size Distribution of US Lower Tail Cities." *Physica A: Statistical Mechanics and its Applications* 444 (2016): 158–162.

Diederiks, Herman., Paul M Hohenberg, and Michiel Wagenaar. 1992. *Economic Policy in Europe Since the Late Middle Ages: The Visible Hand and the Fortune of Cities*. Leicester: Leicester University Press.

Eaton, Jonathan, and Zvi Eckstein. 1997. "Cities and Growth: Theory and Evidence from France and Japan." *Regional Science and Urban Economics*, 27 (4-5): 443-474.

Gabaix, Xavier. 1999. "Zipf's Law and the Growth of Cities." *The American Economic Review* 89: 129–132.

Giesen, Kristian, and Jens Südekum. 2011. "Zipf's Law for Cities in the Regions and the Country." *Journal of Economic Geography* 11: 667–686.

Hohenberg, Paul M., and Lynn Lees. 1985. *The Making of Urban Europe 1000–1950*. Cambridge: Harvard University Press.

Johnson, E. A. J. 1970. *The Organization of Space in Developing Countries*. Cambridge: Harvard University Press.

Knudsen, Thorbjorn. 2001. "Zipf's Law for Cities and Beyond." *American Journal of Economics and Sociology* 60: 123–146.

Krugman, Paul. 1996. *The Self-Organizing Society*. Cambridge: Blackwell Publishers.

———. 1996. "Confronting the Mystery of Urban Hierarchy." *Journal of the Japanese and International Economies* 10: 399–418.

Nitsch, Volker. 2001. *City Growth in Europe*. Berlin: Duncker & Humblot.

North, Douglass Cecil, and Robert Paul Thomas. 1968. *The Growth of the American Economy to 1860*. New York: Harper & Row.

———.1973. *The Rise of the Western World: A New Economic History*. Cambridge: Cambridge University Press.

Ormrod, David. 2003. The Rise of Commercial Empires: England and the Netherlands in the Age of Mercantilism, *1650-1770*. Cambridge: Cambridge University Press.

Portes, Alejandro, and John Walton. 1976. *Urban Latin America: The Political Condition from Above and Below*. Austin: University of Texas Press.

Pred, Allen R. 1980. *Urban Growth and City Systems in the United States*. Cambridge: Harvard University Press.

Richard Blanton, Peter Peregrine, Deborah Winslow, and Thomas Hall. 1997. *Economic Analysis Beyond the Local System*. Lanham, MD. University Press of America.

Robson, B.T. 1973. *Urban Growth: An Approach*. London: Colchester and Beccles.

———. 1981. "The Impact of Functional Differentiation with Systems of Industrialized Cities." In *Patterns of European Urbanization Since 1500*, edited by H. Schmal, 111–129. London: Croom Helm.

Saichev, Alexander, Yannick Malevergne, and Didier Sornette. 2010. *Theory of Zipf's Law and Beyond*. Heidelberg: Springer.

Satterthwaite, David. 2002. "The Ten and a Half Myths that may Distort the Urban Policies of Governments and International Agencies." London: IIED. http://pubs.iied.org/G03188.html.

———. 2005. "Outside the Large Cities: The Demographic Importance of Small Urban Centres and Large Villages in Africa, Asia, and Latin America." Human Settlements Working Paper Series Urban Change 3. London: IIED.

Schivelbusch, Wolfgang. 1986. *The Railway Journey: Trains and Travel in the 19th Century*. Berkeley and Los Angeles: University of California Press.

Soo, K. T. (2012). The Size and Growth of State Populations in the United States. *Economics Bulletin, 32*: 1238–1249.

Subbarayan, A., and G. Kumar. 2016. "Overall Size Distribution of Cities and Towns in India: 2011 Census." *Journal of Applied Sciences* 16: 230–235.

Tilly, Charles. 1964. *The Vendee*. Cambridge: Harvard University Press.

———.1984. *Big Structures Large Processes Huge Comparisons*. New York: Russell Sage Foundation.

Vallabados, Christopher A., and Subbarayan A. Arumugam. 2016. "An Evaluation of Pareto, Lognormal and PPS Distributions: The Size Distribution of Cities in Kerala, India." *Journal of Modern Applied Statistical Methods* 15: 41.

White, Douglas, Natasa Kajzar, Constantino Tsallis, and Celine Rozenblat. 2005. "Generative Modeling of City-Size Scaling Laws, 250 BCE – 2005: Embedded Co-evolution in the Theory of Long-term Geopolitical Dynamics." http://eclectic.ss.uci.edu/~drwhite/pub/DougCmplx9.pdf

White, Douglas. 2006. "Rethinking World Historical Systems from Network Theory Perspectives: Medieval Historical Dynamics 1174-1500." Paper presented at the Annual Meeting of the International Studies Association, San Diego, California, March 2006.

Ye, Xinyue, and Yichun Xie. 2012. "Re-examination of Zipf's Law and Urban Dynamic in China: A Regional Approach." *The Annals of Regional Science* 49: 135–156.

Zipf, George Kingsley. 1949. *Human Behvior and the Principle of Least Effort; and Introduction to Human Ecology*. Cambridge: Addison-Wesley Press.

Chapter 11

Urban Formation: Cores, Flows, and Transformations[53]

Nina Toleva[54]

Introduction

Cities are the jewels of human civilization, crystals formed by millennial overlapping interactions, gems polished by the dynamic flows of the society. Cities, just like all living organisms, grow, change, and evolve. It does not matter if their origin lies in the natural emergence phenomenon or in the practice of intentional planning. The basic laws of society could be easily traced, once the cities are observed as a whole. Gordon Pask speaks of that holistic concept for the first time in his work "Architectural Relevance of Cybernetics" (Pask 1969, 494–496). In that process of holistic observation, we cannot help but notice cities' inhomogeneity, their bright and blind sports, their "flowers" and their "scars", their virtues and their viciousness.

During the evolution of the urban organism, the instruments used for shaping and managing them changed as well. Useful for finding and describing the problematic areas, they also help in discovering the spots and regions with the biggest positive potential, accelerating the process of integration, and lead to improvement of the urban microclimate. These instruments not only delineate and explain the mechanisms of growth and development, but also provide variety of ways for managing the environment, in order to reach optimal conditions for life and urban usage.

Scientific and Theoretical Background

The cities are one of the best, most intricate and extreme examples of man-made complex systems. In favour of exploring them and creating an abstract model of the way they function; a variety of interdisciplinary approaches is required. I use as a background scientific concepts that are considers to be related to the here presented

---

[53] This chapter is an edited version of the essay "Urban Formation: Cores and Transformations" that was first published in *Spaces and Flows: An International Journal of Urban and Extra Urban Studies* 6 (3-50.):
[54] Acknowledgements: The author wants to express her gratitude to her family for their support, and the AUSMIP+ Erasmus Mundus Mobility Program for the wonderful research opportunity.

study. As cornerstones I will use Walter Christaller's work "Central Places in Southern Germany" (Christaller 1966) in which he studied the urban structures as systems of urban structures and combined the concept of self-similarity and Von Thunen's highly abstract core-like model. The model explained the functions in the cities and the process of urban optimization. As other references I will employ Stan Allen's book "Point+Lines: Diagrams and projects for the city" (Allen 1999) in which he examines the cities in terms of field conditions phenomena. Important part of the background is also the work of John Rajchman "Constructions" in which he explores the problems of the future cities (Rajchman 1998).

I think field conditions shape two overlapping systems: the static network of solid urban matter and the dynamic-based layer of urban flows. These two systems are in dynamic interrelated balance, creating, forming, and changing each other. The static network of solid urban matter may be represented as a drawing board on which dynamic based urban flows leave their traces and actually visualize the basic governing principles of society and life itself. The urban flows, on the other hand, have a dual nature. They act both as dissipative particles, and as a fluid substance. This duality leads to a variety of questions and phenomena, for which expanding further the established background is needed, as well as references to the social sciences and even concepts of fluid dynamics in physics are helpful. Thus I place the roots of this paper even deeper in Elias Canetti's work "Crowds and Power" in which he defines the four basic laws of crowd dynamics (Canetti 1984) and links it to Daniel Bernoulli's principle of the relation between pressure and velocity in liquids. This background serves not only as metaphor and inspiration, but also as a solid foundation for creating an abstract urban model which shows new points of view different from already familiar concepts.

Definitions: Urban Fabric, Urban Canvas, Urban Tissue

Even though these terms are usually used interchangeably, I consider that type of usage as rather incorrect and give more precise and suitable definitions of the discussed elements. These definitions are visualized in Figure 1.

Figure 1: Visualization: urban tissue, urban canvas, urban fabric (urban matter).

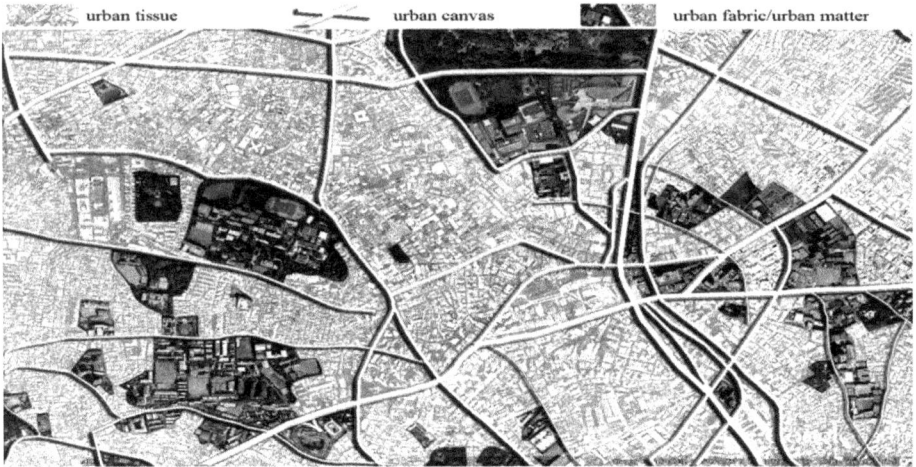

Source: Own Figure.

Urban Fabric (Urban Matter)

The urban fabric (or urban matter) is the actual overall structure of a city; the intricate combination of all elements; the interaction of all layers and functions it accommodates. The fabric is the constantly changing, pulsating, and transforming matter. It is the city as we know and experience it.

Urban Canvas

The urban canvas is the skeleton of the city, formed by the main transportation arteries. It is the higher-level connectivity layer and excludes the lower connectivity levels, as they represent the connections between identical plots or blocks saturated with same functions and similar organization.

In order to trace the canvas, depicting the intersecting the territory routes and ensuring higher level of connectivity is needed. The number of connectivity layers may vary in accordance of the complexity of the city. For example, while in the smaller cities and the villages the connectivity layer are fewer, in the large-scale metropolitan type cities, the number of connectivity layers grows bigger, as the layers of the inter-urban network of the satellite and nearby settlements, actually become part of intra-urban transport system during the process of their assimilation and city expansion.

Urban Tissue

The urban tissue is the layer that provides the primary need for shelter. It is the product of the interaction between personal property plots and the lower hierarchy connectivity layers of the street networks, ensuring the links between every individual plot in areas with same function and similar organization.

Perception of the City

In order to study the city and to try to explain its processes, it is necessary to explore its nature. Cities are aggregate structures; complex systems of overlaid static networks of solid urban matter and dynamic human-based urban flows. I use this abstract representation as a way to intertwine actual concepts in the fields of complexity, networks and field theory, and create a backbone of the model for urban analysis.

In his work Stan Allen (Allen 1996, 24-31) examines the cities as field conditions phenomena and redefines the relation between figure and field. These relations gave the cities their life and shaped their characteristics. Based on this, I will explore two basic types of urban birth in the quest of tracing how the different order of the same figures (or in that case urban layers) may actually change the overall field specifics in the city. The proposed model outlines two extreme examples of urban formation: emergent and planned scenarios. Even though they are highly abstract models, they help to understand the nature of the urban formation and transformations. See Figure 2a and 2b.

Figure 2: Urban formation scenarios: (a) planned (b) emergent.

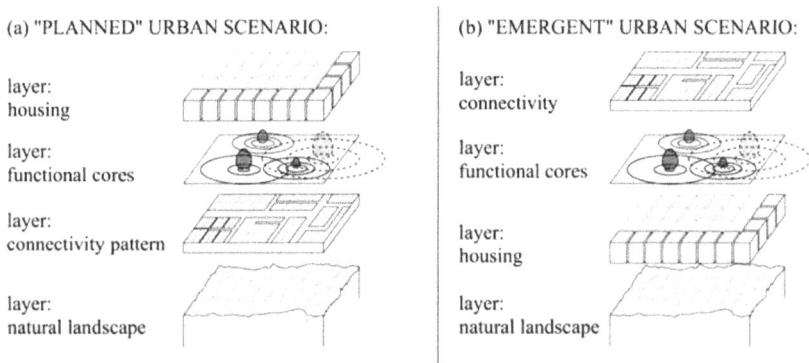

(a) "PLANNED" URBAN SCENARIO:

layer: housing

layer: functional cores

layer: connectivity pattern

layer: natural landscape

(b) "EMERGENT" URBAN SCENARIO:

layer: connectivity

layer: functional cores

layer: housing

layer: natural landscape

Source: Own figure

We will examine Figure 2 in terms of emergence and self-organization, and the definitions for urban tissue, urban canvas and urban matter. In the "planned city" scenario, over the existing landscape, a strictly planned urban canvas is laid on the backbone grid. The functional urban cores are carefully and neatly positioned. The housing facilities are treated as a geometric pattern filling the residual territory. On the other hand, in the "emergent city" scenario, the natural landscape is covered entirely by the housing layer, which satisfies the basic demand for shelter. Later, due to the utilization of the settlement, in the already formed urban tissue, functional urban cores start to emerge. Places for worship, trade, and recreation tend to become particularly active spots, attracting huge masses of visitors. The flows of humans and goods, caused by the activity of the urban cores, are based on the subconscious collective optimization, visualizing the existing field conditions in the city. They leave amplified bright traces, very much like the ants chemical trails, that form highly optimized higher connectivity layer. These connectivity patterns are formed, modified, and shaped not only by socio-cultural characteristics, landscape, and topography specifics, but also by the technological development. They serve as a foundation for expansion and further evolution of the cities.

The actual difference between the two discussed scenarios is the position of the housing and connectivity layers. In conclusion, as in the emergent cities, the canvas network is born from the urban flow, governed by the subconscious use of the city. This way actual optimal connectivity and adaptability are achieved.

The human flows were already mentioned as an important factor in the process of the development of the settlements. They are often conveniently perceived as a single fluid substance, yet they are dissipative systems of single elements, crowd-based systems of complex structures. In the process of study and observation, I concluded that these complex structures actually have a dual nature, and act both as particles and waves. On the other hand, the metaphor representing the society as a flock of birds, or a fish shoal cannot be left aside. Yet the human society is different, mainly because of the huge differences in its lifestyle. The human crowds are govern by four major principles, described by Canetti, which refer to desire for growth; equality between the elements; desire for density; and need for direction (Canetti 1984, 29-30). These simple principles transform the dissipative crowd-system into fluid-like society-substance. Keeping with the metaphor, the author states this substance even obeys the fluid dynamics laws and forms one of the most influencing and matter-transforming urban flows.

Urban Cores and Types of Urban Cores

According to the model, discussed in Figure 2, the urban canvas is formed in the process of interaction between the urban cores. They act as pin-points in the urban field, creating creases, wrinkles, and corridors, that set the preliminary conditions and governing principles of urban fabric evolution. In order to understand the nature of the urban flows and the way they change the city organisms; preliminary study of the urban cores is needed.

In a previous paper, I outlined a multi-disciplinary analysis of the urban cores (Toleva 2012). As the analysis is still ongoing, the preliminary results may be summarized as outlined in Table 1.

Table 1: Urban cores: characteristics

URBAN CORES: CHARACTERISTICS			
1. FUNCTIONAL	2. SPATIAL	3. INFLUENTIAL	4. TEMPORAL
	2.1. location / 2.2. physical characteristics	3.1. influence / 3.2. intensity radia	4.1. stable/static / 4.2. pulsating / 4.3. migrating
1.1. industrial 1.2. administrative 1.3. entertainment 1.4. sport/recreation 1.5. spiritual 1.6. art/cultural 1.7. transportation	2.1.1. central 2.1.2. intra-urban 2.1.3. peri-urban 2.2.1. areal 2.2.2. linear 2.2.3. spot	3.1.1. positive 3.1.2. neutral 3.1.3. negative 3.2.1. walking 3.2.2. public transport 3.2.3. private transport	4.1.1. constant 4.1/2.1. daily 4.2.2. weekly 4.2.3. monthly 4.2.4. annually 4.2.5. planned/chaotic 4.3.1. circular 4.3.2. linear/ directional 4.3.2. chaotic

Source: Own Figure.

The cores can be classified in accordance to their spatial, functional, temporal, and influential characteristics. The functional characteristics are rather easy to define and may vary accordingly to historical, social, and other specifics. According to their spatial characteristics, the cores may be examined from two points of view: in terms of their location in the urban matter, or their physical and spatial characteristics. See Figure 3.

Figure 3: Urban Cores characteristics according to their location (Plovdiv, Bulgaria).

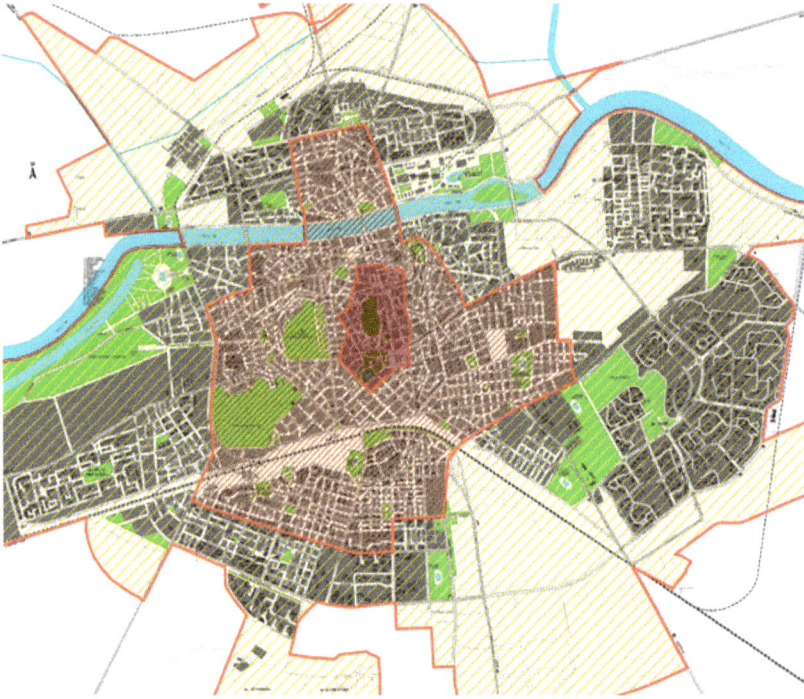

Source: Own Figure.

According to their location, I classify the cores into three basic types. The first type is the central-urban core, located in or in adjacency to the centre of the city. In metropolitan type cities, the central cores are also located near the centres of the compound cities and municipalities. The second type is the intra-urban core, located in the active urban fabric, outside the area of influence of the central zones. The third type is the peri-urban cores, located close to the city physical boundary, yet rather outside of the active urban matter. In the case of the peri-urban cores, some interesting transformations are being observed: as the city grows and integrates new territories and smaller cities to its organism, some of the peri-urban cores transform into intra-urban cores, in accordance to the transformations of the urban matter based on the urban expansion and fusion of active urban areas. According to their physical characteristics (see Figure 4.), I describe the cores as areal, linear, and spot-like.

Figure 4: Urban Cores characteristics according to their shape (Plovdiv, Bulgaria).

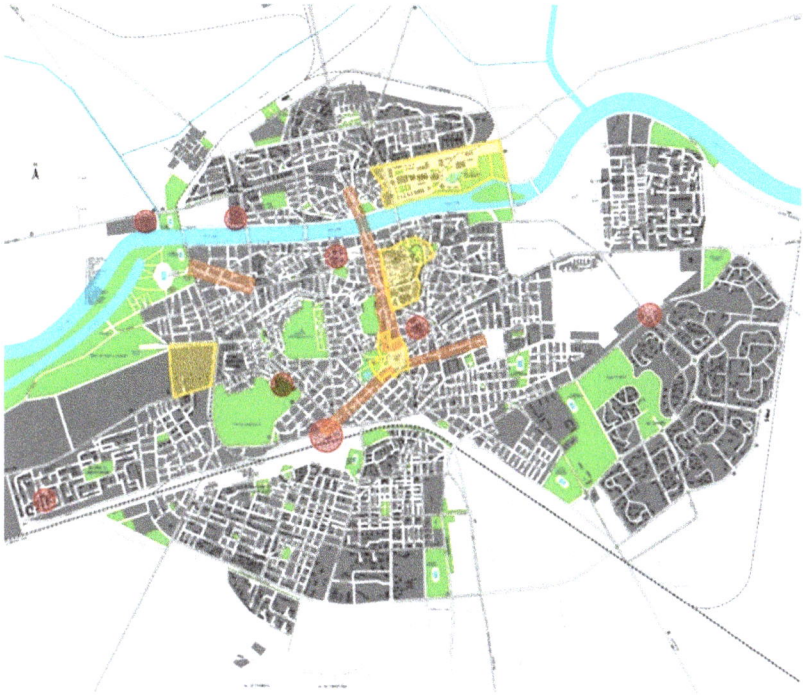

Source: Own Figure.

Examining the city in terms of static extremely complicated network of plots (or nodes), we may conclude that each node has a particular intensity level of utilization based on its function. Some of the nodes have higher or lower intensity levels based on their specifics. This abstraction was necessary in order to explain the nature of the spatial characteristics of the cores.

I define the areal cores as clusters of highly active urban nodes, forming whole active regions, which act like a single core. These cores are either mono-functional or multi-functional. Keeping up with that abstraction, the linear cores are linear-shaped clusters of highly active nodes, forming active core-corridors. The linear cores tend to be formed by nodes with similar function, yet there are examples of linear cores formed by different functions. Respectively, the spot-like cores are very active nodes that have huge impact on the adjacent territory and have the capacity and the strength to become cores on their own. What we observe in that case is that later, smaller clouds of supplementary functions appear nearby, yet they don't always evolve into areal cores.

Each core is emitting positive, negative, or neutral influence waves throughout the urban fabric. It has a specific radius of influence, or rings of intensity, with which it affects the nearby territories. A survey among people from different countries was conducted by the author in order to trace the signs of that core influence. The survey showed not only the specific radia of influence intensity of the urban cores, but also that the core's area of influence consists of several intensity rings depending on the method of transportation, used to reach the core. The intensity rings are shown in Figure 5 and are as follow: 1) Ring of pedestrian transport (Rped) or the distance and/or time respectively the citizens are willing to travel by foot in order to reach the desired core. 2) Ring of public transport (Rpub) or the distance and/or time respectively the citizens are willing to travel with the existing public transportation methods in order to reach the desired core. This ring may split into sub-rings depending on the method of transportation and the average speed of transportation. 3) Ring of personal transport (Pper) or the distance/time respectively the citizens are willing to travel with personal transportation means in order to reach the desired core. Again, this ring may consist of multiple sub-rings depending on the method of transport and its speed (car, bike, roller-blades, scooter, etc.).

What is observed is that the Rpub and Rper may intersect or partially overlap, depending on the chosen transport method (bus, subway, bike, personal car, etc.). In the case of the positive influence cores, the rings are very clear (see Figure 5a.). In the case of the neutral influence cores, they actually lack attractive abilities and are used by the citizens only because they are the closest ones. In the case of the negative influence cores, people actually try to avoid the core. The rings of avoidance are shown in Figure 5b.

Figure 5: Rings of activity: normal and reversed rings.

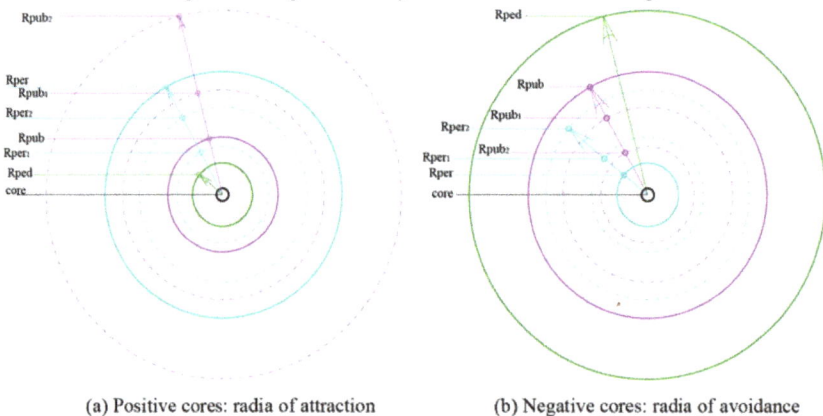

(a) Positive cores: radia of attraction   (b) Negative cores: radia of avoidance

Source: Own Figure.

In all the cases the influential intensity is growing as we approach the core. In the negative cores case the rings are actually reversed. In a previous paper (Toleva 2012), I explored the temporal characteristics of the cores and classified them as stable/static, pulsating and migrating, based on their activity cycles and pulsations (see Table 1, column 4).

Connectivity

The city may be represented roughly as two overlaid layers: the static network of solid urban matter and the dynamic human-based urban flows. While the urban cores pertain to the realm of the static networks, their emitted influence would not be possible if it was not for their connectivity-based interactions. Their influence extends along the network edges. Along those edges multiple urban sub-layers interact in a vast variety of ways, forming, strengthening, using, or growing onto the threads of the urban canvas.

Connectivity between the objects in the city is a feature of utmost importance for the urban life. It stimulates the interaction between the people and their physical environment, eases the accessibility and ensures the circulation of goods, traffic, information, and people. Also, it helps decreasing the criminogenic factors, strengthens the connections, and creates a healthy and active environment. On the other hand, the lack of connectivity usually leads to malfunctioning, deterioration and death of the urban organism. Yet the connectivity has its negative features as well. In some cases, the hyper-connectivity may lead to overcrowding, air pollution, noise pollution, traffic jams, etc.

However, I assume the connectivity is rather positive factor, as it is the basis for the emergence of the urban canvas. It is also the foundation, on which the urban flows act. In that case, the connectivity actually affects the influences, emitted by the cores. It amplifies and spreads further the influence of the positive cores and decreases or restricts the influence from the negative ones. The higher the hierarchy connectivity level, the stronger the influence it has on the overall microclimate. Thus, the connectivity pattern transforms the cores rings into "stars" and "flowers". As the neutral cores do not affect the territory and lack either attractive or repulsive abilities, the connectivity has nothing to change, and thus their influence rings do not exist (see Figure 6.). These transformations in the urban cores influence are actually the origin of the urban flows.

Figure 6: Urban Cores rings: "stars" and "flowers" transformations.

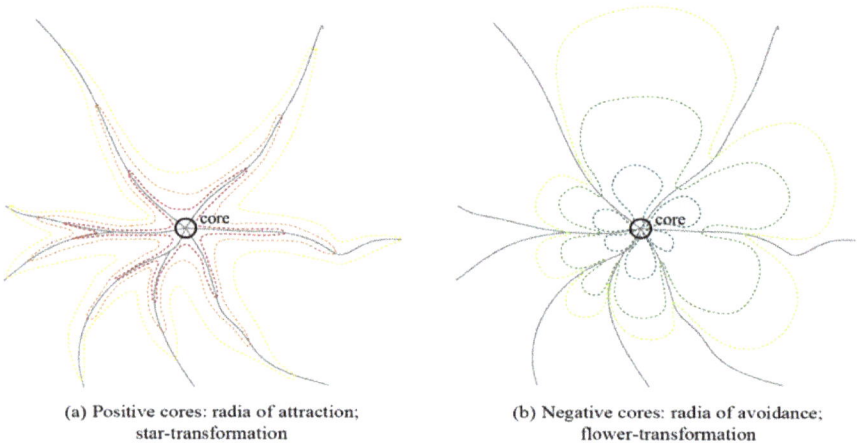

| (a) Positive cores: radia of attraction; star-transformation | (b) Negative cores: radia of avoidance; flower-transformation |

Source: Own Figure.

Exceptions

As the connectivity is not always entirely a positive factor, there are also a few exceptions, which I consider important. For instance, there are cases in which the cores emit both positive and negative influence. Examples for that are shown in Figure 7a (a industrial plant that has negative impact on the adjacent territories, yet it increases the employment in the city and creates positive influence „sleeves" along the major transportation arteries). Other examples are shown in 7b (areas near big transport hub, or subway station, where due to the heavy traffic, a variety of overlapping functions and human flows, a strong negative influence is present mostly for the people living in the adjacent neighbourhoods). In Figure 7c, negative influences (noise and air pollution, etc.) are present along the major urban canvas threads.

Figure 7: Exceptions.

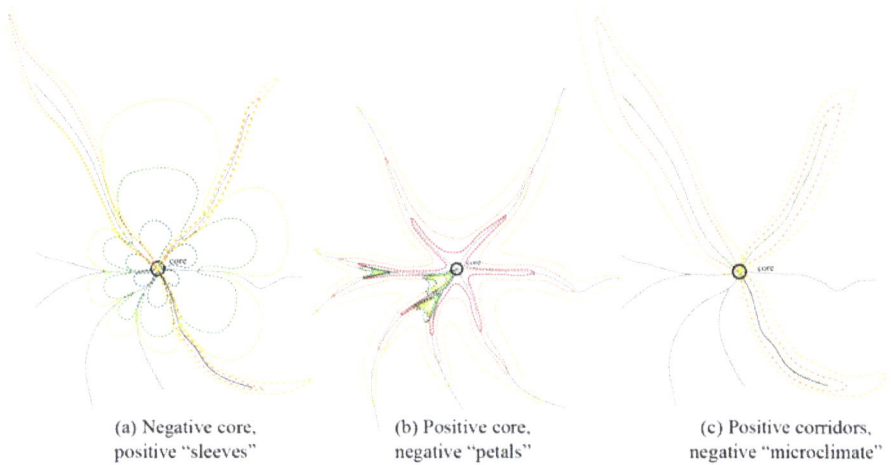

| (a) Negative core, positive "sleeves" | (b) Positive core, negative "petals" | (c) Positive corridors, negative "microclimate" |

Source: Own Figure

Urban Flows. Nature of Urban Flows. Types of Urban Flows

The flows are the dynamic layers that enliven the solid urban matter and create the urban life. They may be born from a variety of features like wind, waterworks, various types of infrastructure; through transport flows, flows of stock and goods, people and even urban wild-life. Yet these flows are just a mere visualization of the actual "master" urban flow the influence flows.

The influence of the urban flow starts from an area with negative or neutral microclimate towards active areas with neutral or positive microclimates. They are very similar to the fluid dynamics that start from area with high pressure towards areas with low pressure. These influences relate to every aspect of the human life: daily activities, work habits, spiritual life, cultural life, recreation and leisure time preferences, vacation travel, shopping, etc. The flows are born not just from human-core interaction, but from the overall urban microclimate established by the cores activity (see also table 2):

Table 2: Urban Flows Characteristics

URBAN FLOWS: CHARACTERISTICS			
1. FUNCTIONAL	2. SPATIAL	3. INFLUENTIAL	4. TEMPORAL
1.1. industrial 1.2. administrative 1.3. entertainment 1.4. sport/recreation 1.5. spiritual 1.6. art/cultural 1.7. transportation	2.1. direction 　2.1.1. central >> intra/peri-urban 　2.1.2. peri/intra-urban >> central 　2.1.3. intraurban 2.2. physical characteristics 　2.2.1. streams 　2.2.2. tides	3.1. influence 　3.1.1. positive 　3.1.2. neutral 　3.1.3. negative 3.2. intensity/operational radia 　3.2.1. walking 　3.2.2. public tranport 　3.2.3. private tranport	4.1. stable/constant 　4.1.1. constant 　4.1/2.1. daily 4.2. pulsating 　4.2.2. weekly 　4.2.3. monthly 　4.2.4. annually 　4.2.5. planned/chaotic 4.3. migrating 　4.3.1. circular 　4.3.2. linear /directional 　4.3.2. chaotic

Source: Own Figure.

The urban flows inherit the characteristics of the urban cores. They also have functional characteristics, according to their specifics and substance, which are actual projection of the master influence, based on their unique features.

In Figure 6 I have already depicted the relation between the urban cores and the urban canvas connectivity patterns. But in the context of the current study I add one more dimension to that model the direction of the influences and their spatial nature. Based on that pattern, I classify the urban flow in two groups: streams and tides. Similar to the definition of an actual stream, the urban streams behave the same way as small, narrow fluid flows running in specified directions. I point out that the urban streams are caused by the positive cores and can be visualized in the already described star-like pattern. On the other hand, the urban tides are rather vast, areal surges of influence or trends and affect the urban tissue in-between the canvas threads, similarly to the spread of the influence emitted by the negative cores.

The urban streams, a rather linear phenomena, can be represented as flows of attraction. In the end a movement away from the core is inevitable, yet the driving force is the attraction. The streams are easily recognized for the intense traffic of goods and people. On the other hand, the urban tides, acting like spatial phenomena, are mostly flows of avoidance, which affect the tissue of the city and establishing a poor microclimate in the affected territories, can be visualized by their devastation radius underpopulation, pollution (streets and air), high crime level etc.

Their temporal characteristics depend on the temporal specifics of the urban cores, in between which they are spread. They act like electro-magnets that are switched on and off, creating changes and disrupt the urban field. Basically, the urban flows can be classified in the same way as the urban cores, yet their interference may create unexpected and even surprising effects.

Interrelations

There are multiple studies referring to the network properties of cities. Among them are the works of Anne Tietjen "Towards an Urbanism of Entanglement", tracing the migration of the active urban regions on a national scale (Tietjen 2009); and the work of Walter Christaller "Central Places in Southern Germany" in which he created a oversimplified model based on twelve extreme assumptions (Christaller 1966).

With the development of complexity theory, such a over-simplified model need to be elaborated and based on more realistic foundation, and to be provided with greater freedom of development. I aim to lay the foundations of a such a more realistic model enabling the study of urban environment. It is based on several concepts, such as: the complexity of social behaviour, the potentials of network theory and informatics, the fluid dynamic properties of the crowd, the emerging self-organizing patterns, and the idea that everything is entangled in one whole, no matter the distance (concept inspired by the scientific breakthrough in the area of quantum entanglement). I consider these concepts to have major role in the process of urban development. The model is based on the mutual influential entanglement between the cores and the way they affect the adjacent territories. The aim is to suggest a way of explaining and tracing the urban dynamics in order to evaluate the microclimate in a particular territory, and to manage and manipulate the process of urban evolution. In order to do so, I have used the following initial assumptions:

> * Assumption 1: Each core emits an influence and affects the nearby territory with different intensity. In the case of the neutral cores their utilization radia are still there, but they have no effect in the adjacent territory and will not be included in the process of territorial assessment as major factor.

> * Assumption 2: Each core has several influence rings, depicted by the study of their individual characteristics and socio-cultural specifics.

> * Assumption 3: The connectivity will be considered only as a positive factor, influencing the interrelated processes and the cores functional connections.

> * Assumption 4: The territory outside the core rings will be perceived as neutral.

* Assumption 5: The rings of the urban cores interfere with each other similarly to the way the physical waves do, amplifying or annihilating the influence they carry.

Also, the model is based on the following observations:

* Observation 1: The negative influence decreases slowly with the distance from the core. It is drastically decreased or even entirely stopped by the urban canvas threads.

* Observation 2: The positive influence is drastically decreased in the urban tissue areas where no higher hierarchy level of connectivity is present. It may vanish within a small radius from the core, when the connectivity and the urban circulation are damaged.

* Observation 3: The territory that is characterized by the intersection of several rings is affected by each of them with an intensity similarly to the intensity of each of the rings and in the same way.

* Observation 4: Another factor affecting the model is which type of urban cores prevail (by number): the positive or the negative ones.

The interactions between the urban cores is the sum of influences. They depend on multiple factors. Thus, the formula for evaluation of the urban territory is (n is the number of the cores, *in* is the influential intensity in each of the core's rings and subrings):

$$In = \left\lfloor \frac{\sum_n In_n}{n} \right\rfloor$$

Formula 1: The negative cores outnumber the positive cores

$$In = \left\lceil \frac{\sum_n In_n}{n} \right\rceil$$

Formula 2: The positive cores outnumber the negative cores

According to those assumptions, observations and formulas, the core-model scheme is presented in two following two schemes (see Figure 9a and Figure 9b):

Figure 9: Abstract model of core interference.

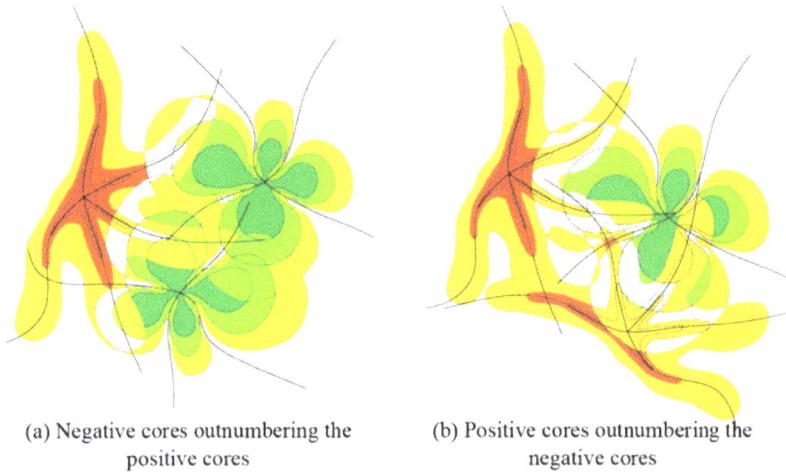

| (a) Negative cores outnumbering the positive cores | (b) Positive cores outnumbering the negative cores |

Source: Own Figure.

Even considering the vast variety of socio-cultural factors, and the different number of cores intensity rings, in accordance to the existing transport infrastructure, the formula can be applied in each and every specific case.

Conclusions

As with all abstract models, there are several complications. Due to the reductionist method every simplification and generalization leads to loss of information. Thus, in order to achieve a better approximation, more factors should be taken in account. This model is applicable without restrictions, for any type or urban organism, yet a thorough investigation is needed beforehand. The rings of influence are different for each particular case. Thus, multiple sociological studies, questionnaires, and observations should be conducted. Another complication that may occur is measuring the radius of influence of the negative cores. While the positive cores may be studied with questionnaires, and observations, in the negative cores scenarios, they may not be a reliable source of information. The negative cores are best studied by long-term surveillance and observance, and with in-depth analysis of the price of the real estates, billboard signs (Radovic 2013), etc. This turns the negative cores surveillance into a hard, complicated, and time-consuming process. On the other hand, there are no clear and non-ambiguous markers for the negative influence. Thus, we may make conclusions based on physical factors, such as lack of maintenance, dust level, garbage level, and utilization of the territory, and conduct field surveys in different daily and monthly cycles. Yet all these difficulties will be overcome with the time and are not in contradiction with the proposed model.

Even though the model is in its nascency, I believe it will become a powerful instrument for urban analysis. It will be proper tool for urban studies in the process of the development of short- and long-term urban strategies. It may be used as a tool for detection and explanation of some of the existing problems and phenomena in the structure of a city. It may be helpful in managing them in a better or even in the most optimal way. This instrument may serve not only the urban planners, but the architects as well. On a smaller scale, they may use it to trace the influences over the plot they work on. The model will provide them with the opportunity to establish suitable conditions and even give them the chance to improve the overall microclimate of the adjacent areas.

Cities are man-made jewels. They are the gemstones in the crown of our civilization. Thus, we need not just to know their properties, but also need to have the most suitable tools to polish them, to shape them in the *most minimal-invasive manner*, in order to extract abd show or enhance their glory and splendour.

REFERENCES

Allen, Stan. 1999. *Points + Lines: Diagrams and Projects for the City.* Princeton Architectural Press

Allen, Stan. 1996. "Field Conditions." In *Architectural Design* 66, 21–21.

Canetti, Elias. 1984. "The Attributes of the Crowd." In *Crowds and Power*, 29–30. New York: Farrar, Straus and Giroux; First edition

Christaller, Walter. 1966. *Central Places in Southern Germany.* Englewood Cliffs, N.J.: Prentice-Hall.

Pask, Gordon. 1969. "Architectural Relevance of Cybernetics." *Architectural Design* (September): 494–496

Radovic, Darko. 2013. *Workbook1 Mn'M: the strength of the city in the city of Intensities in Ten Cities,* Flick Studio.

Rajchman, John. 1998. *Constructions.* MIT Press.

Tietjen, Anne. 2009. *Towards Urbanism of Entanglement: Site explorations in polarised Danish urban landscapes.* Arkitektskolen Aarhus: Aarhus School of Architecture.

Toleva, Nina. 2012. *The Living City: Games, Rings and Fractals*, Proceedings, 70th Anniversary UACEG, International jubilee conference, UACEG 2012: Science & Practice, Volume 1

Chapter 12

The Shopping Centers as Global Public Space: The Case of Istanbul[55]

Nuray Özaslan

Introduction

Urban public spaces have been a place that offers opportunities to the citizens for social gathering in various spatial and real forms. It generated the sense of urban culture. It is located in different forms and functions throughout the history such as the streets, parks, squares, plazas, waterfronts, markets and natural areas in the city. The public space was the place of political freedom and democratic representation of an individual in the Ancient Greek city. Historically, the public sphere contained religious, political and economic functions representing a meaning for the society until the modernity. Following the 18th century, the structure of the city transformed radically due to the industrialization and rapid urbanization according to the prevailing power of economy. Overwhelming development of the new city influenced the studies about the city history in which economic relations claimed to have the major founding role. Max Weber and Henri Pirenne focused on the economic organization of the city in which trade was the main activity for its citizens. David Harvey follows them to understand the city as a reflection of economic and social structures and summarizes the modern situation as "Space cannot be considered independently of money that permits the separation of buying and selling in both space and time" (Harvey 1985,11). The production of a politico-economic space of the bourgeoisie in an abstract form was "the birthplace and cradle of the modern state" (Lefebvre 1991, 279). Habermas categorizes the public sphere that emerged for the first time in early capitalism as a confrontation between the absolutist state and an economic bourgeois individualism (in Hohendahl 1974, 46). For Harvey (1985)

---

[55] This chapter is developed from the conference paper titled "The Shopping Centers as Global Public Space: The Case of Istanbul" submitted at the *International Conference of Constructed Environment*, held in Venice, Italy in 17-19 November 2010. The paper was first published in the *International Journal of the Constructed Environment* 1 (4): 29-37.

contemporary cities were the built environment of the capitalist economic relationships, accumulation of the capital and the labor process.

Henri Lefebvre (1991, 53) explained abstract space in his influential book, *The Production of Space*, as it has been produced by capitalism and neo-capitalism and includes the world of commodities, the power of money and the political state. The new city scape has been formed by the scheme of banks, business centers, manufacturing sites, motorways, airports, immense housing areas, information networks. Contemporary built landscapes replaced the natural landscapes and historic settlements through the production of space which resulted in pulverization of space by the private property (Harvey 1985). During the modernization process, the places of social gathering and communal activity has been varied and consisted of some buildings such as libraries, cultural and leisure centers initiated by the public sector. However, many consumption centers indicate the public/private dichotomy in the urban area. The roots of this dichotomy can be seen in the earliest cities but differs in their nature. Habermas (2010) defines the bourgeois public sphere as the common social activity area in which thoughts and activities for the common good mediates between the private concerns and public life. Sennett (1999) describes the city as the form of public space that give people the opportunity to communicate with others. But he also points out the erasure of a live public space and deterioration of the balance between the public and private domains since the 19th century (Sennett 2002, 37-42).

Postmodern period has also affected the function, location, meaning and architecture of the public sphere. Modernity entered a new phase after the Second World War. Production of industrial goods for excessive consumption was encouraged through various information tools. Together with the development of digital technologies production and distribution of information characterized the postmodern urbanization. Neoliberal economic systems were introduced in the 1980s. It influenced the urban structure and the daily life activities leading to a global city model which has been spread worldwide. Privatization of public investments initiated the profit-oriented operations promoting the consumption economy. Most of the urban areas in the world are filled by privatized so-called new public spaces such as the shopping centers. Saskia Sassen (2005) conceptualized the global city by examining its essential properties which are cross-border global financial markets and specialized services, flow of the capital, the networked economy, global consumer markets, mobility of labor and immigration which create de-facto global system.

As in many countries as well as in Turkey, the state withdrew from the economy and left its place to the private sector following the neoliberal economic policies since 1980. Istanbul has experienced major urban redevelopment schemes compatible with neoliberal policies since the mid-1980s with the desire to join the global cities network. The liberalization of the city through the real estate economy and urban management opened a way to privatization of the urban lands (Bartu and Kolluoğlu 2008). Construction of isolated, secure building developments such as gated residential areas, high rise office buildings, residences and new consumer centers were built extensively in Istanbul which compete with other global cities to attract foreign investment (http-1).

Neoliberal policies also formed new places of social congregation such as social media, virtual platforms and television both of which offer not only geographical, national or local but also a global social network. It offers new types of opportunities for communal activity which might be even independent from the urban culture of the home. One of the global platforms of the civic life is the shopping centers which offer similar characteristics for different lifestyles. One can argue that the contemporary dynamic of social gathering is rather a culture of consumption and shopping centers are well-organized public spaces of the global society. The shopping center is an explicit example for understanding the distortion of urban public space from being a place of communal activity with political, cultural and social aspirations to a place of congregation with the motivation of consumption. Although shopping is a historical and universal experience of cities' daily life and a part of socialization of the public, its postmodern form is transformed into a privatized generic global consumption place.

It is agreed that the new life style since the second half of the 20th century is based on the consumption patterns. Social and economic identities of people are recognized by their consumption habits. Consumption is also the impulse of production in contemporary Capitalism which must create some false needs to maintain the accumulation of the capital (Friedman 1994: 2). The consumption of non-necessities creates demand for the production via the manipulation of the market by advertisers and market researches. Expanding consumption in turn increases the production and vice versa. There emerge some places to exhibit the goods and make people feel that they need the good and buy it. Post industrialism is characterized by the internationalization of economic activities, exchanges of information, newly developed communication and transportation regardless of localities unless they are valued in the market.

New Urban Spaces

The city traditionally used to be the space for communal activities of a society by its traditional public spaces such as squares, streets and markets. They were basically identified by the architecture of its function and its location within the urban fabric. But today the global city consists of different spaces creating a complex, worldwide social environment that sometimes not even need a built environment. Indeed, cyberspace is a typical space created by urban social activity at one level (Magnusson 2006: 257). It offers a virtual platform where people communicate limitless while disregarding the real distances and time differences. The global city relates to the world by offices, hotels, communication and transportation means such as motorways and airports (Magnusson 2006: 257). The global city offers consumption of urban spaces and serves the consumer rather than the citizens. The society realizes the private and social activities and socializes in boulevards, streets, parks, waterfronts, cultural and civic centers, libraries, concert halls and religious buildings.

One of the main reason of this change is again the global economy which is 'disordered' and 'de-centered' comprised of a series of 'flows' of tourists, migrants, ideas, money, information and so on (Lash & Urry 1994 in Stevenson 2003, 95). "Built environments around the world are being shaped and reshaped by the fluctuating global movement of investment capital in and out of the urban economy and the spatial structure" (Stevenson 2003, 96). This new economic reality based on the change in industrial production influenced the society of the city. Immigrant communities, professional-managerial class, low-income groups replaced the traditional working class (Stevenson 2003, 97). One of the results was the flourishing residential, work and consumption spaces of the professional –managerial class. For Saskia Sassen "all the major cities of the developed world are experiencing the 'emergence of the dualities in economic power and cultural representation' which has spatial consequences (in Stevenson 2003, 97). Marcuse argues that cities have become 'quartered' resulting in the division of city (in Stevenson 2003, 44).

Contemporary urban divisions are evident especially both in the residential developments and in the privately owned leisure spaces, "suburban shopping centers which are replacing the 'main street' as the principal shopping spaces of the middle and upper classes in many cities." (Stevenson 2003, 45). The accelerated transformation of urban form leads to a spatial polarization according to the economic status. The essential parameter for an ideal urban environment is the security which generates gated communities with advanced electronic security systems. These fortified residential developments include privatized social functions aiming to create a self-sufficient suburban environment. It includes social clubs, parks, schools and shopping centers. Thus, traditional city centers where all the city dwellers are expected to participate for the communal life are losing their meaning as being the principal urban public space of the city. Privatized urban public spaces are designed as consumption products. 'Shopping' is the essential activity of the contemporary economy. People are motivated for more shopping in the air-conditioned, entertaining and seductive centers. Shopping activity was transformed from being a mere a buying activity for needs to a social gathering. The shopping center became a place for entertaining, shopping, social gathering and exhibition area where people also presents themselves. They are the places of 'spectacle' as Debord (1996) argued for the postmodern society.

Shopping Centers as Contemporary Urban Public Space

The first shopping center was founded in the U.S.A. as early as 1931. It had many shops with a variety of goods in a building (Thorns 2004, 135). By the 1950s, department stores were introduced to the shopping centers. They were designed to attract people to spend more time and hence more money. They need more space for the various activities. Therefore, shopping centers were built outside the historic city centers. They were seductive and began to replace the traditional urban public space. The traditional public space refers to those places (usually in the city center) that are owned and used collectively by the residents. Such places include main streets, public parks and gardens, town squares, cultural precincts, and public buildings such as libraries and civic center (Stevenson 2003, 143). However, shopping centers of the middle- and upper-income classes are replacing the 'main street' as the principal shopping space. It offers a secure and controlled space being a well-organized consumption place.

They are the most popular public space of the contemporary life. They changed the function and the quality of the public space by the transformation of its function, location within the city and architecture. The motivation of social gathering became economic in the contemporary public spaces which are named as shopping centers. The function of public space has turned from being a place where different identities represented equally and individually into a mere consumption area. The former indicated a dialogue between individuals and public socially, culturally, politically and economically the latter reduced its status into an economic life which created similarities and erased the personal differences. Contemporary shopping centers are the public space of postmodern cities all over the world. They offer similar characteristics for different lives.

The argument is supported by the examples from Istanbul which has historical urban public spaces within the city center. Squares, waterfronts, piers, Bazaars, churches and mosques are some of the examples of its rich heritage. However, there are increasing numbers of shopping centers by which one can witness the change in social life. They are located outside the city center as opposing to the traditional public space which is located in the heart of the city. The covered, controlled, secured centers are connected to the city by the transportation means. They are introverted buildings and only a fancy architecture makes them recognizable within the city.

There were 66 shopping centers in Istanbul in 2010 and more were under construction. Today, there are 145 shopping centers in use in Istanbul (http-2). The first modern shopping center is "Galleria" built in 1987 located in Atakoy which is the residential quarter of middle and upper-income classes. Afterwards, the city was introduced to this new social platform and many others were constructed in different parts of the metropolitan city. "Akmerkez" in Etiler (1993) and the "Capitol" in Altunizade (1993) were the early examples having similar establishments such as shops, food court, cinemas and other recreative facilities. Istanbul, in fact, had a strong tradition of shopping activities as being always a city for consumption. The traditional forms of shopping activity such as Grand Bazaar, Egyptian Bazaar and Mahmutpasa Bazaar in the historical peninsula lost their importance for the citizens and transformed into tourist attractions. The traditional ones offer the production, exhibition and shopping activities at the same place. They were usually supported by other social activities such as mosques, baths, tea houses and restaurants and were used not only by the customers but also by the shopkeepers and workers. It was simply a place of social integration and economic activities without offering entertaining facilities. After the construction of modern shopping centers, the social and economic behaviors of the traditional Bazaars were not able to meet the contemporary requirements of the consumer culture. The changing nature of shopping activities in relation to the global parameters in Istanbul will be analyzed by the four outstanding examples of international cooperation to construct the projects with flashy architectures.

The Case of Kanyon Shopping Mall

"Kanyon" is located at Büyükdere Avenue in Levent which is the financial district of Istanbul. The shopping mall is a multi-purpose complex having 160 stores, 30 floor office towers and 22 floor residential blocks with 180 apartment units, fitness centers, and 9 screen cinemas with a capacity of 1,600 spectators and a car park for 2,300 vehicles. Total construction area of the complex is 250,000 m^2 and the shopping center is 37.500 m^2. The clients are the well-known companies of the country, Eczacibasi Group and Is Bank Real Estate Investment. The project was designed by The Jerde Partnership of Los Angeles, USA with collaboration of Tabanlıoglu Architects of Istanbul. Istanbul office of Ove Arup & Partners undertook the engineering and consultancy works and Tepe Construction of Turkey was the main construction company. Kanyon won the 2006 Cityscape Architectural Review Award in the "Commercial Built" category.

The designer of Kanyon is an international design studio founded in 1977 by Jon Jerde and based in Los Angeles. They have 5 more design offices in other parts of the world and also design works all over the world ranging from El Salvador to Russia. They design all sort of buildings but are particularly specialized in designing hotels, casinos, resorts, residential complexes and shopping centers. Jerde Placemaking aims to recreate the communal pedestrian experiences and also to meet the evolving demands or rapid urbanization (http-3). They see each site as a potential economic and social engine that can recreate the urban experience and transform its environment. They focused on making places where people love to go.

The introductory statement of Jerde about the Kanyon project is a clear example of the above argument about the division of the city. "Istanbul's Kanyon, opening in spring 2006, is a city –within –a-city, a diverse mix of residential and office, retail stores, restaurants, and entertainment components designed to provide a stage for "urban theater" and promote interaction among its residents and visitor Entertainment Sphere, Office Plaza, Garden Court and Performance Plaza connected by an interior street, or "canyon", that traverses the site and includes a variety of courtyards and terraces" (http-3).The canyon flows across the project, carving out soft curves through the building forms. (see image 1) It acts as a 'high street' and offers a 360-degree consumer experience with top local and global brands, gourmet restaurants, cafes, and open-air performances (http-4). Every 'social' facility is designed according to the type of consumption and income level.

Image 1: Kanyon Shopping Mall

Source: http://www.kanyon.com.tr (Accessed: 08.11.2010)

The Case of Istinye Park Shopping Mall

"Istinye Park Shopping Mall" is located in Istinye and opened in September 2007 including 300 stores, 12 cinemas, fitness center, restaurants, a car park for 3500 vehicles and a replica of a traditional Bazaar with 20 little shops. The client is Dogus and Orjin Groups and the project designer is Development Design Group Inc., based in Baltimore, USA. They cooperated with Omerler Architecture firm based in Istanbul for the implementation of the project. The project consists of three conceptually and architecturally distinct elements. The Grand Rotunda is a central entertainment space covered by a 75-meter-diameter glass roof. The square under this canopy is a place of social activities such as concerts, fashion shows and performances. There is an open-air plaza housing fashion shops acting as a 'town square' (see image 2). The Bazaar is distinguished from the rest of the center with its stylish Turkish historical facades and scale under the neon lights which attempt to create an effect of daylight. There are groceries, butchers, spice shops and fish shops with restaurants.

Development Design Group Inc. is an international design company aiming for the best use for property (http-5). They design new retail and entertainment concepts, hotels, leisure and resort facilities and residential units. The design firm has multidisciplinary professionals to develop creative concepts for land use to the international clients. One of the firm's projects is Istinye Park which is designed as a vibrant new retail and entertainment destination in the city (http-6). The center housed international fashion shops as well as the local brands. It became a very popular place to shop, to eat and spend time which are the forms of consumption.

Image 2: Istinye Park Shopping Mall

Source: http://www.istinyepark.com (Accessed: 08.11.2010

The Case of Forum Istanbul Shopping and Life Center

The "Forum" is located at the connection point of the E5 and TEM motorways in Bayrampasa on a total construction area of 495.000 m^2 being the biggest shopping and life center in Europe. It was opened in November 2009, housing various local and global brands from IKEA to Zara. There are 265 stores addressing to all tastes and income groups, from electronic technology to pet shops, 34 restaurants, 15 café options provide food and beverages to the visitors (http-7). The Forum has recreation and entertainment facilities such as bowling, cinemas, an ice rink and a massive aquarium which is a distinguishing feature of the Forum. 1.5 million visitors are expected each year for the aquarium. Forum is going to be visited by 25 million people every year.

The Forum is founded by Multi Development Turkey which is a branch of Multi Corporation, a real estate company based in Netherlands and active in more than 17 European countries with projects including shopping centers, offices and residences. The Company has 16 projects in various provinces of Turkey. The concept design of

Forum Istanbul was performed by T+T Design from the Netherlands and is based on the harmony with the city's historical and architectural pattern. Its architectural design was carried out by BDP from England, Chapman Taylor from Spain and ERA from Turkey. An urban square was created between the Metro Station and Forum Istanbul and facilitated with shows, water and light games and an inner court furnished with sitting and activity areas (see image 3). The variety of facilities to motivate the visitors for consumption is much wider in the Forum. It is one of the most popular shopping centers in Istanbul.

Image 3: Forum Istanbul Shopping Mall

Source: http://www.forumistanbul.com.tr (Accessed: 08.11.2010)

The Case of Meydan Shopping Centre

Meydan Shopping Centre is located in Umraniye on the Asian side of the city designed by Foreign Office Architects and opened in October 2007. FOA cooperated with Turgut Alton Architecture (TAM) firm in İstanbul (http-8). Meydan, literally means 'public square' and supports the site planning concept of open access to the public space. The center has vast open spaces and parking lots together with the national and international retail brands in food, furniture, toys and fashion as well as restaurants, cafes, and cinemas (http-9).The project received many awards for its sustainability efforts such as renewable energy use and green roof system and holds the LEED certificate (http-10).

The developer of the Meydan is the international retail company, Metro Group. This explains the commitment to create a public space to challenge the privatized character of other centers in the region (Spencer 2016, 121). Farshid Moussavi and Alejandro Zaera Polo from FOA who split in 2011, are well-known architects of award-winning projects including the Yokohoma International Cruise Terminal in Japan. They had a similar approach and transformed the existing topography, creating a new level of landscape which enclosed the buildings. Zaera-Polo and Moussavi claimed that this is a new prototype based on the traditional urban square that "enables retail-led development to act as a catalyst for forms of urban growth that can accommodate the 'appropriate' mix of urban populations. This is to be achieved through multiple programmed developments and articulated through permeable architectural envelopes" (Spencer 2016, 123). Pedestrian circulation and social gathering of different groups in the central public space is the main outline of the project to make it different from the generic shopping centers in the city (see image 4). Roofs of these retail spaces are designed as gardens and ramps to connect the level of the central square with the roofs, creating a physical continuity and also visual contact between the retail spaces, the roof gardens and the surrounding area (http-11).

Image 4: Meydan Shopping Centre

Source: https://www.metro-properties.com.tr/en/projects/detail/16/ (Last access: 30.06.2020)

Conclusion

The global dynamics of the new economic system influences the living environment throughout the world in the postmodern era. Cities are subjected to global requirements and are shaped by international initiatives. Istanbul is experiencing a development model which sees the city as a valuable commodity. New development areas with high-rise offices, gated communities and shopping centers give an opportunity to the local and global developers to invest to profit. Now, urban land is an issue of real estate and property development rather than being a living environment of a society. Increasing the numbers of shopping centers in the city of Istanbul is one of the ways of real estate investment. Four cases were analyzed in this paper to exhibit the common interest of international cooperation for economic benefits. These developments, however, help the city's polarization into small communities in which security is very important. Shopping centers offer secure and comfortable spaces for middle and upper-income classes. These gated and privatized complexes offer the consumption of goods and leisure in a flashy building. The projects usually have some local references, but they act as islands in the city and connect to it only by transportation means such as metro or motorways. As they are only a real estate development of the postmodern economic activities, they can always be replaced by better investments, but the squares, bazaars and streets of the historic city are irreplaceable.

International economic interests together with the increasing mobility and technological developments strengthened the globalization which disregarded geographical, historical and cultural differences. Generic and fictitious urban developments were imposed into the ancient cities as the contemporary representation of progress disrupting the identity of the place and harming the environment. The shopping centers became new public spaces in the 'global' cities and the temples of consumption culture. The unique past and heritage of Istanbul were overshadowed by the global demands. Privatization of public realm disintegrated the society mainly according to their income. However, recent health crises caused by COVID-19 created a great suspicion about the excessive consumption, privatization of services and spaces and the necessity of vast number of shopping centers in the world. Social distance, online communication, shopping modes and the importance of a clean and healthy environment defines the 'new normal' and this seems to be in the agenda for the near future. Spaces to facilitate massive numbers of shoppers will not work for a while. In this case, the characteristics of publicity and its space should be redefined according to the new conditions. Meanwhile we can also review the meaning of social life and find solutions for a better living way for all in the world.

REFERENCES

Bartu, Ayfer Candan, and B. Kolluoğlu. 2008. "Emerging Spaces of Neoliberalism: A Gated Town and a Public Housing Project in İstanbul." *New Perspectives on Turkey* 39: 5-46.

Debord, Guy. 1996. *Gösteri Toplumu ve Yorumlar* (La Societe du Spectacle). Translated by Ayşen Ekmekci, and Okşan Taşkent. Istanbul: Ayrıntı Yayınları.

Friedman, Jonathan. 1994. 'Introduction.' In *Consumption and Identity*, edited by Jonathan Friedman, 1-17. London: Routledge.

Habermas, Jürgen. 2010. *Kamusallığın Yapısal Dönüşümü* (Structural Transformation of the Public Sphere). Translated by Tanıl Bora, and Mithat Sancar. İstanbul: İletişim Yayınları.

Harvey, David. 1985. *Consciousness and the Urban Experience*, Oxford, UK: Basil Blackwell.

Hohendahl, Peter. 1974. "Jürgen Habermas: The Public Square (1964)" *New German Critique*, Autumn, No. 3, 45-48.

Lefebvre, Henri. 1991. *The Production of Space*. Translated Donald Nicholson-Smith. Oxford, UK: Blackwell.

Magnusson, Warren. 2006. 'The Global City as World Order', In the Global Cities Reader, edited by Neil Brenner, and Roger Keil, 256-258. London, New York: Routledge.

Sassen, Saskia. 2005. "The Global City: Introducing a Concept", *Brown Journal of World Affairs*, Winter/Spring XI, (2): 27-43.

Sennett, Richard. 2002. *The Fall of Public Man*, London, UK: Penguin Books.

Sennett, Richard. 1999. *Gözün Vicdanı: Kentin Tasarımı ve Toplumsal Yaşam* (The Conscience of the Eye: The Design and Social Life of Cites. Translated by Süha Setabiboğlu and Can Kurultay. İstanbul: Ayrıntı Yayınları.

Spencer, Douglas. 2016. *The Architecture of Neoliberalism*. London, UK, New York, USA: Bloomsbury Academic.

Stevenson, Deborah. 2003. *Cities and Urban Cultures*. Milton Keynes, UK: Open University Press.

Thorns, David. 2004. *Kentlerin Dönüşümü: Kent Teorisi ve Kentsel Yaşam* (The Transformation of Cities). Translated by Esra Nal, and Hasan Nal. İstanbul: Soyak Yayınları.

http-1 https://ceoworld.biz/2020/01/09/report-ranking-of-the-globes-100-best-performing-cities-for-2020/ (Accessed 30.06.2020).

http-2 http://www.ayd.org.tr/alisveris-merkezleri (Accessed 30.06.2020).

http-3 http://www.jerde.com (Accessed 08.11.2010).

http-4 http://www.kanyon.com.tr (Accessed: 08.11.2010).

http-5 http://www.ddg-usa.com (Accessed: 08.11.2010).

http-6 http://www.istinyepark.com (Accessed: 08.11.2010).

http-7 http://www.forumistanbul.com.tr (Accessed: 08.11.2010).

http-8 https://www.arkitera.com/proje/m1-meydan-alisveris-merkezi/ (Accessed 30.06.2020).

http-9 http://misavm.com/tr/hakkimizda/meydan-istanbul (Accessed 30.06.2020).

http-10 https://www.metro-properties.com.tr/en/projects/detail/16/ (Accessed: 30.06.2020).

http-11 https://www.farshidmoussavi.com/node/24 (Accessed 30.06.2020).

Note: Information gathered from the web sites of the shopping centers mentioned above may differ according to the time due to economic and administrative changes.

Chapter 13

Urban Surveillance: The Hidden Costs of Disneyland[56]

Timothy Stanley

Introduction

Surveillance is one of the most common experiences we share today. For instance, let's look at something as simple as grocery shopping. Walking in, a TV above your head let's you know you're on camera. Checking out, if you use a debit card your purchase is tracked. If you use a club card each item, you buy is tracked. If you've ever used online shopping for instance, your first visit asks you for your club card number. After entering it the website tells you everything you've ever bought at that store.

Another common experience we all share to one degree or another is the global renovation of urban centers. For instance, during my doctoral studies, I lived in Manchester, England, which was once a harbinger of the industrial revolution. Now however, it has become a consumer tourist center full of trendy shops, museums, theatres and parks. Marshal Mcluhan prophesied this urban transition as the shift from industry to Disneyland. Some 40 years ago now, sitting in the patio of a NY restaurant, he circled his finger around the skyscrapers above his head and proclaimed: "of course, a city like New York is obsolete. People will no longer concentrate in great urban centers for the purpose of work. New York will become a Disneyland, a pleasure dome. You're gonna love Gothamland" (Wolfe 2005).

What is often unnoticed however, is how the Disneyization of cities like Manchester,[57] goes hand in hand with surveillance. Surveillance is often billed as a community building mechanism that will help keep our cities safe and prosperous. What I want to explore are the political and sociological antecedents of the relationship between urban Disneyization and surveillance. Though surveillance is being used in Disneyland, it is also being used in concentration and prison camps.

---

[56] This chapter is an edited version of the essay "Urban Surveillance: The Hidden Costs of Disneyland" first published in *The International Journal of the Humanities: Annual Review* 3 (8): 117-124.
[57] Any number of cities could be cited here, from the largest megacities like London and Los Angeles, to mid-sized cities such as Manchester and Seattle, to even smaller cities such as Newcastle, Australia.

However, the logic of surveillance has been inverted as surveillance has developed from concentration camps to what I will be calling Disney camps. To understand urban surveillance more fully I will briefly explicate the following five points: 1) general definitions of surveillance; 2) political correlations; 3) concentration camps; 4) Disney camps; and 5) the hidden costs.

General Definitions of Surveillance

Firstly, when we are examining surveillance it's important to note that surveillance technologies are focused on personal information. So being caught on camera is one of a plethora of ways in which we are tracked for instance, DNA, fingerprints, retina scans, voice recognition, shopping habits, body mechanics (the way each person has a unique way of moving e.g. bone lengths and joint constructions). Secondly, the personal information being captured will be surveillanced by a machine that is, it's mechanized. As such it is part of what might more broadly be affiliated with the culture of modernity, or something akin to what we might call the machine age.

One of the first machines used for surveillance was an architectural building plan called the panopticon. Jeremy Bentham was one of the first to write about the panopticon which was essentially a round building with an inner tower at its center. The exterior of the building was made up of a series of cells which all faced the central tower. The tower was designed such that someone a prison warden, or an employer could be in the tower and see everyone working in the building from his or her central vantage point. Crucially however, those in the cells would not be able to see if anyone was in the tower or not. Bentham had designed the windows of the tower with a system of shutters so that prisoners or employees wouldn't be able to see if anyone was watching. Bentham elatedly describes his building as follows: "morals reformed health preserved industry invigorated instruction diffused public burdens lightened Economy seated as it were upon a rock the Gordian knot of the Poor-Laws not cut but untied all by a simple idea in Architecture" (1791, i-ii)![58] Bentham wanted to reform morals, make the economy more efficient, and had an overarching political agenda which he believed his machine/building could carry out in the most efficient way possible.

Michel Foucault goes into more detail into the way the panopticon worked by looking at the way it shaped and influenced those who lived or worked in the cells. The feeling of being watched had the ultimate effect of fostering self-discipline in its subjects. Because the experience of being watched was unverifiable, those under the

---

[58] The full title is worth noting: *Panopticon Or, the Inspection-House; containing the idea of a new principle of construction applicable to any sort of establishment, in which persons of any description are to be kept under inspection; and in Particular to Penitentiary-houses, Prisons, Houses of industry, Workhouses, Poor Houses, Manufactories, Madhouses, Lazarettos, Hospitals, and Schools; with a plan of management adopted to the principle; in a series of letters, written in the year 1787, from Crechoff in White Russia, to a friend in England.*

gaze of the tower would police themselves. Because you might be seen, you therefore had to discipline yourself. Foucault argues that this means that the experience of surveillance is interiorized: "an inspecting gaze, a gaze which each individual under its weight will end by interiorizing to the point that he is his overseer, each individual thus exercising this surveillance over, and against, himself" (1980, 155). This interiorization of the gaze creates a certain kind of subjectivity, or to put it more broadly, fosters a form of citizenship. So, surveillance, as it is defined here, encompasses the various mechanized ways individuals are catalogued and managed such that they are aware of it, but unable to verify exactly when it is taking place. This creates the internalized sense in which individual people police themselves.

Political Correlations

The first thing I want to highlight is that alongside the mechanization we've noted in the Panopticon, is the ways a mechanized view of the universe explicated by Newton, informed the mechanized understanding of the human body, and the mechanized view of politics. One of the first and most influential articulations of mechanized politics can be found in Thomas Hobbes's, *Leviathan*. Hobbes was the first to make the shift from an Aristotelian understanding of human beings as political animals, to the belief that human beings were caught up in a political machine. In the introduction to *Leviathan*, Hobbes draws the analogy between a mechanized view of the human body with the heart being like a spring in a clock, and the political body, or commonwealth which in like manner was seen as an automata (1901[1651], xviii). Hobbes stands as a crucial point in western political history because of the influence of the shift he made. As Amos Funkenstein puts it, "the most important political thinkers since the seventeenth century did not reject him outright even if they were profoundly irritated by his claims. Instead, they absorbed the full force of his arguments before transforming them into a different, sometimes even a contrary, theory" 1986, 327).

Such was the case Jean-Jacques Rousseau. Rousseau disagreed with Hobbes's account of humanity as nasty and brutish (Hobbes 1901[1651]) and saw this as a position skewed by a need to justify the rule of a sovereign king. In contrast, Rousseau argued that political problems such as corruption and coercive uses of power are societal. The natural state of human beings was essentially free. As he says, "man is born free, and everywhere he is in chains" (Rousseau 1998[1762], 5). Thus, society was enslaving human beings, and it was society that ought to be changed. Hence, Rousseau emphasized a social contract that individuals could agree upon, and in all agreeing together, be ruled by the sovereignty of their general will rather than a sovereign king. Rousseau argues that when individuals submit their particular wills to a general will they become self-ruled. In Rousseau's words: "In short, each giving himself to all, gives himself to nobody" (Rousseau 1998[1762], 15).

Furthermore, if an individual breaks the contract with the general will, because the rule of all is the condition for freedom, the society as a whole can legitimately compel an individual to be free. Rousseau puts it this way:

In order then that the social compact may not be an empty formula, it tacitly includes the undertaking, which alone can give force to the rest, that whoever refuses to obey the general will shall be compelled to do so by the whole body. This means nothing less than that he will be forced to be free; for this is the condition which, by giving each citizen to his country, secures him against all personal dependence. In this lies the key to the working of the political machine; this alone legitimises civil undertakings, which, without it, would be absurd, tyrannical, and liable to the most frightful abuses. (Rousseau 1998[1762], 18).

However, in arguing for a social contract or the sovereign rule of a general will, a catch 22 emerges in Rousseau's thought. Which comes first, the perfect citizen who creates the perfect society or the perfect society that pops out of the sky and forms the perfect citizen (Matravers 1998, xiii)? If the perfect society causes or draws out inherent human goodness, then who starts it if society is currently riddled with contradictions and evils?

Rousseau's solution is to tentatively posit a benevolent legislator who makes the laws that get the ball rolling. The legislator is epitomized as a dispassionate observer whose happiness does not depend on the citizen's practices but is distanced and selfless (Rousseau 1998[1762], 40). Rousseau says: "Thus we find simultaneously in the work of legislation two things that seem incompatible an enterprise surpassing human powers, and, to execute it, an authority that is a mere nothing" (Rousseau 1998[1762], 42). Both the dispassionate distance of the legislator and the ideal of an authority that functions according to a "nothing" or without the exercise of real force are required by Rousseau so that the legislator doesn't become a sovereign power himself.

Although Rousseau admits that his legislator appears somewhat paradoxical if not completely unrealistic in any way, I'd like to suggest that if we return to the opening pages of Jeremy Bentham's *Panopticon* an interesting correlation can be discerned. "Morals reformed health preserved all by a simple idea in Architecture" (Bentham (1791, i-ii)! By a feat of architecture, technology, and mechanization the paradox of holding individual freedom and a sovereign general societal will together is realized. The general will becomes self-disciplined automata under the panoptic gaze. The legislator is able to be positioned in the center as the omniscient eye who watches and enforces his law through the panoptic element rather than coercive physical force.

Although Rousseau's social contractualism beckons much more detailed explication than I am offering, what is crucial to understand for our purposes here is the fragmenting logic of the Rousseauist panopticism I am describing. First, surveillance atomizes individuals in order to make them a collective. It has to atomize human beings so that they can be identified positively, whether in a cell, or in today's surveillance societies, on camera. As Foucault puts it, surveillance "arrests or regulates movements; it clears up confusion; it dissipates compact groupings of individuals wandering about the country in unpredictable ways; it establishes calculated distributions" (Foucault 1995, 219). Second, however, the way Rousseauist panopticism tracks and sorts is mechanized, and this means it is fundamentally disinterested. Rousseau consistently argues for the rule of the general will of all at the expense of the particular will of individuals. Even when he tempers these statements with the belief that the two wills should coincide, panopticism can easily become a mechanism used to "force individuals to be free." Thus, wherever we see surveillance at work, we will also see these kinds of fragmentation.

Concentration Camps

Bentham actually struggled to get his building built in the early nineteenth century, but the panopticon did eventually take root in Western society. Whether we look at the layout of many prisons or concentration camps, the basic premise of panoptic observation can be discerned. Zygmunt Bauman postulates that the twentieth century may be remembered as a century of camps (2001, 280). In his view the holocaust, while extreme was not an anomaly. It was in fact a continuation of some aspects of the logic of modernity. In his words: "neither the Nazi nor the Communist vision jarred with the audacious self-confidence and hubris of modernity; they merely offered to do better, and more ruthlessly (but more speedily in its result), what other modern powers dreamed of, perhaps even tried, but failed or did not have the guts to accomplish" (Bauman 2001, 274). In orderly systematic fashion the Holocaust carved strangers out as the abnormal dissidents of society, corralled them into ghettos, and systematically exterminated them. Camps were the Rousseauist belief in order and perfect humanity brought into a more radicalized and brutal reality. The panopticon was used as the chief means to force society's outcasts to be free, and if, as in the case of the Jews under Nazi rule, they could not conform to the general will then they could be discarded. Surveillance was employed to create the general will and the great society not through the logic of the dungeon, but through the logic of self-discipline. The outcasts that were deemed not to conform to the sovereign rule of all were separated out for purification.

In order to understand surveillance in the form of a concentration camp we need to look at the experience of those under its gaze. What kind of people are these camps shaping and influencing? What status do citizens have in the concentration camp? To answer these questions, I want to explore what Giorgio Agamben refers to as *homo sacer* the sacred human whom "the people have judged on account of a crime. It is not permitted to sacrifice this man, yet he who kills him will not be condemned for homicide" (Agamben 1998, 71). *Homo sacer* is a somewhat paradoxical term in that it makes individual subjects sacred, un-sacrificable, and yet open and bare before the threat of death. Agamben traces the genealogy of this contested category (1998, 71ff; Cf. Zizek 2002, 100ff and Milbank 2003, 90ff). It nonetheless represents an interesting insight into the logic of the concentration camp. Echoing Bauman's concern Agamben also notes that "today it is not the city but rather the camp that is the fundamental biopolitical paradigm of the West" (Agamben 1998, 181). The sovereign power of the general will of the collective is formulated in the workings of the panoptic machine which seeks to ideologically inculcate individual subjects into its whole. Each subject is related to each other like cogs and springs designed to work together to produce the perfect society for all at the expense of those forced into the camp.

What is key about *homo sacer* however, is that this term creates a space of exception, a no-man's-land where human life as a citizen is reduced to biology. Thus, biopolitics is born in the conflation of bare life with sovereign power such that nothing becomes impossible, nothing becomes illegal (Agamben 1998, 159). This helps make sense of how the holocaust, and in Agamben's latest work, Guantanimo Bay, can become possible. Those under the panoptic gaze take on a unique form of subjectivity. Those deemed to be *homo sacer*, to be bare lives without humanity, can, in the name of the general will, be "made to be free" in a state of exception where "the care of life coincides with the fight against the enemy" (Agamben 1998, 147). *Homo sacer,* as the societal outcast, experiences the full brunt of surveillant power concentrated in the experience of the camp. The perfect society exists outside the camp, made possible by the expulsion of the outcasts who are being disciplined, rehabilitated, interrogated, or simply removed, full stop. The concentration camp represents one of the most pervasive uses of surveillance over the past century and continues today, but it is at this point that I want to turn to look at how the logic of the concentration camp has been inverted in today's urban Disneylands.

Urban Disney Camps

Urban life and culture have undergone dramatic changes over the last fifty years. The cities of the nineteenth and early twentieth centuries were largely industrial powerhouses of capitalist manufacturing. Over time social patterns allowed people to move from the center of cities out into suburban areas. As the metropolitan area of cities expanded, industrial businesses relocated and the inner cities slowly disintegrated. The industrial center became dirty, corrupt, and crime ridden which only accelerated urban flight (Burgess 2002, 245). In response, there have been a series of urban renewal projects designed to rebuild and refurbish new "fantasy cities." Disneyland is by and large the best correlate of this new urbanism. In fact, "Disney parks have been taken to represent 'a whole approach to urban planning'" (Bryman 1999, 27, citing, Warren 1994, 90). The Disney approach has also produced museums, theatres, restaurants, and shopping venues themed around experiential entertainment like Hard Rock Café, Nike Town and various other shopping venues like the West Edmonton Mall (Hannigan 2001, 305-324).

However, the Disneyization of urban centers functions in the wake of the city's dark and derelict past. The rise of terrorism only compounds the concerns new urban dwellers have when moving to, and shopping within, the city center. In facing these circumstances citizens and politicians alike have tended to grab at the most economical and efficient means of alleviating what Zygmunt Bauman calls their "ambient fear" (Bauman 2001, 205). The ambient fear works itsm way out as an insatiable quest for a safe clean community. As a result, even though the Disney city appears fantastical, chaotic and pluralistic "underneath the chaos there are orders; the fragmentation is not random" (Marcuse 1995, 244; Cf. Koskela 2001, 137). And it is for these reasons that surveillance is such a popular partner of Disney cities.

David Lyon, a prominent commentator on surveillance notes that the connection between "Disneyization with surveillance is seldom made, and yet this is the very mechanism that realizes the power of social control. Disneyland itself is safe and squeaky clean because it is patrolled by innocent looking extras who maintain constant surveillance" (Lyon 2002, 55-56). Various forms of surveillance watch and maintain order in the Disney city as in gated communities and shopping malls which are increasingly modelled after principles of Disneyization (Shearing and Stenning 1984, 342). In the growing phenomenon of gated communities (Gorringe 2002, 177), people feudalistically pay for the protection of their land, possessions and the "freedom" to consume. The principles of consumerism have taken on particular influence in shopping centers and cities modeled on Disneyization.

In many cities, "it is only residents' capacity to consume that is viewed as in any sense significant or important" (Bryman 1999, 27, citing Warren 1994, 27). Once inside the confines of the surveillanced space social theorists have found that, "one must always look as if one has bought something, or is about to buy" (Shields 1989, 160). Presumed non-customers (such as the homeless or teenagers) "will be asked to move on or will be thrown out" (Judd 1995, 149). The spaces of consumption become "aestheticized" by exclusion and (Duncan 1996, 129), as with the disembodied experience of much telecommunication today, the urban experience is sanitized and 'purified'" (Sibley 1995, 78). The Disneyized city no longer holds to the vision of the general will of all, but rather has settled for the safe community for those who are willing to act and look the part of consumer tourist. The various surveillant apparatuses still exist as they did in the modern internment camps, but now individual subjects choose to enter and be watched in the hopes that the presence of the camera and sensors will protect them from the strange outcasts they fear.

What I want to highlight is how the logic of panopticism has been inverted in this new urbanism. The social outcasts are no longer quarantined off to be rehabilitated in an intensified experience of surveillant self-discipline. Rather, if the social outcasts don't fit the profile the camera is looking for then they are simply filtered out of view. The mechanization of surveillance is no longer for the outcast, *homo sacer*. Rather, the perfect society for all has been replaced by the safe society for the consumer elite who can afford to maintain a presence in camp Disney.

As with concentration camps, to understand them fully we need to look at the forms of citizenship being fostered in camp Disney. To this end, I want to suggest that in this new urbanism *homo sacer* becomes "the invisible flâneur" (Wilson 1995). The flâneur is the wanderer who experiences the alienation of the city in an intensified way. Instead of playing the game according to the rules of the machine, he becomes the man of the street. In Elizabeth Wilson's discussion of the flâneur she picks up on Walter Benjamin's study of Charles Baudelaire (Benjamin 1973). "Baudelaire aligned himself with all the marginals of society with the prostitutes, the ragpickers, the drunkards. It is not unusual for a rebel of his class to identify with the 'lumpen' part of society" (Wilson 1995, 73). The flâneur is in some ways a less threatening way to name the *homo sacer* of the concentration camp. He wanders due to the isolation and anomie he experiences.

He doesn't fit the norms. His life is one of marginalization. Yet, paradoxically the flâneurs, by their nature, seek out the crowd to secure their own isolation.

> The flâneur only seems to break through this "unfeeling isolation of each in his private interest" by filling the hollow space created in him by such isolation, with the borrowed and fiction isolation of strangers. "The pleasure of being in a crowd is a mysterious expression of the enjoyment of the multiplication of numbers" (Benjamin 1973, 58, citing Badelaire 1931, 626).

Ironically this is the crime for which they are most guilty in camp Disney. Rather than become special or concentrated inside a camp, they are pushed to the margins and made invisible outside them. If they will not conform to the panoptic machine, then they will be relegated from the gaze altogether. Crucially, the inverted panopticism of camp Disney intensifies the isolation and anomie of the flâneur.

The Hidden Costs

"Safety, security and social order are all seen by most people as positive accomplishments. Who would not wish to walk without fear on a street after dark" (Lyon 2002, 53)? Urban centers are often reliant upon tourism and consumerism which in turn relies on wealthy people entering the city with the feeling of safety and security. We live in a world of terrorism and real crime that cannot be overlooked and must be taken seriously. City councils and local governments are therefore under pressure to provide the environments necessary to foster safety not only for the tourism and shopping industries, but in light of the most recent terrorist event after September 11th, 2001. Often the government and private sectors collude to foster safe urban spaces (Davis 1990, 242).[59] The means of responding to the perceived threats seem to be seamlessly extending surveillanced boundaries throughout metropolitan

---

[59] Davis discusses the Haagen Development firm's redevelopment of the Martin Luther King Jr. Center in Watts district of Los Angeles. Following the completion of the King Center "he won the bid for the $120 million refurbishing and expansion of the Crenshaw Plaza in Baldwin Hills, followed by a County contract to create a shopping complex in the Willowbrook area just south of Watts. In each case the guarantee of fail-safe physical security was the *sine qua non* in persuading retailers and franchises (and their insurers) to take up leases" (Davis 1990, 242; Cf. Lyon 2002, 61). Davis points out the way in which local governments play a key role in colluding with private industry to create these surveillant centers.

areas to create zones of safety and no-man's-lands in between. You can find these no-man's-lands in most major cities around the world. Throughout most urban centers you find pockets of undeveloped un-Disneyized sections where outsiders congregate. Sometimes these are clear ghettos like Skid Row in LA, but also the fenced off sections or condemned buildings, alleyways or under bridges. The no-man's-land is no longer policed and surveillanced, rather the safety zones are. The boundaries which mark the difference between the two are often hard to discern. By choice, for security, individual subjects choose to enter the camp and be "free."

In the process of Disneyization, urban centers are fast becoming blinding simulacra a matrix of images, symbols and glass that give the appearance of transparency when in fact they blind urban citizens from the dystopic life of the flâneur. Safe clean "'community' is nowadays another name for paradise lost but one to which we dearly hope to return, and so we feverishly seek the roads that may bring us there" (Bauman 2000, 3). But at what cost? Surveillance apparatuses are being employed in ever greater numbers and in ever diverse ways in camp Disney and I'd like to suggest that the hidden cost is filtered out of view. Do we still have an obligation to the outcasts we cannot see? Can we develop further strategies of integration which counter the fragmenting nature of urban surveillance? Of course, the answers to these questions are beyond the scope of what can be accomplished in an essay such as this, but I hope that any future conversations will take into account the political and social processes any use of surveillance entail.

REFERENCES

Agamben, Giorgio. 1998. *Homo Sacer: Sovereign Power and Bare Life.* Translated by Daniel Heller-Roazan. Stanford: Stanford University Press.

Baudelaire, Charles, and Y. G. Le Dantec. 1931. *Oeuvres.* 2 vols. Vol. 2. Paris: Biblioteque de la Pleiade.

Bauman, Zygmunt. 2001. *The Bauman Reader.* Edited by Peter Beilharz, *Blackwell Readers.* Oxford: Blackwell Publishers.

———. 2000a. *Community: Seeking Safety in an Insecure World.* Oxford: Blackwell Publishers.

———. 2000b. *Modernity and the Holocaust.* Ithaca: Cornell University Press.

Benjamin, Walter. 1973. *Charles Baudelaire: A Lyric Poet in the Era of High Capitalism.* Translated by H. Zohn. London: New Left Books.

Bentham, Jeremy. 1791. *Panopticon.* London: Reprinted and sold by T. Payne.

Bryman, A. 1999. "The Disneyization of Society." *The Sociological Review* 47.1: 25–47.

Burgess, Ernest W. 2002 "The Growth of the City." In *the Blackwell City Reader,* edited by Sophie Watson, 244–250. Oxford: Blackwell Publishers.

Davis, Mike. 1990. *City of Quartz: Excavating the Future in Los Angeles.* London: Verso.

Duncan, N. 1996. "Renegotiating Gender and Sexuality in Public and Private Spaces." In *Bodyspace: Destabilizing Geographies of Gender and Sexuality,* edited by N. Duncan, 127–145. London: Routledge.

Foucault, Michel. 1995. *Discipline and Punish: The Birth of the Prison.* 2nd Vintage Books ed. New York: Vintage Books.

———. 1980. *Power/Knowledge: Selected Interviews and Other Writings, 1972–1977.* Edited by Colin Gordon. New York: Pantheon Books.

Funkenstein, Amos. 1986. *Theology and the Scientific Imagination from the Middle Ages to the Seventeenth Century.* Princeton: Princeton University Press.

Gorringe, Timothy. 2002. *A Theology of the Built Environment: Justice, Empowerment, Redemption.* New York: Cambridge University Press.

Hannigan, John. 2001. "Fantasy City: Pleasure and Profit in the Postmodern Metropolis." In *Readings in Urban Theory,* edited by Scott Campbell, 305–324. Oxford: Blackwell Publishers.

Hobbes, Thomas. 1904[1651]. *Leviathan.* Edited by Alfred Rayney Waller. Cambridge: Cambridge University Press.

Judd, D. R. 1995. "The Rise of the New Walled Cities." In *Spatial Practices: Critical Explorations in Social/Spatial Theory,* edited by Helen Liggett and David Perry, 144–166. Thousand Oaks: Sage.

Koskela, Hille. 2001. "The Gaze without Eyes: Video Surveillance and the Changing Nature of Urban Space." In *Virtual Globalization: Virtual Spaces/Tourist Spaces,* edited by David Holmes, 134–156. London: Routledge.

Lyon, David. 2002. *Surveillance Society: Monitoring Everyday Life, Issues in Society.* Buckingham: Open University Press.

Marcuse, Peter. 1995. "Not Chaos, but Walls: Postmodernism and the Partitioned City." In *Postmodern Cities and Spaces,* edited by Sophie Watson and Katherine Gibson, 243–253. Oxford: Blackwell.

Matravers, Derek.1998. "Introduction." In *the Social Contract: Or Principles of Political Right,* ix-xv. Ware: Wordsworth Editions Limited.

Milbank, John. 2003. *Being Reconciled: Ontology and Pardon, Radical Orthodoxy Series.* New York: Routledge.

Rousseau, Jean J. 1998[1762]. *The Social Contract: Or Principles of Political Right.* Ware: Wordsworth Editions Limited.

Shearing, Clifford D., and Philip C. Stenning. 1984. "From the Panopticon to Disneyworld: The Development of Discipline." In *Perspectives in Criminal Law: Essays in Honour of John Ll.J. Edwards,* edited by Anthony N. Doob, 335–349. Aurora: Canada Law Book.

Shields, R. 1989. "Social Spatialization and the Built Environment: The West Edmonton Mall." *Environment and Planning D: Society and Space* 7: 147–164.

Sibley, D. 1995. *Geographies of Exclusion: Society and Difference in the West.* London: Routledge.

Warren, S. 1994. "Disneyfication of the Metropolis: Popular Resistance in Seattle." *Journal of Urban Affairs* 16: 89–107.

Wilson, Elizabeth. 1995. "The Invisible Flâneur." In *Postmodern Cities and Spaces*, edited by Sophie Watson and Katherine Gibson, 59-79. Oxford: Blackwell.

Wolfe, Tom. 2005. "Pleasure Principles." *New York Times*, June 12.

Zizek, Slavoj. 2002. *Welcome to the Desert of the Real!* London: Verso.

Chapter 14

Urban Citadels of Security and Safety: The Proliferation of Gated Communities[60]

Stefan Litz

Introduction

Urban studies and urban sociology both focus on the specifics of urban agglomerations and social life: the overarching theme highlights the contingencies of human interaction in the specific context of the large city. The characteristic feature of social life in urban agglomerations includes high density of humans, anonymity, reduced social control, and social as well as cultural heterogeneity of the urbanites (cf. Wirth 1995). Within this context, questions concerning how to maintain social order and security as well as safety and about consequences resulting from the fragility of public order are paramount. This topic gained, partly as a result of increasing crime as well as increasing fear of crime, in many large cities around the world much attention. Politics and urban planning seem therefore, at least in some large cities, meanwhile almost obsessed with the question how to ensure safety and security for its inhabitants and visiting tourists (Sorkin 1992, xiii).

Next to social, psychological and biological factors, human life is always impacted by the specifics of the culturally designed habitat. Interaction unfolds in a specific haptic, visual and olfactory environment. This assumption implies that the architectural design of the built urban environment may have a certain impact on the experience of social life in the city. Architecture and urban planning, that is, "control by design" (Lofland 1998, 180), can influence social interaction and therefore social development. On the other hand, the design and architecture of urban habitats can also be perceived as a visible and physically manifested result of social development. The latter interrelationship is expressed in light of increasing fear of crime by the principle "form follows fear" (Ellin 1999, 167 pp).

---

[60] This chapter is an adapted and translated essay with permission by Springer Nature originally published in, *Berliner Journal für Soziologie*, "Die Zitadellengesellschaft: Soziale Exklusion durch Privatisierung und Befestigung urbaner Lebenswelten", Stefan Litz, Copyright 2000.

Hand in hand with at least punctually increasing crime rates, but especially with increasing fear of crime, some architectural and urban planning trends are emerging in large US American cities and, meanwhile, also in other industrial nations that may give a hint how our urban landscape may develop in the future[61]. As a consequence of the experience of an increasingly hostile and therefore an urban condition that is perceived as threatening and dangerous, many cities witnessed a wave of privatization and fortification of territories and buildings. The fortification with walls, fences, ditches and the surveillance of the access points to such secluded urban residences, promoted a new form of radical segregation of a specific group of the population. The principles of ancient fortification, supplemented by modern electronic monitoring and security technology, are employed for designing residential areas, shopping malls, museums, offices, and recreational facilities etc. It is meanwhile possible to basically live a life in only such fortified and secluded facilities that restrict access to the wider public and, as one may need to move between them, to use cars that look more like tanks and are made bullet proof–just like Tesla's Cybertruck presented to the public first in 2019.

This chapter will specifically focus on fortified communities that are called "gated communities". This term refers to fortified subdivisions or villages that are separated from the surrounding areas by fortifications and normally publicly accessible space (that is collectively used only by the residents) is privatized. Access is strictly monitored and only granted to residents, their visitors and staff or servants while promising heightened safety and social-cultural security within a deteriorating and hostile experienced public space. The proliferation of such compounds creating what may be called the "citadel society", a term coined by Otto Karl Werckmeister, became in the second half in the last century in the United States of America especially notable. In citadel societies, a large if not the largest portion of the population is living in social misery while the other wealthy part is mentally and spatially severing its ties more or less radical from the other part (Grill 2000, 16).

In other parts of the world, this development received not much attention and such fortified and secluded developments of gated communities are still rare to find. On the other hand, it is almost needless to say, that the United States are not necessarily facing significant different problems than many other countries. However, those problems (as the experience so far indicates) are emerging only earlier and are much more pronounced. The movement to fortify private space and territory also took hold in some European cities and in other parts of the world. Therefore, it seems important to summarize the results of the discussion that focuses on gated communities in order to get a better idea of the driving forces and consequences of privatization and fortification. This chapter will critically discuss types and forms of the fortification of private space and the possible social, cultural, mental, and political

---

[61] For a discussion of the privatization and fortification of urban agglomerations in less developed countries see, for example, Caldeira (1996) and Grill (2000).

consequences resulting from the proliferation of those "citadels of safety and security".

The Social Reality of the Postfordist and Postmodern Metropolis

The specific social conditions provide the main impetus for the privatization and fortification of human urban habitats in the contemporary American large metropolis. Due to the revolutionary change of the communication and information technology, a postindustrial or postfordistic society has emerged in which products are specifically tailored to match the particular demands of individuals who may perceive themselves as belonging to different nations, regions and ethnicities etc. This change of the philosophy of production and the praxis of production is reflected in the postmodern culture that avoids standardization as well as repetition and emphasizes diversification and differentiation (cf. Gartman 1998). Social heterogeneity, pluralization, and flexibilization of life and career planning (cf. Beck 1986) seems to be trends that are supported and desired by many.

In the public space of the postmodern city individuals encounter various individuals and social groups. In fact, the public realm is characterized by the very fact that encounter of individuals from a plurality of social groups with different ideas about life and politics is possible. It is a place of social life outside of the private circles of the family and friends and enables interaction with acquaintances and strangers (Goheen 1998, 479). Ariés (1977) views the public space as a place of socialization of diverse individuals and social groups while, at the same time, their interaction is governed by law and conventions. For debates, the exchange of ideas and for the discussion of political and social issues, individuals and social groups need places that are publicly accessible and that are also permitting larger gatherings and demonstrations. Every citizen therefore needs, in principle, to be affirmed that public space is accessible and can be utilized as long as the law is not violated. In Germany, for example, access and the use of public space, like piazzas and streets, is guaranteed by Art. 2 II (1) and Art. 11 I to individuals and, for groups, by Art 8. I of the *Grundgesetz* (basic law) is applicable. Only unrestricted access to public space enables communication and interaction of a wide variety of culturally and socially different individuals[62]. The exposure to other individuals and ideas–a plurality that is only possible because of the anonymity and reduced social control in the context of large cities–is the motor propelling the evolution of urban culture and therefore, in the end, the social development of societies. Public spaces that are inclusive and do not,

---

[62] It should be highlighted that communication and interaction is increasingly becoming virtual and unfolds, next to classical means, in the internet.

in principle, exclude anyone from accessing and using it are pivotal for this to happen (Flusty 1994, 12)[63].

Together with the emergence of the postfordistic production system (especially in the United States) the welfare state was, step-by-step, replaced with a neo-liberal state (Harvey 1989, 166 pp.). Economic differences are only marginally if not at all addressed by social-political intervention and programs with the primary aim to generate and maintain social and civil peace. Instead, existing socio-economic disparity and differences between rich and poor are dynamically further enhanced. The cleavages between the socio-economic winners and haves and have-not in the postmodern service and information society is increasing. In addition, the US is facing an enormous ethic pluralization due to mass immigration and the likelihood to belong either to the wealthy upper-class or the lower class or "urban underclass" seem to strongly correlate with ethnic categories. Extreme cultural and socio-economic heterogeneity alone may be perceived by many individuals as a threatening situation since they are confronted with different value systems. In addition, a high or increasing crime rate (or one that is perceived as high and threatening) often exaggerates fear from often stereotypically perceived different social and cultural groups (Jencks 1997, 217).

In fact, until the early 1990, the crime rate in the United States increased but reached in 1991 its temporary peak. Afterwards, the crime rate historically as well as by international comparison stabilized first on a high level. It decreased afterwards partly due to stricter law enforcement and punishments, deployment of additional police forces, and due to an increasingly better economic situation for many. According to the Federal Bureau of Investigation (FBI), the decrease in crime since 1991 was the longest continuous decrease of the crime rate since the 1930s. However, this does not mean that everything is fine since, for example, from 1992 to 1996 in Chicago alone more than 3000 individuals were killed with guns while during the same time in Toronto (a city of similar size in Canada) "only" 100 killings involving guns were recorded (cf. Anderson 1999). However, the statistically demonstrated decreasing crime rate does not change anything when it comes to the "culture of fear" (cf. Glassner 1999) that actually grew over many years and seems to be omnipresent in the United States. According to many in the United States, crime remains one of the most important and pressing social problems in the country (Helsley and Strange 1999, 80). Blakely and Snyder (1997a, 150p) stressed that some opinion polls revealed alarming trends: In an opinion poll conducted in Orange County, a county predominantly inhabited by individuals belonging to the wealthy upper middle class and upper class, 44 percent of the respondents were worried about becoming victimized near their own residence, 39 percent were worried about crime that may happen in public parks, and 31 percent were afraid of crimes occurring in shopping

---

[63] The higher valuation of the private sphere viz-a-viz the public sphere seems to have begun in the 19th century (Sennett 1983).

malls and centers. A poll in 1995, conducted by Time and the TV station CNN, revealed that 89 percent of Americans feel that the crime rate, contrary to the statistically indicated decrease, was actually increasing and 55 percent were afraid of becoming victimized.

For some time, moving from the city center to the suburbs was deemed by many to be sufficient to escape the virulent social problems of many inner cities in the US. The physical distance between the social groups in the context of limited access to private and public transportation was ensuring separation. In fact, by restricting density, building structures, as well as by zoning and rezoning, urban planning could deliberately create and maintain territorial separation of various social groups (Blakely & Snyder 1997a, 8). Once the social problems of the inner cities though became problems of the suburbs (as mobility and heterogeneity of space utilization increased in the suburbs) and since a significant part of the wealthy suburbanites moved back into the inner cities due to gentrification, this traditional strategy of spatial separation became fragile. The "paradises and hells in the urban area of Los Angeles are located 'next to each other', Malibu, Beverly, Bel Air, Brentwood contra South and East Central (…). White wealth versus 'Mexamerica; or the 'ganglands'"[64] (Henning 1998, 54). Due to the proximity of different social groups potentially explosive conflict herds emerged. Once public space became populated by homeless individuals and drug-addicts and increasing crime rate was recorded, the desire for territorial separation and exclusion increased. The value of private space and the existing tendency of spatial exclusion of specific social groups was growing. Xenophobia and paranoia triggered cries for establishing solid physical boundaries. Some radical solutions relying on fortification and technology were proposed and adopted. "Without the buffer of distance between suburbs and city that characterized the city of the Fordist economy, but also without the fine-grained mix of uses that characterized the city of the early 19th century, many self-contained residential neighborhoods are defining their territory with a wall" (Luymes 1997, 190). Traditionally public space became at the same time privatized space for a group of individuals who had, in accordance with legal regulations, the exclusive right to use this territory. The privatization and fortification of pockets of the urban lifeworld or the creation of "quasi-public spaces" seemed for many a viable and pragmatic way out of the described misery. Mike Davis (1994, 262) highlights that public space is less and less appreciated and carefully maintained.

In order to minimize contacts with strangers and individuals who are not welcome, unmonitored public space becomes depreciated while monitored and controlled private space becomes appreciated. The controlled private space seems to foster some kind of social homogeneity of users and better physical and cultural integrity. The generation of security and safety by means of fortification and control is not only a way to protect and reduce crime but also an approach to protect inhabitants

---

[64] Translation from the German original by S. Litz.

from other perceived social problems, like, for example, juvenile youth, homeless people and, generally, potentially dangerous strangers (Blakely and Snyder 1997b, 88). The emergence of fenced or walled artificially created communities that are featuring gates and monitoring facilities–likewise shopping malls, parks and theme parks that restrict access–can be understood as a response to fear of being exposed to strangers in uncontrolled environments (Sennett 1997, 25). The similar socio-economic structure of the inhabitants of such communities or buildings should at the same time, as a highly welcome side-effect, ensure a faster appreciation of the land value and the prices of dwellings. Davis (1999b, 277) reports that realtors estimated that the fortification of space may ensure that the value of homes located in gated communities will increase within 10 years by more than 40 percent.

A completely different argument that is used to justify the radical spatial separation by means of gated communities and fortifications seems to be the desire by some individuals to seek and enjoy social community. A community is, according to Toennies (1887), characterized by organic solidarity including strong emotional or affective ties. Community rests on a strong sense of belonging and mutual interdependence between individuals who interact continuously for a prolonged time. Society, on the other hand, is the modern, more rational and instrumental form of interaction. The term 'community' implicates a shared perception of space, time, experience and tradition. Communitarist like, for example, Etzioni (1994), demand social and territorial structures that enhance community building. The proponents of gated communities argue that social interaction is enhanced between those who live in such places since access is only permitted to identifiable and often personally known individuals. Since access to the territory is clearly regulated by means of exclusion and control, those who share the restricted territory with others are considered to be more trustworthy and belong to some kind of community. The development of higher social cohesion, a community, should therefore emerge in gated communities. The necessary cooperation of the inhabitants in order to address common issues in a form of self-governance or, to use a different term, in strata councils, is seen by proponents of such community forms as another argument in support of gated communities (Blakely and Snyder 1997a, 129pp).

Whatever the factors that are triggering the proliferation of such fortified communities, the construction industry has responded to the increasing demand with the supply of such "citadels of security". The term "citadel" was originally referring to a smaller town or city (*citadella*). Later on, the term was used to indicate a fort or fortification that was placed within or next to a town or city. It was structurally separated from the rest of the town by fortifications in order to better defend it (Flusty 1994, 32). Marcuse (1997a, 247), who focuses more on the social characteristics of the inhabitants, highlights that "*a citadel is a spatially concentrated area in which members of a particular population group, defined by its position of superiority, in power, wealth, or status, in relation to its neighbors, congregate as a means of protecting or enhancing that position*". A visible territorial separation by fortifications is, to him, not a necessary feature of a citadel. For the purpose of this essay, however, only such structures that have some measures in place allowing social exclusivity and control are considered "citadels of security".

Privatization and Fortification of Residential Communities

The tendency in the US to privatize public space and fortify urban territory stands, in fact, in sharp contrast to the traditional principles and practices in urban planning and architecture. Attempting to generate wide open and green spaces, according to the principles of Le Corbusier and Olmstedt, was, for decades, the central guideline for modern urban planning in the US (Jencks 1997, 218). This central principle proposes that clear demarcation of functions and property borders of private and public spaces should be avoided. In many areas in the US, for example, no fences or other clearly visible signs of demarcation are differentiating between private property and public space. This practice, however, has been criticized by Oscar Newman in 1972 by his influential book with the programmatic title *Defensible Space*. Newman's proposition to separate and fortify space became, step-by-step, more influential in urban planning and architecture. It became a key ideological justification for those who supported the fortification movement. The idea to maintain open spaces and prohibit or limit clear demarcation of ownership and function of space was, according to Newman, the key factor for the abuse of space and buildings. Newman campaigned for an architecture that clearly indicates private property and separates it from public space by fences and walls or other means like ditches etc. Surveillance cameras and private security guards can further enhance the separation of private from public space and help to control the use of space (Jencks 1997, 218). Next to protecting the physical integrity of the residents, these mechanisms should also help to develop close-knit social networks and ties between the residents. The emergence of a specific and clear social identity seems to be indispensable for the creation of a feeling of community. Clearly indicating inclusion and exclusion by the built environment is, according to Newman, the *conditio sone qua non* (Kaliski 1994, 4) for the development of a sense of community.

Inspired by Newman, the idea of visible territorial separation and fortification of private property was proposed in the US in the late 1970s: first and foremost by the so-called "Los Angeles School of Architecture". The representatives of this school developed different visions and ideas about urban planning and architecture assumed to be better aligned with the changing social reality of the urban situation in a large metropolis or megapolis. Architecture should respond to the social problems that emerged due to increased social differentiation, cultural heterogeneity, collective violence or social unrest, and design territories and buildings accordingly (Jencks 1997, 218). Hidden, fortified, inaccessible, monitored, exclusionary residences and other types of buildings emerged. In order to characterize this development, Flusty (1994, 16) spoke of the creating of "interdictory space".[65]

Radical territorial separation may instrumentalize various strategies (Flusty 1994, 16pp). First of all, buildings can be camouflaged or hidden in such manner that they either cannot be easily seen or it will be difficult to reckon the function or purpose of the buildings. This principle is often employed for hiding "public spaces" behind walls or in the backyard of a building. Access to buildings or space may be made complicated or hidden or require the use of long and complicated access paths. A building or territory becomes, in consequence, a space that is difficult to access. In addition, some individuals can be excluded from accessing a specific space it becomes inconvenient to be used. For example, entrance areas of buildings and stores may have sprinkler systems that are triggered by a randomized time-schedule or that may start spraying water after a certain time if sensors discover human body temperature. Similarly, facilities that irrigate grass and plants according to a randomized schedule are intended to make it unpleasant for homeless persons or others to use a park during certain times (Davis 1995, 363). Access to space can be also regulated by employing clearly visible and deterring surveillance systems. Private property is monitored by CCTV and, in addition, private security guards may patrol the premises to deter individuals who are not welcome. Due to the identifiable monitoring and security guard presence, not-welcome individuals are likely avoiding loitering in those territories and trespassing. Modern surveillance often employs Jeremy Bentham's (1995) panopticon principle. Walls, fences, and ramparts, including monitored access points with strict access controls, seem to be instrumental in order to achieve exclusion and inclusion. Those who have the right to access and use the territory are clearly defined and limited–and access is controlled and monitored. Exclusion is not achieved indirectly or covertly but, quite the opposite, it is explicitly signaled and enforced. Often, the various strategies that were mentioned so far are combined in order to achieve and ensure the intended exclusion.

Fortification architecture that developed into a refined art (as many remaining forts from the 17th, 18th and 19th century demonstrate) focuses on building interdictory spaces in a particular territory. In this sense, buildings are constructed with the explicit objective to maximize social exclusion and the ability to defend the space. Some of the modern building structures may remind us of forts that were constructed during the colonialization period while much of the territory that belongs today to the USA was conquered. Such buildings have extremely strong walls, their windows are

---

[65] Additional means next to the privatization and fortification of urban life that can only be briefly pointed out here is the visual and acoustic surveillance and monitoring of public space and crime hot spots. Davis (1999b, 268) terms this monitored space *Scanscape*. Oc and Tiesdell (1998) coined in this context the notion 'panoptical city". The CCTV and monitoring strategy is used to some degree in various countries. In Germany the use of CCTV is, compared to the USA and Great Britain or other countries like South Korea, used very restrictively. Even though, since 1996, in and around Leipzig main railway station, more than 100 CCTV cameras are monitoring the area.

highly secured and difficult to access and especially vulnerable and exposed areas have few or no windows or doors at all. Normally, those buildings also feature a particularly refined alarm system and are video monitored (Flusty 1994, 20p). Less elaborated, but applying the same principles, buildings of the less affluent population are often also fortified. For example, windows are equipped with protective grilles, halogen flood light, and fences and gates are installed. These measures provide at least some protection against unwanted intruders and some petty criminals (Flusty 1994, 20). Elements of the fortification architecture are also visible at public buildings, for example, at the public library of Hollywood after its renovation in 1985 by Frank Ghery.

> This is undoubtedly the most menacing library ever built, a bizarre hybrid (on the outside) of dry-docked dreadnought and Gunga Din fort. With its fifteen-foot security walls of stucco-covered concrete block, its anti-graffiti barricades covered in ceramic tile, its sunken entrance protected by ten-foot steel stacks, and its stylized sentry boxes perched precariously on each side, the Goldwyn Library (influenced by Ghery's 1980 high-security design for the US Chancellery in Damascus) projects the same kind of macho exaggeration as Dirty Harry's 44 Magnum" (Davis 1994: 239).

However, the most influential defensive structure designed by Ghery is probably the fortification of the city center of Cochiti Lake in the US state of New Mexico that was enclosed in 1973 by a wall (Davis 1994, 276). This urban design may have served, to some degree, as the prototype for the modern fortification of collectively used urban space and living areas. By secluding traditional public space like streets, squares and parks from actual public use, a collective yet private world is generated. The general public is no longer able to use these "public spaces". No longer only individual houses are fortified and made defensible, but complete quarters, small villages, and even complete small towns (Blakely and Snyder 1997a, 65 pp) may be (re)defined as interdictory spaces. For the inhabitants of those fortified communities, physical safety and security (a central motive for the fortification of towns and cities in the medieval times) became the key criteria for home purchase (Blakely and Snyder 1997b, 85). Fortified communities offer some kind of privacy and some protection from crime and bumping into strangers that may by chance stroll around the neighborhood. Those communities offer (even though only to a limited degree) a sphere of mental relief from the omnipresent fear of becoming victimized. It does not seem to be surprising that the popularity of gated communities increased at times of rising fear from crime and social unrest (Blakely and Snyder 1997a, 75).

It was assumed that, in 1997, approximately 20.000 of such fortified or gated communities with around 3 million households existed in the USA. According to these estimates, around 8 million US-Americans were, at that time, seeking refuge in such compounds from social problems of urbanization and a social reality that is perceived to be dangerous (Blakely and Snyder 1997a, 7). However, it is difficult to provide precise data about this development since the number of such establishments and their inhabitants changes all the time (Blakely and Snyder 1997, 180). The dynamics of the change in the built environment becomes clear, however, as in 1988, for example, around 1/3 of all of the 140 master-planned new communities located in Orange County (greater Los Angeles) were fortified gated communities. Within only five years, the number of gated or fortified communities had doubled (Blakely and Snyder1997a, 7). Meanwhile such gated communities became in urban and suburban areas in the USA quite ubiquitous features. Smaller towns regularly feature such secluded, fortified communities. Gated communities are located all throughout the United States, but they are especially concentrated in the South-West, South and South-East. California, and Florida as well as Texas feature a particularly large number of such developments (Blakely and Snyder 1997b, 87). According to estimates, in 1994, more than 500.000 individuals resided in such fortified or gated communities (Blakely & Snyder 1995, 46). It is clear, that gated communities and the fortification architecture are atavisms of the past (Helsley and Strange 199, 102). Gated communities were omnipresent in the distant past once permanent settlements emerged, as the reconstructed stone age gated community located at Lake Constance in Germany illustrates. Life was dangerous and villages and towns needed to be fortified. The proliferation and concentration of modern versions of gated communities like, for example, in the North of San Antonio, are reshaping the build environment as, for example, "in the rapidly developing north-central corridor of San Antonio, at least 16 separate gated neighborhoods have been built in the past 10 years, forming a landscape dominated by continuous walls and controlled access on either side of the arterial roads that cross the area" (Luymes 1997: 197). Those fortified and gated communities emerged first in the urban areas in the US (Blakely & Snyder 1997a, 5) and their concentration tends to be higher in or close to large urban agglomerations.

After the fortification of the urban periphery the fortification of buildings and living quarters of the inner urban cities started to take place. Apartments, condominium and town home developments in the inner cities are supposed to become, as they feature walls and access controls, more attractive (Rosen 1993: F1). Mike Davis (1999a, 286) describes in his book the example of how an approximately 178 acres facility with urban town houses and apartment complexes in which singles, retirees and families reside has been redeveloped as interdictory space. The property owned by Forest City Enterprise is called "Park La Brea" and located in Los Angeles. It was fenced in order to enhance "social control" (Davis 1999a: 286). In addition, individual condominiums in the inner cities are to some degree build or refitted to resemble small forts. In Westwood, located in larger Los Angeles, the condo "The Wilshire" offered secured suites ranging from 600.000 – 3.9 Mio US Dollars. It boasts CCTV, electronic fences, private elevators to individual suites and security guards plus a heliport (Henning 1998, 60).

Living in gated communities was in the US, for most of the time, though only a reality for particularly privileged groups and individuals. The first fortified community in the US, in which traditionally public space was privatized, was likely the suburb of Tuxedo Park built in 1885 near New York. The wealthy inhabitants attempted by creating their own microcosm to remove themselves from the ugly side of the rapid urban industrialization. Within the 20th century, similar facilities were inhabited by those who belonged to the new American aristocracy in New England and, later, in Hollywood, where the new caste of movie celebrities resided (Blakely and Snyder 1997a, 4). The walls, fences and monitored gates symbolize the socio-economic status of the inhabitants and serve at the same time as structures that are intended to reduce or prevent crime. The main purpose of those facilities is to implement social inclusion or exclusion: likeminded individuals and socio-economically similarly households prefer to live in the same neighborhood. Today, a majority of the newly constructed modern citadels of security in the US are though for those who belong to the middle class. They are for executives, professionals as well as wealthy retirees and often feature, next to monitored entrances and fences or walls, common facilities like swimming pools or tennis facilities etc. (Blakely and Snyder 1997a, 91). However, an increasing number of gated communities or fortified communities are also built for those who belong to the lower income class.

Next to newly constructed fortified settlements, some existing residential quarters applied to build walls or fences and/or erect street blockades to separate themselves from their surrounding areas (Blakely and Snyder 1997b, 86). In Los Angeles alone, in 1994, approximately 147 applications that may have resulted in some street closures were in the final round of the decision-making process (Flusty 1994, 22). But there was also some resistance, for example, the planned enclosure of "Whitley Heights", part of the film and artist residential community of Hollywood was met with opposition. Gradually, the area around the Hollywood Boulevard, below "Whitely Heights", that is located on a hilly area, had deteriorated to a place where prostitution and drug dealing flourished. Therefore, in 1986, the community of "Whitley Heights" petitioned to close off their streets and fence their residential area. This desire was less driven by a rapid increase of actual crime in the residential neighborhoods but rather by the desire to better control the territory. However, many individuals who lived in the shadow of the residences on the hill rallied against it. The group CAGE ("Citizens Against Gated Enclaves") filed a lawsuit against the community being fenced off. Since the courts declared the streets and walkways located in "Whitely Heights" to be public space, requiring public access, the already installed gates were at the end not permitted to be closed (Blakely & Snyder 1998a, 104 pp). In other suburbs, like in the San Fernando Valley, some communities and residential blocks were also fenced long after they have been built. Davis (1994, 286) mentioned that a single developer fenced and fortified more than 100 living quarters and emphasized that the demand for more safety and security seems not to decrease. According to Davis, the demand for gated and fenced communities is threefold compared to demand for residential developments that are not sealed off.

Where it is difficult or impossible to enclose and regulate access to a particular community or territory due to legal and economic reasons, the residents themselves tend to hire private security guards to patrol the neighborhood and/or establish a neighborhood watch program. Those programs are intended to enhance monitoring and reporting suspicious behavior to the police in order to increase the subjective feeling of safety and security (Davis 1999b, 275). Los Angeles alone features several thousands of such neighborhood watch program associations. Often, such neighborhood watch areas are featuring signs that threaten criminals with "armed response". Individual homes are equipped with flood lights; in addition, private security guards patrol the area and monitor, of course, those homes who pay a fee for it (Flusty 1994, 9). Even though access to traditionally public space like piazzas, sidewalks, and streets is not exclusively reserved for the inhabitants, the "militarization" (Davis 1994, 259) of space is also a strategy to limit public use.

Gated communities are not only found in the US though: next to approximately 50+ gated communities in Canada (Helsley and Strange 1999, 81), similar developments may be identified in large metropolitan areas all around the world. In England, for example, several of such gated communities, called compounds, exist. Still, so far, especially compared with the development of such facilities in the United States, few examples of gated communities exist in the UK. The so called "Bryant Mills" complex in Bethnal Green, a former factory that has been transformed into gentrified luxury lofts, qualifies rather as a larger condominium. Similar developments may be found in the London Docklands (Oc and Riesdell 1997, 160). In the West of London, however, at least one community may be found that does qualify as a gated community. Behind fences several large homes are clustered together. Access to those homes is via one access point that has a security booth and is monitored. Next to some streets and a "public" square that the inhabitants share, however, no other amenities are shared by the residents in this compound. It should be emphasized that the phenomenon of gated communities or the radical fortification or urban life is so far, at least compared with other modern industrialized countries, especially proliferating in the US: but it is not an exclusive feature of that country.

Independent from historical, geographical and cultural contingencies, fortified urban residences and communities are characterized by some specific features. Those features can be instrumentalize to develop a typology of community fortification. Based on the stringency of access control (strict vs. loose) and degree of seclusion (radical vs. indicated) Luymes (1997, 198) developed a typology of fortified and privatized urban space. Hand in hand with increasing control and fortification, the degree of perceived security and safety increases and–at least according to the theoretical assumptions–the sense of community should also be increasing. Normally, the degree of seclusion and fortification increases with the prices for the units located in such compounds. It correlates with economic wealth and the desire of the residents to feel safe and secure. Even within one and the same gated community different degrees of safety, exclusion and fortification may be found. For example, in one gated community near San Antonio (US), especially expensive and exclusive residences are located in a sub-area that is separated from the rest of the gated community by a wall and it features stricter access controlling and monitoring. The whole gated community is surrounded by a perimeter, but access to the whole compound is not monitored by private security guards in contrast to the sub-development within the gated community (Luymes 1997, 198 pp).

Blakely & Snyder (1997b, 89 pp) also differentiated various kinds of gated communities–focusing on the primary motives of their inhabitants–in order to generate a one-dimensional typology of fortified space. In so called "*life-style*" communities, retirees and individuals who share a passion for a particular lifestyle or sports, like golf, seek to find some kind community and separation from outsiders. The purpose of such communities is to primarily control the social composition of the neighborhood. Many of the wealthy residents live only for some time in such communities as it is often only their second residence. In gated communities for seniors, age restrictions of ownership as well as gates and walls create exclusive cocoons for retirees. For example, for "Leisure World" in Silver Springs, Maryland, private security personnel is monitoring public buses that serve the compound in order to ensure that unwanted individuals are not using the public buses. The perimeter of "Leisure World" features some walls, fences, ditches, barricades and gates. Some of such compounds, like "Leisure World", feature hundreds of inhabitants that reside in homes that are master planned and intended for a particular section of the population who share a specific life-style and that comes with clubs and activities that are exclusively reserved for the inhabitants (Blakely and Snyder 1997a, 49p). Other fortified communities that are more exclusive attract especially wealthy individuals who enjoy a particular fancy lifestyle. A prototypical compound of such a gated community may be "Blackhawk" near San Francisco. It features, next to several club houses and other community amenities, like Tennis courts and a Golf range, homes that vary in price from several thousands to several million US dollars. Residents are top athletes, computer professionals and executives. "Blackhawk" features also three particularly exclusive and heavily fortified and monitored sub-divisions. Some have their own gates that are monitored by security guards while access to others is only electronically controlled (Blakely and Snyder 1997a, 58). In so called "*elite communities*" on the other hand, individuals who belong to the wealthy upper class, celebrities and top executives or highly paid professionals, usually are not much interested in shareing leisure facilities. Some Hollywood celebrities or top athletes and other members of the new American aristocracy reside in such kind of very exclusive gated compounds. In addition, Blakely and Snyder (1997a, 74 pp) also mention that some gated communities are especially attractive for top-earning doctors and lawyers. More recently, gated community developments are also targeting the lower middle class. In such compounds, access is often regulated with electronic gates, and homes are often sold in a range between app. 150.000 – 250.000 Dollars.

The last type of such fortified enclaves distinguished by Blakely and Snyder (1997a) are termed by the authors "*security zones*". Individuals belonging to the upper lower class and lower middle class are driven to fortify their homes or residential block retrospectively with barricades and other simple means of fortifications due to their virulent fear of crime. In addition, poorer living areas in the inner cities or residential blocks who employ various means to deter drug dealers and prostitutes or attempt to prevent random drive-by shootings (Blakely and Snyder 1997a: 100) belong to these types of security zones.

Based on this typology, it is obvious that access to different types of gated communities primarily depend on the net-worth of individuals who live behind those gates and fences. Wealth correlates in the United States, however, still strongly with specific ethnicities. According to Blakely and Snyder (1997a, 148) individuals who seek refuge behind walls, gates and fences seek primarily a place safe from crime and want to be separated from the wider public. It is clear that different kinds of individuals are concentrated in different types of gated communities.

Implications of the Proliferation of Gated Communities

Since access to citadels of safety and security, i.e. gated communities and fortified condos and other buildings, is only available for those who pay for it, physical safety is redefined as a private good. In accordance with this privatization tendency, non-marketable rights seem to decline at the same time. An urban society is developing that Davis (1994, 260) characterizes as being split in fortified pockets of glittering wealth and derelict areas where the police is crashing down on the criminalized poor. The proliferation of fortified space has had a significant impact on social interaction. Sections of the urban space become "interdictory spaces" that are, like a patchwork carpet, dotting the city map. Mike Davis (1999b, 227) elaborated on a new political geography of the urban metropolitan area using the example of Los Angeles. Los Angeles may be considered, according to Davis, as the archetype of the large metropolis of the future. It is characterized by various zones of citadels of security, from "gang free parks" to "drug free zones" and areas with "neighborhood watch" as well as "armed response" signs and "gated affluent suburbs". Those citadels offer, at various spots in the large city, zones of relative security and safety within a deteriorated public space, accessible only for those who are able and willing to pay for it. It may be an exaggeration to call them private little paradises within a wider area of hell, so to speak, but these terms highlight the stark contrast between the perception of living inside or outside of the "citadels of security".

The result of this tendency to redesign space to defend social status and physical integrity leads to the spatial segregation of individuals into groups based on their financial means and socio-economic status (Flusty 1994, 46). This phenomenon is, however, not really a novelty. But since security and safety needs to be purchased, the basic principle of any democratic state and the social contract upon which it is build is being undermined. The state must guarantee every citizen, independent from the economic situation and participation in the production and consumption process, at least one basic good: the physical integrity or safety of the person. Hobbes (1965) perceived the task of the state first and foremost in ensuring internal peace–this is the main reason that individuals have agreed to the social contract. The state claims the monopoly of legitimate physical force and protects the physical integrity of its citizen while prosecuting those who may violate this basic right. The social consequences of the proliferation of interdictory spaces have been explained from the perspective of the social contract by Blakely and Snyder (1997b, 85 p) as follows:

> The forting-up phenomenon has enormous policy consequences. By allowing some citizens to internalize and to exclude others from sharing in their economic privilege, it aims directly at the conceptual base of community and citizenship in America. The old notion of community mobility is torn apart by these changes in community patterns. What is the measure of nationhood when the division between neighborhoods requires armed patrols and electric fencing to keep out other citizens? When public services and even local government are privatized, when the community of responsibility stops at the subdivision gates, what happens to the function and the very idea of democracy? In short, can this nation fulfill its social contract in the absence of the social contract?[66]

The privatized and fortified communities are intended to provide autonomously and independently from state authorities for their security and safety, as well as collective services like, for example, street maintenance and garbage collection within their walled-in area. In some of those gated communities, an extensive privatized system exists that may include private schools, playgrounds, parks etc. promising safety for all those who can afford to pay extra for it. The less affluent are excluded from these services and remain dependent on the public services that are, often, at least in the USA, considered or in fact inferior to private services. Not surprisingly, the inhabitants of gated communities often request to be exempted from certain taxes they have to pay to the city. The rationale for this demand is their claim that they are not using some of the services provided by the public authorities. A so called "cocoon citizenship" (Henning 1998, 52) emerges that is characterized by the fact that individuals share little with their neighbors outside of the walls and fences or little with the whole social and political system. This undermines the very concept of the civil society, the organized interaction with other citizens as well as social responsibility and solidarity (Blakely and Snyder 1997b, 95).

It is also problematic that the potential interaction of individuals belonging to different social and cultural groups is inhibited or even completely eliminated as a result of this development. The public is the realm for interaction, conflict, confrontation, and stimulation of life in the context of exposure to different ideas and perspectives (Bickford 2000, 257). Rowe (1991, 39) therefore claims that the spatial separation of individuals make it more difficult to take the perspectives of others. He points out that this is not only detrimental for individual development but also problematic for social development.

---

[66] Smith et al (1997, 324), however, see this development way less dramatically than Blakely and Snyder.

Life in so called citadels of security can in fact result in or correlate with mental trauma. Blakely and Snyder (1997a, 138) wrote:

> In socially isolated environments, social distance leads to stereotyping and misunderstanding, which in turn leads to fear and even greater distance. A resident in one of our focus groups exemplified this dynamic when she told us that she never left her downtown San Francisco office building, even for lunch, for fear of the people on the streets. Her building is located on a central street of department stores and offices populated at lunch hour mainly by businesspeople and shoppers. But because it is a public space where anyone may go, it is too uncontrolled for her comfort, too unpredictable. Unlike her gated suburb, its openness increases the vulnerability she already feels to an unacceptable level.

Even though this may be an extreme case, many individuals may develop similar pathological attitudes. Due to fear from being exposed to physical and cultural danger (agoraphobia) they avoid public and uncontrollable spaces. Life in gated communities has a self-reinforcing impact on existing fear of public space. The compulsory fixation on security and safety increases fear since the walls and other fortification mechanisms reinforce the assumption that the outside world is potentially more dangerous than the secured world within the compounds. "In such bunker-style communities, the walls, moats, guarded gates, and security cameras convey an impression of a fortress and of a menacing presence beyond the walls. A fixation on security amplifies fear" (Judd 1995: 161).

However, the luxury to enjoy private wealth behind walls and gates while, at the same time, others need to share and use deteriorating public space, comes with a loss of freedom of mobility. A relative secure and safe life appears to exist only in fortified spaces and buildings. The various "citadels of security" that exist at different places in the city (e.g. for consumption and recreation) are interconnected by highways and skyways. However, travelling between those islands of safety may be dangerous. Individuals may be warned not to stop even at red traffic lights in some "no-go-areas" in some of the cities in the United States. A portion of the population accepts that their mobility is limited in exchange for assumed safety and security. Others are, due to the creation of interdictory spaces, robbed of their constitutional right of freedom of movement and assembly. It results in a territorial inequality in which the rich can buy access to small "paradises" while the poor have no choice but to use impoverished public space (Flusty 1994, 15). The constructed environment with "citadels of security" contributes to segregation and a modern version of territorial apartheid emerges. The vision of public space that Olmstedt and others shared is carried to its grave: public parks and space should bring individuals from different social classes, groups and ethnicities together and serve as a social safety valve. It is not surprising that Davis (1994, 263) points out that the USA today looks rather like Victorian England when it comes to social mobility and that, in Los Angeles at least, real democratic room shared by all has become a rather rare phenomenon (Davis 1994, 263).

The question emerges whether the cultural, mental, social and political costs are at least from a functional perspective justified. Since gated communities create clearly visible boundaries and collective issues are addressed by the owners within the so called CIDs[67] (common interest developments) groups, it has been argued that a sense of community and shared identity should emerge. Some empirical studies had, therefore, the objective to see whether such a sense of community in fact actually emerges. In a study conducted by Blakely and Snyder (1997a, 130 pp), focusing on those who live in gated communities, 64 percent of the respondents indicated that they view their living situation as comfortable. However, only 8 percent felt that there was particular close social interaction between the residents. An astonishing 28 percent indicated that there are no social and emotional ties and that everyone is basically only caring about themselves. Only 1/3rd of the respondents felt that the sense of community in the gated compounds is more intense than outside of their community. These results therefore contradict the assumption that territorial exclusion is intensifying the sense of community of those who live together behind fences or walls.

Blakely and Snyder (1997a, 15 pp) also revealed that, if one compares the development of the market values of the properties in gated communities and other properties, the assumption that real estate value in gated communities is higher, is not necessarily reflected by the numbers. The authors have compared the value of comparable homes outside of gated communities within a diameter of app. 4 kms of gated communities in Orange County from 1991-1995. According to their study, no significant differences in the sales values were found and, in fact, homes that were located in gated communities showed even a somewhat lower value appreciation. There was also no significant effect in terms of greater price stabilization for properties in gated communities during a time of decreasing property value.

The primary purpose of the fortifications, however, is to protect the physical integrity of the inhabitants and their property. Based on microeconomic modelling, Helsley and Strange (1999, 82) argued, that the fortification of gated communities

---

[67] So called "common interest developments" (CID) are characterized by the fact that quasi-public places and other facilities are private yet common property. Much of what is permitted in the community is strictly regulated and buying a property means that one is accepting the regulations. In order to manage these communities, so called strata-councils exist, organized by the developer, and membership in the CID group is mandatory (Bickford 2000, 359). MacKenzie (1992, 19 pp) assumes that, in the USA, around 150.000 of such strata organized communities exist with more than 32 Mio. residents. According to an estimate by the Community Association Institute (CAI), the USA featured around 190.000 of such communities in 1996 (Blakely and Snyder 1997a, 180). The master planned versions of the gated communities are therefore a sub-set of the CIDs. Gated communities can therefore be also called "enclaves". An enclave is "*a spatially concentrated area in which members of a particular population group, self-defined by ethnicity or religion or otherwise, congregate as a means of enhancing their economic, social, political and/or cultural development*" (Marcuse 1997a, 242).

should reduce the crime rate in those compounds as the potential costs for conducting crime is increasing due to enhanced monitoring and therefore a higher chance of law enforcement. Therefore, crime should relocate to the surrounding areas in which conducting a crime seems to be less potentially "costly" for the perpetrators. However, there is no evidence that the privatization and fortification of space is actually reduce crime. Where fortification in fact may have a prohibitive impact on crime, the crime and violence may be simply happen in less protected private spaces and public spaces in nearby areas (Flusty 1994, 38). A comparison of crime from 1988-1993 between some fortified and some non-fortified residential quarters showed in fact very similar results. Crime that occurred in 1991 in a cluster of gated communities outside of Las Vegas included, for example, 5 robberies, 3 rapes, 3 murders and a series of sexual harassment of children for which all the residents of the gated communities themselves were found to be responsible for (Flusty 1994, 23p). Fences and walls are not impermeable for criminals and they cannot prevent crime that is caused by the inhabitants of those gated communities. However, territorial separation and fortification seems to have at least a positive impact on the experience of fear of becoming victimized. In a study reported by Blakely and Snyder (1997a, 126pp), 70 percent of the respondents of gated communities felt that their residential compound had less crime than the surrounding area. 80 percent of those 70 percent felt that the reduction of the crime is a result of the fortification. It is obvious that, with increasing safety measures, the subjective perception of security of the inhabitants of the gated communities seems to increase.

The assumption that the best criminal prevention policy is a good social policy is difficult to object though. The growth of individual wealth should therefore always correlate with increasing collective wealth (Flusty 1994, 50). Walls are in fact only the "second-best solution" (Marcuse 1997b, 105) to deal with social problems.

Conclusion

Will societies in the US and in other western industrial nations emerge that are characterized by radical spatial exclusion and social autism, where various islands of wealth and affluence and security are floating in an ocean of deteriorating public space? Looking at the fate of Victorian so called "private roads" in London, predecessor of modern citadels of security, may be instructive. The establishment of such "private streets" triggered resistance by the public and caused social uproar. Around 1895, those developments were widely challenged and eventually came to a halt (Atkins 1993, 274). A political debate focusing on the relationship of private and public goods and rights emerged. Perhaps, the scientific analysis of the fortification of urban life and a fundamental critique will be able to trigger once more a wider debate about the relationship and value of public and private space, public and private rights, and collective and individual wealth. It is certain that social wealth is not only determined by the individual private fortune and capability to consume but also by public goods like, for example, security and a healthy social and ecological environment (cf. Galbraith 1958).

The fortified communities in Southern California and other urban agglomerations in the US are by now though often common features of culture, building practices and urban space fragmentation. A public debate, putting aside a few debates that revolve around fencing of some public parks and residences, barely takes place (Blakely and Snyder 1997a, 141). For example, in San Diego, some urban planners who tried to oppose the construction of further gated communities were literally fighting alone. Their call to prohibit the development of additional gated communities was opposed by a coalition of homeowners, developers, and the majority of city councilors. In addition, the urban planners eventually realized that the larger public actually strongly supported the idea of spatial fortification and exclusion (Smith et al. 1997, 417 p). Is a kind of "privatopia" (MacKenzie 1994) emerging in which economically wealthy individuals can enjoy a relatively clean, safe, comfortable and private space, while the social and economic deprived need to live in an increasingly dangerous and desolate public space? Is a "fortress mentality" (Blakely and Snyder 1997b, 95) emerging hand in hand together with this urban development?

From the perspective of democracy theory, Bickford (2000) emphasized that "common interest developments" and "gated communities" should be strictly limited for the benefit of democratic public life: "Certainly this would mean infringing on some people's ability choose to live in a privately, precisely controlled environment. But when some people's pursuit of a purified notion of privacy has significant impact on others and on the public realm, it is surely a matter of concern for a democratic public" (Bickford 2000. 369). Perhaps, the idea that a sustainable and peaceful life is only possible, in the long run, if society is characterized by solidarity and tolerance, may prevail at one point. One can hope that Blakely (1994, 46) concluded a bit too early, that the new form of radical spatial separation indicates that the great American experiment of social integration was, at the end, not very successful. European nations will increasingly face similar challenges related to the integration of socially diverse individuals and groups–if they want or not. It will become clear at some point if they will experience a different or a similar development of increasing fortification and privatization of space especially in urban agglomerations.

REFERENCES

Anderson, Nick.1999. "Serious Crimes Continue to Drop in U.S.". *Los Angeles Times*, 22. November.

Aries, Philippe.1977. "The Family and the City". *Daedalus* 106: 227-235.

Atkins, P.J. .1993. "How the West End was Won: The Struggle to Remove Street Barriers in Victorian London." *Journal of Historical Geography* 19: 267-277.

Beck, Ulrich. 1986. *Risikogesellschaft. Auf dem Weg in eine andere Modern.* Frankfurt a.M.: Suhrkamp.

Bentham, Jeremy. 1995. *The Panopticon Writings.* London: Verso.

Bickford, Susan. 2000. "Constructing Inequality: City Spaces and the Architecture of Citizenship." *Political Theory* 28: 355-376.

Blakely, Edward J. .1994. "Fortress America." *Planning*, January: 46.

Blakely, Edward J., and Mary G. Snyder .1997a. *Fortress America: Gated and Walled Communities in the United States.* Washington D.C.: Brookings Institution Press.

———. 1997b. "Divided we Fall: Gated and Walled Communities in the United States." In *Architecture of Fear*, edited by Ellin Nan, 85-100. New York: Princeton Architectural Press.

Caldeira, Teresa P. R. .1996. "Fortified Enclaves: The New Urban Segregation." *Public Culture* 8: 303-328.

Davis, Mike. 1994. The City of Quartz: Ausgrabungen der Zukunft in Los Angeles. Berlin: Verlag der Buchladen Schwarze Risse/Rote

———.1995. "Fortress Los Angeles." In: *Metropolis. Centre and symbol of our times*, edited by Philip Kasinitz, 355-368. New York: New York University Press.

———. 1999a. *Ökologie der Angst.* München: Verlag Antje Kunstmann.

———. 1999b. Los Angeles: Ökologie der Angst., In *Kursbuch Stadt. Stadtleben und Stadtkultur an der Jahrtausendwende*, edited by Stefan Bollmann, 263-284.

Ellin, Nan. 1999. *Postmodern Urbanism.* New York: Princeton Architectural Press.

Etzioni, Amitai.1994. *The Spirit of Community: The Reinvention of American Society.* New York: Simon & Schuster.

Flusty, Steve. 1994. *Building Paranoia: The Proliferation of Interdictory Space and the Erosion of Social Justice.* Los Angeles: Los Angeles Forum for Architecture and Urban Design.

Galbraith, John K. .1958. *The Affluent Society.* Boston: Houghton Mifflin.

Gartman, David. 1998. "Postmodernism; or The Cultural Logic of Post-Fordism?". *Sociological Quartely* 39: 119-137.

Glassner, Barry. 1999. *The Culture of Fear. Why Americans are Afraid of the Wrong Thing.* New York: Basic Books.

Goheen, Peter G. 1998. "Public Space and the Geography of the Modem City." *Progress in Human Geography* 22: 479-496.

Grill, Bartholomaus. 2000. "Paranoia im Paradies." *Die Zeit* Nr. 21, 18. Mai 2000: 15-20.

Harvey, David. 1989. *The Condition of Postmodernity.* Oxford: Basil Blackwell.

Helsley, Robert W., and William C. Strange. 1999. "Gated Communities and the Economic Geography of Crime." *Journal of Urban Economics* 46: 80-105.

Hennig, Eike. 1998. "Fortress L.A. = Die Engelsburg?" *Vorgänge. Zeitschrift für Bürgerrechte und Gesellschaftspolitik* 37: 52-61.

Hermann, Ulrike. 1993. *Herkunftswörterbuch. Etymologie und Geschichte von 10.000 interessanten Wörtern.* München: Orbis.

Hobbes, Thomas.1965. *Leviathan oder Wesen, Form und Gewalt des kirchlichen und bürgerlichen Staates.* Reinbek: Rowohlt.

Jencks, Charles. 1997. "Hetero-Architecture for the Heteropolis: The Los Angeles School." In: *Architecture of Fear*, edited by Ellin Nan, 217-226. New York: Princeton Architectural Press, S. 217-226.

Judd, Dennis R. 1995. "The Rise of the New Walled Cities." In: *Spatial Practices: Critical Explorations in Social/Spatial Theory*, edited by Liggett, Helen, and David C. Perry, 144-166. Thousand Oaks: Sage Publications.

Kaliski, John. 1994. "Liberation and the Naming of Paranoid Space." In: *Building Paranoia: The Proliferation of Interdictory Space and the Erosion of Social Justice*, edited by Steve Flusty, 4-7. Los Angeles: Los Angeles Forum for Architecture and Urban Design.

Lofland, Lyn H. 1998. *The Public Realm- Exploring the City's Quintessential Social Territory.* Hawthorne, NY: de Gruyter.

Luymes, Don 1997. "The Fortification of Suburbia: Investigating the Rise of Enclave Communities." *Landscape and Urban Planning* 39: 187-203.

MacKenzie, Evan 1994. *Privatopia: Homeowner Associations and the Rise of Residential Private Government.* New Haven: Yale University Press.

Marcuse, Peter 1997a. "The Enclave, the Citadell, and the Ghetto. What has Changed in the Post-Fordist U.S. City." *Urban Affairs Review* 33: 228-264.

———. Marcuse, Peter 1997b. "Walls of Fear and Walls of Support." In: *Architecture of Fear,* edited by Ellin Nan, 101-114. New York: Princeton Architectural Press.

Newman, Oscar. 1972. *Defensible Space: Crime Prevention through Urban Design.* New York: Macmillan.

Oc, Taner, and Steven Tiesdell. 1997. "Housing and Safer City Centres." In *Safer City Centres. Reviving the Public Realm,* edited by Taner Oc, and Steven Tiesdell, 156-169. Thousand Oaks: Sage.

Philip Kasinitz, ed. 1995. *Metropolis. Centre and Symbol of our Times.* New York: New York University Press.

Rosen, P. 1993. "Houston Residents Retreat Behind Walls and Barricades." *Houston Post* 5. Dezember 1993, S. Fl.

Rowe, Peter. 1991. *Making a Middle Landscape.* Cambridge M.A.: MIT Press.

Sennett, Richard. 1983. *Verfall und Ende der Öffentlichkeit. Die Tyrannei der Intimitat.* Frankfurt a.M.: Fischer.

———.1997. *Fleisch und Stein.* Frankfurt a.M.: Suhrkamp.

Smith, Larry J., Mary M. Ross, Robert D. Pritt, Brian Woram, John Witt, and Terrence S. Welch. 1997. "Gated Communities: Private Solutions or Public Dilemma?". *The Urban Lawyer* 29: 413-426.

Sorkin, Michael (ed.). 1992. *Variations on a Theme Park: The New American City and the End of Public Space.* New York: Hill & Wang.

Toennies, Ferdinand. 1887. *Gemeinschaft und Gesellschaft.* Leipzig: Fues.

Weichert, Thilo. 1998. Audio- und Videoüberwachung im Öffentlichen Raum. In: *Vorgänge. Zeitschrift für Bürgerrechte und Gesellschaftspolitik* 37: 62-71.

Wirth, Louis. 1995. "Urbanism as a Way of Life." In: *Metropolis. Centre and Symbol of our Times,* edited by Philip Kasinitz, 58-82. New York: New York University Press.

Contributors

Dr. Kalpana Bora Barman, Lecturer at Cotton University, Assam (India). *Research Interests*: Narratives of the Urban, Theories of Space, Postcolonial Literatures and writings from India's North East.

Dr. Tommaso Durante, Associate Lecturer in Global Media Studies at School of Culture and Communication, Faculty of Arts, The University of Melbourne (Australia). *Research Interests*: Aesthetics of Globalization, Globalization and Mediatization, Theories of the Social Imaginary, Theories of Ideology, Visual Methodologies.

Prof. Nick Dunn, Chair of Urban Design & Executive Director, ImaginationLancaster, Lancaster University (UK). *Research Interests*: Future Cities, Nocturnal Cities, Urban Design, Speculative Design, More-than-Human Design.

Dr. Stefan Litz, Associate Professor in Management and International Business, Schwartz School of Business, Saint Francis Xavier University (Canada). *Research Interests*: Globalization, Organization Theory, Corporate Social Responsibility, Business Ethics, Human Resource Management.

Dr. Marcella Livi, German and French instructor at various Universities and Colleges and currently German Language 9-12 High School Teacher (USA). *Research Interests*: Literature with a designated emphasis in Critical Theory.

Munehito Moro, PhD Candidate, International Christian University Tokyo (Japan). *Research Interests*: Popular Culture, Science Fiction, Film Theory, Globalization.

Dr. Andrew M. Marton, Professor, Department of Pacific and Asian Studies, University of Victoria (Canada). *Research Interests*: Urbanization and Regional Development in China, Chinese Society, Culture and Creativity in China, Chinese Education.

Dr. Terry McGee, Professor Emeritus, Department of Geography, Former Director of the Institute of Asian Research, University of British Columbia (Canada). *Research Interests*: Sustainability of Asian Mega-Urban Regions, the Southeast Asian City, Urbanization in Malaysia.

Dr. Rohini Mokashi-Punekar, Lecturer at the Indian Institute of Technology Guwahati (India). *Research Interests*: Translating medieval Varkari poetry from the Marathi and English translation of Phule's play "Tritiya Ratna".

Dr. Steven A. Nardi, Adjunct Faculty, The College of Mount Saint Vincent (USA). *Research Interests*: Harlem Renaissance, Modernism, Contemporary Poetry and Poetics, Formalism, Children's Literature.

Dr. Nuray Özaslan, Professor of Architecture, Faculty of Architecture and Design, Eskisehir Technical University (Turkey). *Research Interests*: Urban and Architectural History and Theories, Urban Design Theories, Globalization, Future Cities, Architectural Education.

Dr Daniel Pasciuti, Assistant Professor of Sociology, Georgia State University (USA). *Research Interests*: Global Urbanism, Urban Governance, Political-Economy and Global Development, Quantitative and Comparative-Historical Methods, and Housing and the Courts.

Adishree Panda, Research Associate, Transport & Urban Governance Division, The Energy & Resources Institute (TERI), New Delhi (India). Graduate of Development Planning Unit, University College London. *Research Interests*: Urban Governance, Sustainable & Inclusive Cities, Mainstreaming Climate Action.

Dr. Timothy Stanley, Senior Lecturer, School of Humanities and Social Science, The University of Newcastle (Australia). *Research Interests*: Philosophy, Religion, Technology, Intellectual History.

Dr. Maciej Stasiowski, Independent Scholar, Graduate of the Faculty of Management and Social Communication at the Jagiellonian University, Cracow (Poland) and frequent collaborator of the London Centre for Interdisciplinary Research (UK). *Research Interests*: Architecture, Urbanism, Film, New Media, Visual Arts.

Arch. Nina Toleva-Nowak, Chief Expert in the Culture and Cultural Heritage Department, Plovdiv Municipality (Bulgaria). *Research Interests*: History and Theory of Architecture, Urban Theory, Preservation of Architectural Heritage, Interdisciplinary Research Approaches and Natural Sciences.